Sociology for Music Teachers

Sociology for Music Teachers: Practical Applications, Second Edition, outlines the basic concepts relevant to understanding music teaching and learning from a sociological perspective. It demonstrates the relationship of music to education, schooling and society, and examines the consequences for making instructional choices in teaching methods and repertoire selection. The authors look at major theories and concepts relevant to music education, texts in the sociology of music, and thoughts of selected ethnomusicologists and sociologists. The new edition takes a more global approach than was the case in the first edition and includes the application of sociological theory to contexts beyond the classroom.

The Second Edition:

- Presents major theories in ethnomusicology, both traditional and contemporary.
- Takes a global approach by presenting a variety of teaching practices beyond those found in the United States.
- Emphasizes music education in a traditional classroom setting, but also applies specific constructs to studio teaching situations in conservatories (with private lessons) and community music.
- Provides recommendations for teaching practices by addressing popular music in school music curricula, suggests inclusionary projects that explore musical styles and repertoire of the past and present, and connects school to community music practices of varying kinds.
- Contains an increased number of suggestions for projects and discussions among the students using the book.

Hildegard C. Froehlich is Emeritus Professor at the University of North Texas, Denton, Texas, USA.

Gareth Dylan Smith is Research Fellow at the Institute of Contemporary Music Performance, London, UK.

Sociology for Music Teachers

Practical Applications

Second Edition

Hildegard C. Froehlich and
Gareth Dylan Smith

Routledge
Taylor & Francis Group
NEW YORK AND LONDON

Second Edition published 2017
by Routledge
711 Third Avenue, New York, NY 10017

and by Routledge
2 Park Square, Milton Park, Abingdon, Oxon OX14 4RN

Routledge is an imprint of the Taylor & Francis Group, an informa business

First edition published by Routledge 2004

Library of Congress Cataloging-in-Publication Data
Names: Froehlich, Hildegard C., author. | Smith, Gareth Dylan, author.
Title: Sociology for music teachers : practical applications / Hildegard Froehlich and Gareth Smith.
Description: Second edition. | New York ; London : Routledge, 2017. | Includes bibliographical references and index.
Identifiers: LCCN 2016049120 | ISBN 9781138224506 (hardback) | ISBN 9781138224513 (pbk.)
Subjects: LCSH: Music—Instruction and study—Social aspects. | Music—Social aspects. | Educational sociology.
Classification: LCC MT1 .F79 2017 | DDC 306.4/842—dc23
LC record available at https://lccn.loc.gov/2016049120

ISBN: 978-1-138-22450-6 (hbk)
ISBN: 978-1-138-22451-3 (pbk)
ISBN: 978-1-315-40234-5 (ebk)

Typeset in Times New Roman
by Apex CoVantage, LLC

Contents

Acknowledgments and Dedications

Hildegard: Even more than was the case in the first edition, many acknowledgments are necessary. Next to expressing enormous gratitude to my co-author Gareth, I most of all owe a word of thanks to those readers of the first edition who provided either solicited or unsolicited feedback since 2007. I hope to have responded in kind to all of them, always being aware, of course, that each of us has only a limited way of seeing the whole. In particular I wish to thank Dr. Adria R. Hoffman from the Department of Curriculum, Instruction and Special Education, University of Virginia for directing me to many valuable sources in the field of sociology of education. Finally, I maintain the dedication expressed in the first edition, simply expanding it now to students and colleagues worldwide whom I have met since retiring from my university job in 2002.

Gareth: I am grateful to Hildegard for inviting me to co-author the present volume. As an emerging voice in music education scholarship, it has been a privilege and a challenge to contribute; I hope I shall be judged to have been up to the task. Whenever I write I feel that my work is mostly that of so many others, just nudged a millimeter forward or sideways as I add a little of my own perspective. I am, therefore, profoundly grateful to all who have mentored, criticized, and discussed with me, enabling me to start finding my own voice. In particular, I must thank Professor Lucy Green for her invaluable guidance and wisdom in this regard.

We both wish to thank Constance Ditzel, Senior Editor, Music (Acquisitions) at Routledge, Peter Sheehy, and Kevin Kelsey for their support and assistance throughout this project. We also thank the blind reviewers for invaluable feedback on sample chapters and, later, the entire manuscript. We know that the changes we made on the basis of the reviewers' recommendations have strengthened what we wanted to convey. We also know, however, that there is always room for further improvements, which can come about only through ongoing dialogue and constructive discourse.

Hildegard C. Froehlich and Gareth Dylan Smith

Figures

Preface

The collaborative efforts of the book's co-authors began with a conversation at the 9th International Symposium on the Sociology of Music Education in the summer of 2015, at Loyola University in New Orleans. It appeared that the first edition of the book had piqued the interest of colleagues far beyond its principal target audience in the United States. We wished, therefore, to broaden the scope of the text to include a wider range of perspectives and practices that might increase the book's appeal to a larger readership. We were working on writing this second edition of *Sociology for Music Teachers: Perspectives for Practice* while politics internationally were becoming more divisive, polarized, and nationalistic than we had witnessed in the "West" for decades. During the same period, the Olympics took place for the first time in South America, a sign that international cooperation continues its course, and values of pursuing excellence through hard work and lifelong dedication are shared among nations. We asked ourselves, then, where in the worlds of political macro events and everyone's daily teaching duties this edition would have its place. Better yet, does it have a place?

Goals

This book makes the case that sociologically savvy music educators can more successfully than might otherwise be possible see the world from their students' points of view. Encouraging beginning and experienced teachers to incorporate their students' musical perceptions and life experiences into all curricular decision making, the book:

- Addresses students and licensed, certified, or degreed music teachers who are institutionally immersed in the worlds of music and schooling.

- Explores identities of self as musician-performer, musician-producer/composer/songwriter/improviser, and educator-teacher, and how these derive from diverse racial and ethnic, personal and professional contexts.
- Looks at teachers' communication with students, colleagues, parents, administrators, and others in the workplace.
- Considers teachers' balanced pedagogical decision making in repertoire choice, teaching and delivery style, and collegiate conduct as socially situated acts.
- Discusses music teachers as social and cultural value educators.
- Embraces core music teaching practices as having the potential to lead to transformative and empowering learning for students.
- Invites readers to articulate and reflect on their social and musical selves in light of insights from sociological perspectives.
- Asks readers to formulate questions derived from those insights, answer them for the pedagogical contexts relevant to her or him, and act (or be ready to act) in the classroom.
- Exhorts readers to examine and modify their assumptions (and established teaching practices, where applicable and appropriate) in light of insights developed from and inspired by this book.

New to This Edition

The expanded focus of this new edition includes:

- Specific pedagogies pertinent to popular music.
- A greater emphasis on suggesting strategies by which to compare diverse musical styles and repertoires with one another.
- A more international outlook.
- New and more varied tasks and assignments for classes and small groups.
- A focus on issues concerning inclusion and equality in the classroom.
- Updated, professionally relevant literature reflecting the expanding body of knowledge in sociologically informed music education scholarship.

Because new perspectives do not necessarily render older sources (out-)dated or superfluous, one of the main challenges for us in preparing this edition was to decide what sources to retain, which to take out, and—most important and key to this edition—how to broaden the scope of the book's content to reflect teaching and research contexts beyond those of the United States (the almost exclusive focus of the first edition). Linking such suggestions to the larger social issues of inclusion and equality in the classroom poses perhaps the greatest challenge for music teachers today. We address this challenge more directly than was possible in the first edition, while acknowledging that the broader scope of this edition also brings about new challenges for us, the authors. As we look at music teaching and sociology through a wide-angle lens, zooming in on details in one context may obscure or distort knowledge of another. However, while aware of local, regional, national, and international differences in teaching style, and specifics of musical repertoire and practices, we have attempted to show how such differences can be explained and understood through an orientation to sociological perspectives.

Introduction

Why Sociology for Music Teachers?

The introduction provides:

- Who are *we?*
- Premises, Purpose, Objectives, and Themes
- A Brief Chapter Synopsis and Structure of the Book
- The Book's Bibliographical Context

"What in the world does sociology have to do with music teaching?" Stated differently, how can the study of society at large speak to what musicians do in their roles as music teachers in school classrooms, private studios, or other public or private spaces? Like the first edition attempted to do for music teachers in the United States, this revised and expanded edition seeks to answer both questions in ways that speak to music teachers beyond the United States alone. It is for you, the reader, to decide whether what you deal with in your own workplace is subject to forces, structures, and system similar to those addressed in this book.

Of course, sociologists do not generally provide recipes for *how* to teach music (or, for that matter, any other subject). But sociological thinking can help a teacher place himself or herself into the *why*, *what*, *how*, and *for whom* of music teaching in particular social contexts. Choices in repertoire and pedagogy can be reasoned within those contexts and make apparent how classroom actions are situated in particular socio-geographic and political realities. Sociologically informed musician-educators, therefore, are likely to see themselves and their own actions as reflections of societal macro structures. Changes in personal choices have the power of impacting those macro structures just as macro structures impact what a teacher does in a particular classroom (the micro structures).

As you embark on reading this book, you are probably already familiar with one of the *leitmotifs* among good music teachers anywhere: know your learners! It is, indeed, essential for your success as a teacher. Of equal importance, however, is to know yourself. As sociologist Ben Agger (2004) suggested to his American readership, sociology should begin and end "with the self, the person who lives in Arlington, Texas or Arlington, Virginia, Eugene, Oregon, Topeka, Kansas, Toronto, Canada" (4). We now embrace that statement by saying that sociology should begin and end with *you*, wherever you live and prepare to or already work as a music teacher. To this end, we ask you to fill in the blanks in Figure 0.1 that refers to your own geographical locale. We will come back to it later.

With the geographical "coordinates" provided, we ask you next to consider the larger social network of family, friends, peers, colleagues, co-workers, and employers with whom you interact on a regular basis (see Figure 0.2). In other words, we invite you to step back from your own self and view your actions from the vantage points of those around you.

I, __________________________,

live in ____

and work in ____

as a ____

Figure 0.1 Your "Self" in Geographical Context

Your family members

Your friends

Your colleagues

Your administrative support staff (if any)

Figure 0.2 Coordinates for Your Social Self

Humans are embedded in a complex system of many selves, all shaped by diverse economic, socio-political, and cultural experiences and values. Australian Margaret Barrett explained, "Context and setting are integral to the constitution of human thought and activity. . . . In short, we cannot separate mind and cognition from culture and context, values and beliefs, and a culturally mediated identity" (2011, 3). The connectedness of mind, thinking, culture, beliefs, and identity is a thread that weaves through nearly everything said in this book. It impacts the theories you will read about, the references we have selected to describe them, the examples we give to illustrate the theories, the choices we make in tasks and discussion materials, and the tone of voice with which we present them.

Who are *we*?

Hildegard was born and raised in Germany (what then used to be known as West Germany) and has lived for more than forty years as a naturalized citizen of the United States with teaching duties as a music education professor in Texas. Gareth was born and raised in the United Kingdom and is based in London, where he works as a drummer, educator, scholar, and writer. Clearly, each biographical background continuously impacts our teaching, scholarship, and musicianship—not necessarily in that order. Our respective experiences and shared interests are reflected in this book and its construction. We ask you, therefore, to read this book as if you were in conversation with us: challenge and correct where you think we have got it wrong, think about examples that add to the ones we have provided or that weaken their validity. Ask questions about unresolved issues and, inspired by your reflections, test and explore new ideas on your own and with others in your ongoing growth as a music educator.

While you think about your own story and compare it with ours, keep in mind your everyday life and how this is shaped by the values that make up and are informed by the socio-cultural norms and traditions of your country as a whole. Not everyone in the country shares equally in those norms, values, and traditions, but they are the basis for the laws of the land and are upheld as well as acted upon by local and state governmental agencies. In certain countries, those agencies have a say in matters concerning the arts and arts education; in other countries they do not. In Figure 0.3 we ask you to re-create the table and fill in details about your own schooling, the school "system" of which you were a part (private, public, boarding school, home schooling), the place of the arts (and especially formal music instruction) in it, and what you know about the relationship between what happened to you in your music education and what you know about any local, state, and/or federal government policies that made that education possible.

My schooling:		
Primary	Secondary	College (tertiary)
My schools:		
Urban	Large	Small
Rural	Large	Small
The music instruction I received:		
In school		Out of school
What I know about government and the arts in my country:		
Local level	State/regional level	Federal level

Figure 0.3 My Schooling and How It Relates to the Society in Which I Live

When you engage in the previous exercise, you are likely to encounter problems with terminology because hierarchies of decision-making bodies in governmental systems around the globe have many different labels. Sociological analyses, however, identify those hierarchies despite differences in what they are called. Therefore, avoid becoming sidetracked by what sounds unfamiliar when reading this text and replace the unfamiliar with the familiar. For example, if the terms "school principal" or "school district" mean little to you, replace them with "headmaster" or *Schulbehörde*. Differences in terminology pale in the sociological analysis of what they have in common. Their meaning is nearly always embedded in a host of prior decisions and assumptions about societal and educational norms and values, policies, and political realities. To uncover those is the purview of sociological theory in education.

Sociology connects many fields of study by examining possible relationships between how and what people think, how they interact with each other in society, and how the societal macro system relates to micro structures within it. Applied to music as a school subject, personal choices of music making and listening meet education as a public, political mandate. However, rarely are the intersections between various micro structures and the larger macro system free from perceived or actual incongruities or even conflict. Because the same can be said for the worlds of music and education, applying sociological lenses to those incongruities and conflicts can explain their origins and possible resolutions in any of those worlds. For instance, there are identifiable reasons why music artistry and musicological scholarship seem so often incompatible with specific institutional pedagogies, theories of curriculum and instruction, educational philosophies, and cultural policies. Once these complex causes are identified and named, conflict resolutions are more readily visualized and implemented.

This book is designed to guide you, the reader, in the challenges of respecting differences in musical tastes and preferences and accepting that these can be vehicles of social affirmation for one person and exclusion for another. Although those challenges are often beyond a teacher's control, being aware of them and incorporating that awareness into your pedagogical actions can go a long way to make you a sociologically savvy music teacher. For anyone, the term "music" triggers very particular sounds in the mind, mixed with specific texts, memories, and emotions. Without those connotations, the term by itself means little because it is unspecified (non-contextual). Because there are so many forms of music, all of which have originated in and come from different traditions, locales, and modes of creative engagement, you will find us often use the plural for the generic term of music. We have done this in an effort to point to the many experiences both teachers and students can have in their respective worlds of musics.

To match personal musical experiences with what goes on in the classroom, numerous efforts over many years by scholars in education, sociology, and music have resulted in the increased use of multi-ethnic and multi-cultural repertoire selections. Popular musics of many different styles, too, have become commonplace in many music curricula, although the uncritical inclusion of popular music to the exclusion of other traditions continues to be under scrutiny as well (Christophersen and Gullberg 2017; Hebert, Abramo, and Smith 2017; Scruton 2000). Furthermore, varied resource materials on numerous styles and genres of music (both in print and on the Internet) have become available for teachers in affluent countries. Such resources clearly can enrich any curriculum in multiple ways, but the challenge for music educators nearly everywhere continues to lie in determining what might constitute well-defined, socially equitable, and inclusive curricula in music education. Sociologically informed thinking can prove helpful in addressing this challenge.

Premises, Purpose, Objectives, and Themes

Three premises underlie the purpose, objectives, and themes of this book:

1. A music teacher's work is continuously shaped and re-shaped by numerous social and cultural parameters that impact what a musician-educator does or does not value and how such values affect pedagogical decisions.
2. Each teaching situation is unique to a particular institutional context that is shaped by its locality, purpose, population, and history. Sociological

theories can uncover similarities across even the most disparate educational settings and contexts.

3. Teachers should provide learners with the tools for asking questions, critiquing unexamined values, and celebrating diversity in informed and mature ways.

The overall purpose of this book is to guide both aspiring and experienced music teachers in making sociologically informed decisions in curricular matters and when communicating with students and colleagues. To accomplish that purpose, our objectives are (1) to introduce our readers to perspectives from sociology that can be applied to music, education, and music education; (2) to encourage our readers to apply what they have learned about those perspectives to their own realities of music teaching in terms of repertoire choice and pedagogical decisions; and (3) to use sociologically informed reasoning as a sharpened tool for skills in critical thinking. After all, being or becoming a successful music educator should include understanding fully one's place in the macro system of those political actions that govern a community at the state (regional) and/or nation-state level. Such understanding, coupled with musical knowledge and fine-tuned pedagogical skills, might well define the *ideal* music educator.

This edition's purpose and objectives are intentionally kept broad and applicable to many music schooling situations, especially in industrialized nation-states. However, despite geographic, economic, and cultural differences separating those nations, we believe that even more commonalities connect them:

1. Where they exist, licensed, certified, or degreed music teachers in many industrialized nations are institutionally and professionally bound to the worlds of schooling and music.
2. Diverse racial and ethnic, personal, and professional contexts impact teachers' identities as musician-performers and educator-teachers and also shape their instructional styles and communicative skills.
3. Understanding *teaching* as socially situated, pedagogic acts turns student *learning* into socially situated acts as well, documented by levels of engagement and achievement. For learning to be perceived as positive experiences by all learners, pedagogical decisions about curricular content and delivery style become crucial tools in effective music teaching.
4. Pedagogical decisions reflect the social and cultural meanings music teachers as transmitters of agreed-upon knowledge and skills attach to their actions. Pedagogic choices, therefore, symbolize values a teacher transmits to the students and their parents as well as to school leaders, and—in some countries—taxpaying citizens who require fiscally responsible schools. Each music teacher is also a value educator.

5. Transmitting social and cultural values by way of a particular music curriculum requires responding to the meanings that learners attach to such mandated knowledge. Weaving together learners' meanings with those the teacher brings to the pedagogical process is, we argue, at the core of all teaching practice. This complex activity, if carried out with full awareness of teachers' power as socializing agents, has the potential to transform and empower each student.
6. Thinking sociologically about music and education processes should lay the groundwork for sharing common questions and assumptions about teaching practices in music. Such sharing can then provide a common language across countries, policies, and mandated curricula around the world.

Reality Check 0.1

Before you read on, please check for yourself whether you agree with each of the six themes listed. If not, where do you believe our thinking differs from yours, and why? How would you re-word or reconsider our assertions?

With the previous themes—modified or not—in mind, we ask you, our readers (whether school teachers, college instructors, students, or scholars), to articulate, reflect upon, and (most important) act on insights gained from this text. Ask yourself how what you read either confirms what you already know or raises questions for further scrutiny. Whether what you are interested in pertains to specific curricular and pedagogical choices in repertoire, teaching and delivery styles, and/or how you communicate with non-music colleagues and parental clientele, we give all these considerations equal importance in your work as a music educator.

A Brief Chapter Synopsis and Structure of the Book

The material covered in this book is vast and required from us a careful selection of what to include in each chapter. Given that this is an updated edition, we opted to follow the format introduced with the first edition, but expanded it to focus on a more inclusive list of references and a larger number of interactive tasks for readers.

Chapter 1 (following this Introduction) begins with *you*: How have you become the musician-educator you are or wish to become? How and why did your own musical and educational values evolve in the ways they did, and how have those processes continued to shape and influence your actions as musician and educator?

Chapter 2 places into critical perspective what shapes teachers' and students' identities as musicians, compulsory schooling in general, and school music in particular. The chapter makes the case that music as a curricular subject will—by necessity—be, look, and sound different from music learning in other contexts, especially when—as some leading (music) educators advocate with increasing urgency—informal learning may be incorporated into the formality of school music pedagogies.

Chapter 3 contains a somewhat chronological review of research since the middle of the last century on the occupation of "school teacher" among other occupations. The chapter especially considers such variables as social status, work autonomy, and perceived and/or actual decision-making authority.

Chapter 4 provides a summary of what various music scholars (ethnomusicologists, music sociologists, cultural theorists, and music educators) have said about music and the other arts as socially situated acts. A diversity of viewpoints, or lenses, is made available in that regard. Hailing from many parts of the globe, all perspectives offer sociological constructs for understanding the world and our roles in it.

Chapter 5 extends what Chapter 4 began, by focusing exclusively on the sociology of education as the provider of lenses that allow either close-up views or wide-angle examinations of particular issues common to education as a societal mandate in most countries. The chapter then highlights what likely impacts all music teachers' work just as much as it does that of math, science, and reading teachers: (1) the ever-present gaps in achievement and opportunity common in classrooms, and (2) the fact that classroom discourse can convey messages not necessarily intended that way by the teacher (a phenomenon also known as the hidden curriculum).

Chapter 6 looks at music teachers as value educators. Although sociologists of music have addressed the value of music in its own right, only a few of them have directly addressed the role of music teachers as value educators and/or "culture workers." To do so, we examine how a teacher's role changes when focusing on the *art* of music for its own sake as compared with teaching music as social construct. Because of the aforementioned ambiguity of the term music, the chapter is also about relative and absolute musical values and music learning as self-selected leisure or a teacher-directed, formalized musical undertaking. These practices differ significantly across music schooling in different locales and for different purposes, but all have social significance.

Chapter 7 summarizes the previous chapters and reiterates the importance of viewing music learning and teaching as social acts that should be equally informed by the artistry of those involved in those acts and how the actors live in the world. The chapter is about the music educator who knows how to make connections between apparently disparate musical and social phenomena and thinks beyond the seemingly obvious. By embracing such a way of thinking, the realities that shape compulsory schooling in many parts of the world may begin to look more alike than different from each other. Forces of power, choice making, and hierarchical structuring of institutions interact with each other in all places. Understanding these systems can be empowering and presents new opportunities for exploration and learning.

Structure of the Book

Each chapter is interspersed with suggestions for conversations and dialogues about concepts presented. Identified as small group discussions, writing tasks, reality checks, observation and interview projects in addition to questions for class discussion, the tasks are intended to facilitate opportunities to critically examine accepted teaching and learning modalities and, where appropriate, to affirm "the tried and proven." These discussions should preferably take place outside of class, perhaps in bars, pubs, coffee houses or other "third Place" hangouts (Oldenburg 1999) over good food and beverages of your choice. That is where your interviews should start: beginning with each other and expanding from there into what might become semester-long assignments. Who knows, perhaps they could become the beginning of actual research projects?

Similarly, decide carefully on which of the tasks to engage in. But also be reminded that all tasks are suggestions only; others may be substituted. We consider it essential, however, that you engage in at least one hands-on task while working through the book either in its entirety or in parts. To set the tone for any of the tasks suggested, we, the authors, present our own thoughts in dialogue at the start of each chapter and elsewhere. We do this to demonstrate that there are far fewer right or wrong answers than there are points of view stemming from contexts uniquely our own.

The Book's Bibliographical Context

Because this new edition is structured to reach a more international readership than was the case for the first edition, the book's bibliographical breadth has grown considerably. Whether articulated by sociologists, social psychologists, or philosophers, social theories about music, education, and music education abound. They come from thinkers of various nationalities with their particular linguistic and academic traditions and backgrounds. The French school of sociology, for instance, continues to differ from Russian, Anglo-American, and German socio-cultural approaches. Many more perspectives have also been added by scholars in countries of South America, the Middle East, and Asia. Feminist scholarship from different parts of the world, too, brings renewed energies to long-standing questions and multiple answers about social welfare, justice, and equality in education and the arts. However, despite such richness in perspectives and sociological understandings available since the middle of the last century, culture critics John Shepherd and Kyle Devine concluded that only now—in the twenty-first century—the sociology of music has reached a moment "in which the distinctiveness of a sociological approach to music has become apparent" (Shepherd and Devine 2015, 15). But they also called the contributions that have aided in reaching this goal "scattered and fragmented scholarship" (2015, 15).

Given that it is possible to view music education as its own distinct field, albeit embedded equally in the sociology of education and the sociology of music, this book provides a snapshot of a continuously growing body of literature in all three fields. Coming from many parts of the world, the body of knowledge reflects a wide array of sociological lenses, already described in detailed handbooks, readers, monographs, and articles. Specific to music education, for example, several English-language publications provide encapsulating status reports of prevailing ideas (e.g., Bontinck 1999; Froehlich and Green 2014; Green 2008b; Kelly 2009/2016; Laurence and Urbain 2011; McCarthy 2002; Vulliamy and Shepherd 1984; Wright 2010, 2014; see also selected articles in *Action, Criticism, & Theory for Music Education*). It would require a handbook (or reader) all of its own to show the academic distinctiveness of a sociology of music education similar to Shepherd and Devine's (2015) text on the sociology of music.

The distinctiveness of a sociology of music education would lie in the necessity to wed theory with practice as an ongoing imperative for music educators. Always thinking in application to practice, teachers tend not to be satisfied with the articulation and examination of theoretical constructs alone. Instead, they want to know what constructs do for taking actions toward improving learning and teaching processes. We aim in this edition to contribute to answering that query.

Reality Check 0.2

Compare your responses in Figures 0.1 to 0.3 to those of your classmates and explore "otherness" as observable facts among those present in the entire class.

Key Sources (for full information see References)

We suggest you look at the titles of these publications and select ONE that piques your interest. Write a short paragraph on why the title intrigues you and what you expect to find when reading the book.

Ball, Stephen. 2004.
Ballantine, Jeanne H. and Floyd Hammack. 2009.
Froehlich, Hildegard C. and Lucy Green. 2014.
Green, Lucy. 2008b.
Hallinan, Maureen T. 2000.

Kelly, Stephen. 2009.
Laurence, Felicity and Olivier Urbain. 2011.
McCarthy, Marie. 2002.
Shepherd, John and Kyle Devine. 2015.
Smith, Gareth D. 2013a, 2015.
Wright, Ruth. 2010.

1

The Musician and Teacher in You

A Matter of Multiple Identities

This chapter follows up on and expands your group discussions from the Introduction:

- Processes of Socialization
- Identity Research on Musicians

Hildegard: From second grade on I knew that I wanted to become a teacher (the reasons not always fully clear to me), but only when I graduated from high school did I seriously consider enrolling in music education as my field of study. As much as I loved singing, playing, and listening to music (and have continued to do so all my life), teaching has always been my first interest and I have found great joy in interacting with students about many subjects in education, music, sociology, and research. Most important, however, I discovered that one has to be a lifelong learner in all of these subjects to call oneself a professional (music) educator.

Gareth: Although I have long had an interest in teaching, my route into becoming an educator grew out of a firm commitment to being a rock drummer. I began teaching music in a primary school after graduating with a classical music degree, in order to pay rent while pursing my rock 'n' roll dream. I soon enrolled to study music education so I could learn to do my teaching job better. I found teaching—and learning and thinking about education—to be incredibly creative, understanding I was actually a teacher when a parent of a student addressed me, "Mr. Smith"! I feel a constant urge to develop my art—as educator, scholar, and musician.

Hildegard: My performer colleagues have often claimed that once you have been trained in the classical music tradition you can play any musical style thereafter. I have never quite believed that and have certainly found for myself that I am very afraid of branching out into musical styles that are not classically based. Gareth, what has been your experience in that regard, and do you think the issue is instrument specific? Were/are my colleagues correct?

Gareth: Prior to and alongside my formative years as a drummer in the popular and musical theatre styles that have been my professional musical home for decades, I trained as a classical clarinetist. Growing up in the UK this meant studying for graded exams 1 to 8, playing in a concert (wind) band at weekends, in orchestras at school and in the community, and then studying classical music for my undergraduate degree at the Royal Welsh College of Music and Drama. As I transitioned through music college and as my career took turns toward drumming and more popular styles, I found that I called upon my classical training less and less. In terms of instrumental technique as a drummer, the rock and punk music that I mostly played was much louder than classical music, so required far greater physical stamina and the development of different, much bigger movements. For singers, classical technique can be a significant hindrance, especially if they try to apply it in popular styles (as Australian singer and researcher Diane Hughes has repeatedly shown). With the possible exception of recently emerged sub-genre "symphonic rock," the sound of a *bel canto* vocal is antithetical to nearly all non–Western classical musics. Other disadvantages of classical training, in my experience, include over-reliance on following instructions and on reading sheet music (a form of following instructions)—skills that, although helpful up to a point—can alienate musicians in communities that value democratic collaboration and aural musicianship. One major advantage of classical training that I have noticed is the discipline that it instills, including arriving on (before) time to rehearsals and concerts, practicing your instrument for excellence, and knowing when not to play in rehearsals.

Introduction

With the backdrop of the conversation you just read, here is a scenario in which you may recognize part of yourself: feeling reasonably competent as a performer, you go to the music conservatory, university, or music college during the day, hold a part-time job that pays your bills, possibly even playing gigs that provide some extra income and connect you with other musicians. In your mind, there seems to be no reason why the situation should change significantly once you graduate, except perhaps that becoming educated may be replaced by educating others. You envision having musically talented pupils who are as serious about their music study as you were about yours. Then you receive your degree and/or teaching certificate and find your first full-time employment as a music teacher. You soon discover that teaching is a demanding job that makes it difficult to practice and be "on call" for regular music gigs. You may find that not all of your students are as devoted to the study of music as you were at their age and that your work schedule as a teacher often requires a twelve-hour or more commitment per day. You may want to find a partner for life and start a family. In short, you have to make adjustments to your ideals and professional aspirations. Dependent upon a variety of factors, the process of making those adjustments can be easy or difficult. All factors have to do with (1) the view you have of yourself as an aspiring musician, (2) how your training either has reinforced or thwarted your personal and musical hopes and dreams, and (3) how the people you associate with most closely respond to you and your career progress. Thinking about the learning and teaching of music in this way triggers important questions:

- How have you become who you think you are? Who influenced you?
- How do you interact musically with others around you either in personal face-to-face contacts or through the Internet?
- How do you react to those people around you who think unlike you or do not share your interest in music?

Answering these questions honestly will likely lead to some heightened awareness about what it means to think sociologically. In practical teacher terms, the awareness helps you get a grasp of "otherness" around you: why some of your students think unlike you, reject the repertoire you select for them, or continue to seem bored when you try hard to engage them in activities and conversations. You may also begin to understand why your school administrators, your students' parents, and the school community at large often attach different values to music and the arts in society than you do.

As early as 1991, the former editor of the *Music Educators Journal*, Charles Fowler, foresaw "troubled waters" for music as a curricular subject in the United States because of a continuous waning of public support for the arts as classically trained artists defined them (Fowler 1991). This trend seems to be ongoing despite efforts to propose new approaches to curriculum revisions and pedagogies. But changes in curricula and instructional imperatives require changing the minds of others. To do this successfully requires knowing your own socio-musical roots so that you discern social and cultural differences between yourself and those with whom you work on a daily basis. Becoming conscious of such differences makes it easier to communicate with other-minded students, parents, school administrators, and non-musician colleagues in ways that are familiar to them. When placing someone's socio-economic and cultural background into your own understanding of their societal contexts, you consider what has become known as an individual's socialization process. This chapter first describes that process briefly before focusing on one particular phase within that process, called occupational socialization (sometimes also referred to as professional socialization).

> **Small Group Discussion 1.1**
>
> Introduce yourselves to each other and talk about your respective family, musical, and educational backgrounds. Address the bulleted questions from the Introduction to this chapter, and include in your discussion experiences inside and outside of school that you believe had a bearing on your choice of studying music and/or becoming a music teacher.

Processes of Socialization

Beginning with infancy and continuing well into adulthood all the way into old age, your socialization processes reflect how you see yourself in light of who you believe you are at various stages of life. Three such stages have been "officially" recognized for a long time, but it is quite possible to name more. The primary socialization occurs during infancy in the interactions with your most immediate caregivers (parents, guardians, or other primary providers). The secondary socialization generally begins as you enter the phase of compulsory schooling and is usually assumed to last from pre-school or kindergarten onward all the way into high school and possibly even college. Once you make decisions about professional goals and your job training, the tertiary (adult) phase of socialization sets in, of which your occupational socialization is but one ongoing, critical part. In many nations, of course, the increasing emphasis on training for jobs and careers can blur the lines between the secondary and tertiary socialization phases.

Sociologists and social psychologists alike have been interested for a long time in knowing how (1) musicians acquire norms and values that contribute to their occupational belief systems, and (2) how working musicians uphold and hone those beliefs along with musical skills and knowledge throughout their careers (Heyer, Wachs, and Palentien 2013). Often on the basis of long-term observations of musicians at work, researchers have reported how musicians view their own roles and statuses in the organization(s) that hired them, their relationship to other members in the workforce (ensemble) and the conductor or bandleader, and what it means to be a hired hand in the music world. The studies talk about expectations of artistic and creative independence on the one hand and experiences as workers and replaceable "numbers" on the other. It is a conflict that can cause alienation from the workplace and—eventually—lead to burnout.

One does not, of course, need to belong to a union or professional members' organization, or even necessarily think of oneself as a "professional," to assume the identity of "musician." Fewer rather than more children and young adults pursue the study of music in order to find work later; rather, many who pursue excellence in music performance seek work in music because it affirms their musician identity, central to who they are or want to become. Nonetheless, the progression from dedicated music novice to accomplished music teacher tends to be slow when one moves from self-perceived musician to musician-teacher and from there to school music teacher and school employee.

From Musician to Musician-Teacher

You probably know from firsthand experience the close connection between early involvement in the making of music and the choices that eventually led to your decision to pursue music professionally. You remember the impact family members, teachers, and peers have had on those choices, and you can recall what engaged you in music so much that you opted to make it your livelihood. For many, going this route requires applied music lessons, playing in ensembles, and taking courses in music theory and musicology. These and obligatory "basic" courses fulfill or fulfilled a person's formal music education (and degree/certification/licensure) requirements. However, the act of making music itself is likely to contribute most directly to the image young people have of themselves as musicians, including images of becoming professional musicians.

One-to-one lessons and/or other modes and contexts of learning in Western classical music, jazz, or other styles of music each bring with them certain forms of expected conduct, contributing to musicians' senses of who they are. The identities of choral singers, orchestral musicians, "bedroom players," YouTube artists, or producers/composers working on laptops and tablets are similarly constructed—either through being part of face-to-face and online communities or through deep and dedicated learning processes of varying kinds (Green 2002; Smith 2013a). Each and every one of these music learning communities and situations functions as a powerful socializing agent.

There is likely nothing more sustaining than being a member in an ensemble of musicians who unite in the common purpose of making music—music that they write or have written or co-written, or music that they are "just" playing. As an integral part of a community of practice, an ensemble or even an online community of musicians becomes a system of enculturation. It affirms and strengthens a participant's identities as a musical and social person, one more reason why spending time alone in the practice room or at a digital audio workstation (DAW) may feel like a more tangible sign of belonging to a community of musicians than is typical for being enrolled in large academic classes either in education or other subject matter areas.

Apart from occasional teaching assignments in schools and on-site classroom visitations, for instance, most teacher education classes, frequently required for college music students seeking teacher certification, do not commonly allow for one-to-one mentoring processes similar to those provided by studio teachers. Sitting in the library, reading about educational policies, or debating curriculum theories does not usually compare favorably to the "formalized informal" peer-learning that playing in small ensembles can provide (Lebler 2008; Smith and Shafighian 2013). Thus, preparing to become a school music teacher might involve socialization experiences quite different from those that are typical of becoming a performing musician in a conservatory or a music academy setting.

From Musician-Teacher to School Music Teacher

Compulsory schooling, mandated by many industrialized nations, does not always include music as a curricular subject. Where it does, either as an elective (optional) or required course for a specified period of time, expectations vary with regard to what is being taught and learned: acquiring a repertoire of patriotic and/or seasonal songs in earlier years, studying one or more instruments in later years, and performing in choral and/or instrumental ensembles. At a more advanced level, music classes may provide instruction in the rudiments of music reading and music history, provide the intensive study of an instrument (or voice), and give opportunities for personal creativity through improvisation and composition. In some instances, schools may provide room for all of these and more activities, whereas other schools may not offer any such opportunities. It is this wide range of curricular expectations across countries, regions, and locales that signify the rather tenuous status of music as a curricular subject and may also impact the transition from aspiring musician to school music teacher. The tenuous status as a curricular subject reflects on the tenuous social status of those who teach music to children. Although the study of music may be considered an appropriate and welcomed activity for leisure pursuits of children and young adults of all social classes, the arts as a serious career choice tend to be less favorably viewed.

The Social Standing of the School Music Teacher

American cultural and literary historian Paul Fussel (1983/1992) observed for the United States that American families of the affluent upper-class and the "top out-of-sight" class tended to look down on the socio-economic standing and social class of individuals who pursue the formal study of music in preparation for an occupation. Thus, although socially and academically advantaged students (possibly not only in the United States) may enroll in music performance classes in high school, they are not generally encouraged by their families to continue their studies for professional purposes. According to Tom Parkinson and Gareth Dylan Smith (2015), this discouragement is also present in other countries, reinforced by mainstream media representations, and it may be even more prevalent for those musicians who study popular music.

On the one hand, then, more affluent students interested in the professional pursuit of music education may find such choice economically and socially counterproductive to their upholding their social status while, on the other hand, less affluent students may find private music study as a prerequisite to music teacher preparation courses prohibitive. From an economic standpoint, this is all the more troubling because teaching as a career may be perceived by individuals of lower socio-economic status as an upward-bound occupational move, but the choice of music as the teaching specialty may lessen that perception in some instances (Elpus and Abril 2011; Stewart 1992). Therefore, the combination of music as a leisure activity, perceived low professional prestige, and comparatively low to mid-level earnings in many countries, may override the vision of a teacher's job as being economically secure and stable. Such may not be the case, however, in countries where newly graduated teachers receive tenure (either as lifelong employees or employees with civil servant status) after stringent apprenticeship years of service and/or where music teachers are also experts in at least one other subject matter (Lindqvist, Nordänger, and Carlsson 2014). It is a demand, however, that moves the musician identity further into the background while the educator identity is placed into the foreground.

Reality Check 1.1

Consider the schooling environment in which you grew up. Talk with each other about this and the schooling environment in which you will likely work or already work and identify what you would consider the greatest differences/similarities between contexts.

Music Teaching as a Career in the Macro View of Occupations

Where does music teaching as a career fit into the hierarchy of other professions? Your own answer likely depends on where you grew up and now live and work. For sociologists, the answer lies in a combination of national census reports, local surveys, and individual interviews. Together, these sources can provide an overall picture of what it means to be a music teacher among many other occupations. For example, a national, comprehensive report for the United States, titled *The Changing Nature of Work: Implications for Occupational Analysis* (1999), piqued our interest. Jointly produced by the Committee on Techniques for the Enhancement of Human Performance: Occupational Analysis, the Commission on Behavioral and Social Sciences and Education, and the National Research Council, the report provides the following categorizations: both teachers and musicians are listed under Professional Specialty, but musicians are grouped under "Writers, Artists, and Entertainers" and teachers together with librarians and counselors, that is, individuals working as staff members. Apparently, music teachers fall somewhere in the middle of these two descriptors: somewhat autonomous musicians and decision makers in the classroom and staff members within a larger employment system. For part-time and freelance music teachers, the chasm between the two worlds may be even greater. Teachers—along with doctors and lawyers—were labeled as doing "interactive-emotion work" (156), a description equally applicable to musicians. However, no teacher group in the report, including that of music teacher, was singled out by specialty area, nor did the authors allow for multi-faceted or portfolio careers, whereby individuals may work in multiple roles. In this regard, Dawn Bennett (2008) presented a compelling case for re-conceptualizing "musicians" as more than only performers or composers. After all, for musicians, teaching often forms one of multiple income streams (Dolloff 2007; Musicians' Union 2012; Rivas-Caicedo 2017).

The non-specified job expectations typical of school music teaching as a career, as well as the variety of activities that fall under a school subject called music, may well reflect the somewhat precarious place of music as a valued skill and knowledge set in a particular society. This precariousness impacts the music teacher's occupational identity and his or her standing as an "education worker" among other employees, most of whom have other specialty areas. All such "education workers" are part of a system, however, that, depending on size and locale, imposes educational rules and regulations far removed from what teachers (music teachers included) have foremost on their minds when working in a classroom setting. Fitting into such a system takes knowledge of oneself and one's limitations and strengths, as well as of those with whom one interacts professionally. This kind of experiential learning falls under what sociologists call a person's occupational socialization. Although academic knowledge cannot replace lived experience, it can prepare you for it, as can details about what it means to choose music teaching as a career. It can inform you about expectations others have of you and what you should know when communicating with anyone who may not be certain of what it is that you do for a living.

Music Teachers as Subject Matter Experts and Staff Members

Music teachers' work commitments become visible through their dedication as musicians and pedagogues. Both types of commitment affirm and deepen a teacher's sense of being a professional music educator. Interestingly, though, the two sets of commitment can be (and often are) at odds with each other when characteristics unique to the chosen field of music can hinder a teacher's adjustment to the norms governing the workplace of school. Although well skilled as a highly trained performer and/or composer, producer, or musical director, a teacher's deep immersion in those skills and knowledge may potentially distract from instructional needs mandated by the learners present in the classroom.

Within the range of professional commitments that define a teacher beyond subject matter expertise and pedagogical skills are membership in educational and subject matter–related organizations, volunteering for certain duties in- and outside of school, and seeking contacts with colleagues for the purpose of advancing one's work as an artist, educator, or citizen in the world. Further commitments may also include various duties of providing and keeping in order (virtual) paper trails for pedagogical actions taken, raising funds for curricular or extra-curricular projects, filing funding reports, keeping records of student learning and remaining in touch with parents, preparing students for taking (standardized) tests, and being available for meetings and consultations as called by school administrators or governing boards. Experienced teachers usually have learned to accept these duties as integral to their job description. Novice teachers, however, tend to consider them as extraneous to their jobs. It is a sign of having become fully socialized to the norms and values of the teaching profession to accept such duties as component parts of one's occupation.

Thus far, relatively little is known about the roles the arts play in school curricula across the globe. In some countries, music and the arts are included in political conversations and public discourse about education and teacher training; in other countries, the arts are exempt from those debates. Therefore, the relationship between a teacher's function as subject matter expert (musician) and education expert (pedagogue) remains under-researched on a comparative, international scale. Locally, that is, specific to a particular country, the number of studies has continued to increase steadily since the end of the twentieth century (e.g., Austin, Isbell, and Russell 2010; Chong, Low, and Goh 2011; Hammel 2011; Isbell 2008, 2009; L'Roy 1983; Roberts 1991a and b, 1993; Swennen, Volman, and van Essen 2008; Vogt, Heß, and Rolle 2012).

It could be argued that efforts must now be made to obtain a fuller picture of school music teachers around the world and, along with such a picture, to formulate a comprehensive policy framework across countries (Cooper and Alvarado 2006). In that regard, it might be of value to ascertain the extent to which, especially, female teachers see themselves more as artist or as educator, or find the roles inseparable. After all, the view individual teachers have of themselves impacts directly on what their learners take away from schooling experiences. Similarly, the view a teacher holds toward the roles of musician, pedagogue, or both also affects his or her interactions with teaching colleagues and school administrators.

Interview Project 1.1

Select three to five classmates for outside-of-class conversations about the choices they made to enroll in music, major in music education, and/or pursue advanced degrees in music education. Compare your classmates' stories with your own and discuss how your respective stories might impact your future work.

A Music Teacher's Occupational Norms and Values

Hardly any sociological dictionary defines the terms "norm" and "value" without referring also to their interdependence. Social norms are rules or principles of behavior that define a particular social group and determine the values that are shared by the individuals in a group. Applied to the normative behavior of professionally trained musicians, their values stem from embracing musical traditions, conventions, and expectations that, as Gruhn (1999) suggested, accept music "as an art form" first and only secondarily "as a mode of expression." Although Gruhn applied this distinction specifically to the study of classical music, we believe it to be an apt one for all musicians who are in serious pursuit of their art and craft. This is not to say that music as an art form cannot also be or become a mode of expression, but the demands in terms of skills and ongoing practice and study may differ.

Not all students who enter into formal education at conservatories or music schools are prepared for facing the demands of professional preparation as a musician, among them stamina, endurance, creativity, repetition, entrepreneurship, analytic awareness, and the tenacious willingness to work through disappointment and even failure. Furthermore, listening to music with analytic clarity and score in hand is a different form of listening than immersing oneself emotionally in favorite songs or instrumental compositions. The critical study of music theory and history as two sub-disciplines in the larger discipline of music demands a similarly intellectual approach to what so frequently is referred to as purely "emotive" work.

Acknowledging distinctions that individuals and societies make between music as an art form and as a mode of personal expression is crucial in understanding why societal values for music and the arts are not necessarily the same as those shared by highly trained musician-artists. The distinction has also led to important philosophies about music and the arts, all of which bear on what music educators do. Clearly, though, becoming socialized to the role of a professionally trained musician means to engage in those activities that other professionally trained musicians have established as the norms of the musics they perform and the careers they pursue. However, upon graduation and beginning their first teaching jobs, novice music teachers often enter new normative cultures—those of the schools that have hired them. Here, advancing musical skills in the students ranks likely second to institutional demands of contributing to the learning of basic, functional skills, maintaining discipline among the pupils, keeping pace with administrative routines, and fitting in with the rest of the teaching staff. Inexperienced teachers, usually still unfamiliar with those role expectations, may encounter what sociologists call *role distance*. It is a feeling that can ultimately lead to role conflicts in the workplace (see Goffman 1959/1973; Scott and Marshall 2009). Music teachers may face these conflicts when dealing with who they are as musicians and as employed educators. Whether perceived or affirmed by others, it is often those conflicts that make it difficult for music specialists to become fully integrated members of the teaching and wider school staff.

For many years, thinkers have seen the value and purpose of school music education in enhancing leisure pursuits (e.g., Elkington and Stebbins 2014; Kaplan 1951; Keil 1966/1991; Stebbins 1992). It is an idea that has gained renewed momentum among more recent music educators (e.g., Higgins 2012; Mantie and Smith 2016; Mantie and Talbot 2015). Many authors champion music learning for the betterment of people's lives in more general terms (e.g., Green 2002, 2008a, 2011; Partti 2012; Wright 2010). Looking to set free the empowering musical potential of all individuals by democratizing education, music is seen by such writers as having the potential to help de-marginalize minority students and teachers, setting a course for a socially just society, and enabling a lifelong pursuit of musical interests to enhance every citizen's quality of life.

Identity Research on Musicians

As long ago as 1969, American sociologist Charles Kadushin used the term *professional musician* to indicate an individual wanting to perform rather than teach music for a living. Joining the musicians' union, getting paid for one's work, and the winning of competitions were the deciding factors for seeing oneself as a member of the occupation "professional musician." The students interviewed by Kadushin were enrolled in the Manhattan and the Juilliard schools of music, institutions without music teacher education programs. However, later studies with students in locales that featured music education as a degree choice yielded similar results.

Music students preparing to become music teachers showed a strong allegiance with full-time performers while their identities as future music teachers/educators remained weak. Furthermore, exposure to the teacher role did not necessarily lead to a stronger sense of self as an educator. More recent research on pre- and in-service music teachers in English-speaking countries has made similar suggestions, following comprehensive summaries of pertinent literature in the contexts of their own original investigations (e.g., Austin et al. 2010; Ballantyne 2005; Ballantyne, Kerchner, and Aróstegui 2012; Berg and Miksza 2010; Haston and Russell 2012; Russell 2012; Scheib 2006). Other researchers have contended that the label of "musician" has often been reduced by music conservatories and in the public consciousness to meaning "performer" rather than keeping the term wide open to include being a teacher, composer, producer, entrepreneur, and occupying myriad other roles (Bennett 2008; Hallam and Gaunt 2012; Smith 2013b). In their view, being called a musician signifies a lifestyle, not only an employment or career choice, or exclusively what one does when playing an instrument or singing for pay.

British social psychologists and musicians Raymond MacDonald, David Hargreaves, and Dorothy Miell (2002) looked at the relationship between an individual and the music-making process, the resultant identities being called musical identities. It is a social-psychological way of examining a broad social construct. In North America, sociologists with an interest in music and musicians with an interest in sociology generally focused on how musicians:

- Saw themselves as members of a workforce (e.g., Becker 1976, 1982; Coffman 1971; Etzkorn 1966; Faulkner 1971, 1973; Frederickson and Rooney 1988; Kamerman and Martorella 1983; Kealy 1974, 1980; McCall and Simmons 1978; Nash 1954, 1957, 1961; Nielsen 1999; Rumbelow 1969; Stebbins 1966, 1964, 2010).
- Prepared to enter the workforce (Kaplan 1966; Kingsbury 1988/2010; L'Roy 1983; Martin 1995, 2005, 2006; Nettl 1995; Roberts 1991a, 1993, 2007).

Other such efforts beyond English-speaking countries will be addressed in later chapters.

Identity scholarship clearly bridges sociological and psychological perspectives, thereby often being labeled social-psychological research and making it difficult to see where one approach ends and the other begins. However, we concur with Brian Roberts's (2007) sociologically reasoned assertion that one might want to refer to identity construction rather than development. At the same time, we also agree with authors MacDonald et al.'s (2002) social-psychological position that music identities inseparably connect social and musical selves at the most individual (and, thus, psychological) level. As Lucy Green (2014) observed, sociologists consider identity (among other things) as a phenomenon both *constructed* and *construed.* This relationship is partly explained by Smith's (2013a) model of the Snowball Self. As with all metaphors, this necessarily comes from particular realities; balls of snow are, of course, likely unfamiliar to people who live in warmer climates. Hopefully, though, the snowball imagery can illustrate some of the processes inherent in what Smith called identity realization.

A Model for Identity Realization

The Snowball Self (see Figure 1.1) is a model that presents the self—*who a person is*—as a figurative, autonomous snowball, rolling down a mountainside gathering form and shape in the process. Thus does the self as it takes form while moving down the "piste" of life. Identities in this model are portrayed as existing at three "levels"—(1) the overall concept one has of one's (snowball) self; (2) separate and overlapping, intersecting identities within this larger self, such as musician, teacher, writer, sibling, parent (see Figure 1.2); and (3) contextual identities, which are the identities that we realize day to day, hour to hour, and minute to minute as we navigate and negotiate who we are in different areas and moments of our lives.

Figure 1.1 Showing the Snowball Self

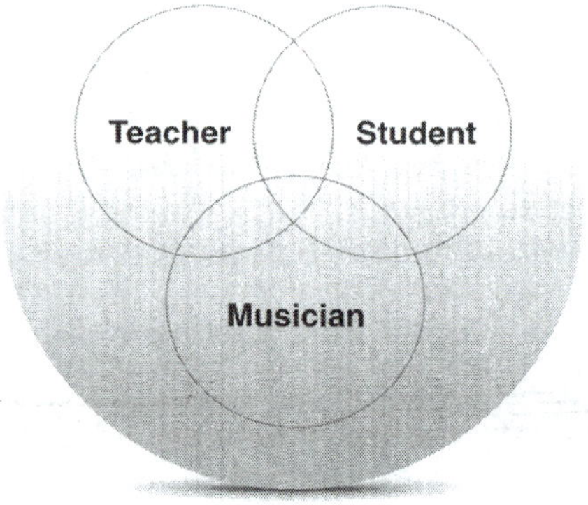

Figure 1.2 Showing Intersecting Identities within the Snowball Self

The model is based on two "realizations"—identity and learning. Two meanings of the verb "to realize" become important: (1) to make something real or make it happen, and (2) to understand something, to "get it." The first is an active doing; the second a more passive process of awareness.

- **Active identity realization** refers to any instance of someone going about being or trying to become, for instance, a musician. This involves immersing oneself in musical traditions, communities and activities and acquiring the necessary attitudes and skills. Active identity realization follows and leads to passive identity realization.

- **Passive identity realization** refers to understanding who you are, for example, feeling like a musician or seeing yourself as a teacher; this may happen during and after key life moments such as a successful concert performance, creation of a satisfying production in a DAW, or (as in Gareth's earlier example), being recognized by others as a teacher.
- **Active learning realization** refers to all the ways in which people seek to learn things and the ways in which that learning takes place, for instance, taking lessons in voice or an instrument, watching online tutorial videos on how to use a DAW, or jamming with friends in a band learning songs.
- **Passive learning realization** refers to recognizing or understanding that you have learned something unintentionally, for instance, realizing in a concert band rehearsal that all the musical decisions are being made by the conductor and the composer and you have no creative autonomy there as a clarinetist; discovering through relentlessly practicing jazz chops that you're really a better rock or hip-hop drummer; or (as in Hildegard's earlier example) discovering through your work as a teacher the immense joy derived from interacting with students.

Learning realization and identity realization work together as follows. Passive identity realization is a moment of discovery, of learning. Active identity realization requires active learning realization (one cannot be a musician or teacher without developing appropriate skills and attributes). Passive learning realization is a by-product of active identity realization and active learning realization. Active identity realization and active learning realization lead to passive identity realization and passive learning realization, which, in turn, can lead to active identity realization and active learning realization.

All realization of identities and learning contributes to the realization of one's overall Snowball Self (Smith 2013a, 21; see Figure 1.3). Learning and identity realization are not only symbiotic and mutual but also often amount to and are experienced as the same thing. Learning about oneself, therefore, is both learning realization and identity realization, and people never, ever stop learning, being, and becoming all the time they're alive.

Learning realization and identity realization occur in each of our discrete identities and across them as they overlap. What is being learned while actively realizing one's teacher identities can equally apply to what is being learned while making music, and vice versa. The main "takeaway" from this model is that, as Lucy Green (2002) emphasized, learning and identity are so intertwined as to be inseparable. This is one of the threads present in each of the following chapters.

When people begin teaching full-time, they can find themselves "juggling" this job among other musician-related work. Some seem to keep all their "plates spinning," but this can easily lead to "burning your candle at both

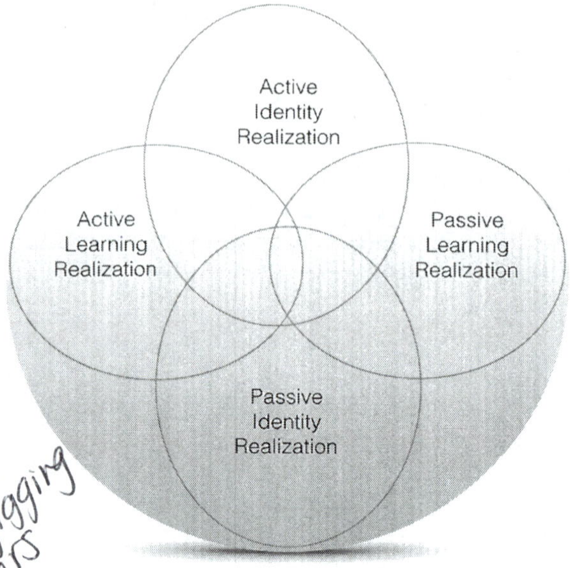

Figure 1.3 Showing Intersections of Identity Realization and Learning Realization

ends." Everyone needs to rest, "chill out," and sleep. You may *actively realize* your music teacher identity while *passively realizing* say, primarily your performer, composer, or producer identities. In addition, there also may be identities of parent, sibling, and/or colleague. All need to be paid attention to either passively or actively. Time away from teaching may be spent attending to family, writing music, performing at open-mic nights, or rehearsing music with others either professionally or as amateurs. You *actively realize* other musician and/or non-musician identities while *passively realizing* your teacher identity.

None of this identity movement and realization is fixed, and you may eventually replace some identities with others; this applies across job roles, career trajectories, and other life changes large and small. When thinking pluralistically about such identity shifts as a music teacher, you do not necessarily replace one set of abilities and attributes with another but learn to frame your various roles and responsibilities (including responsibility to yourself) and multiple obligations (including deadlines) as "career creativities" (Bennett 2013). Engaging in those creativities can reveal a music educator's many contributions to society. They certainly benefit those students who might begin seeing you, their teacher, not as a one-dimensional but a dynamic and multifaceted human being.

Small Group Discussion 1.2

1. Discuss your memories of classmates who participated in the same high school ensemble(s) you took part in but who made it very clear that going into music professionally "was not for them." Try to recall their reasons and how you reacted to them at the time.
2. Recall instances of each of the types of realization explained in this chapter: passive identity realization, active identity realization, passive learning realization, and active learning realization.
3. Do this for your identities as musician and teacher and consider the extent to which these could be one and the same.

Further Thoughts from Gareth and Hildegard about Their Respective Occupational Socialization

Hildegard: Gareth, would you make the same career choices again that you made years ago?

Gareth: Yes. I have made a point throughout my career of enjoying myself (and I realize I have been very fortunate to be able to make this choice, over and over again). The things I like doing most are making music, writing (blogging, academic writing, and limericks), and teaching. — It's okay for music to not be the thing you love most at all times

Hildegard: You mean, in that order?

Gareth: The order varies, partly because I have a low boredom threshold (maybe I'm just very impatient), and because all music making, writing, and teaching experiences are not equal; sometimes a bad gig can provide high-quality cathartic blogging or classroom material; less-than-perfect teaching or writing moments can make a performance all the more rewarding. I have worked hard to ensure I always maintain a shifting but tolerable balance between these necessary (to me) activities. The choices that led me to study music, to learn about education, and to undertake doctoral and post-doctoral research have made me who I am, and I get to learn and develop every day. Life is exciting and good. What about you, Hildegard?

Hildegard: Although I sometimes wished that, early in my career, I had explored much more seriously than I did, other professional options and avenues in addition to teaching music, life continues to be exciting and good but I am not sure that it is due to music education as my career choice. It is true that I have never regretted doing what I have done throughout my career: teach, make music, think about it, listen to it, and write about what it means being a music educator and scholar. I am not sure, though, that, as a group, music educators have been very successful in strengthening the position of music as a subject in the hierarchy of other school subjects. We still have work to do.

Key Sources (for full information, see References)

Becker, Howard. 1976, 1982/1984/2008.
Bennett, Dawn E. 2008.
Berg, Margaret H. and Peter Miksza. 2010.
Chong, Sylvia, Low Ee Ling, and Goh Kim Chuan. 2011.
Elkington, Sam and Robert A. Stebbins. 2014.
Green, Lucy. 2014.
Kaplan, Max. 1966.
Kealy, Edward R. 1974, 1980.
Roberts, Brian A. 1991a, 1991b, 1993, 2007.
Russell, Joshua A. 2012.
Stebbins, Robert A. 1992.
Swennen, Anja, Monique Volman, and Mineke van Essen. 2008.
Vogt, Jürgen, Frauke Heß and Christian Rolle. 2012.

2

Music Learning and Teaching as Socially Situated Acts

This chapter addresses how societal macro realities connect to micro pedagogical decisions in terms of:

- Music as a Subject in the Social Realities of School
- Compulsory Schooling as Transmitter of Societal Values
- Authenticity of Musical Engagement and Pedagogic Authority
- Pedagogical (Re-)Orientations to Adolescents' Learning Needs

Gareth: When I was hired to teach music in an independent north London primary school in September 2001, I was comforted to know that the headmaster appreciated my fondness for folk-rock and protest music from the 1960s and 1970s (although I don't recall how the subject cropped up in my interview for the position). Taking this empowering message into my teaching, I based much of my curriculum and the content for the twice-yearly concerts around music with which I was familiar, and I set about improving my skills as a guitarist to help pull it all off. I also worked with individual children to help them sing songs that they liked and which they knew from listening to music at home. I quickly came to realize that many parents of students at this school liked what I was doing. The parents were mostly close enough to my age at that time that there was considerable crossover in terms of our musical tastes and, therefore, the musical preferences with which those parents had instilled their offspring. Were I to find myself teaching elementary school general music again, I wonder how I might go about the job. Would I place (perhaps more consciously this time) similar value on the musical preferences of the headmaster, and how far would (or could) I go to develop the knowledge and skills necessary to ascertain the "best" music education experience for the children? How would I locate my music classroom, and the experiences I enabled and curated there, in the complex social context of the school with its multiple stakeholders and overlapping interests and agendas?

Hildegard: Most of my years of teaching took place in higher education, but the main question that has been with me for my entire career continues to be: how do we make choices as the experts we profess and others believe us to be, and how do those choices impact those around us? Whether teaching a third grader to play the recorder or a doctoral student to engage in doing research, what are the messages our learners take with them? How do the things we do and suggest they do, fit into their worlds? How well did I know those worlds, and how different was mine from theirs?

Introduction

What do you understand to be the aims of music education? Where does that understanding come from, why do you think the way you do, and what might be reasons you do not think something different? Regardless of your personal answers to these rather general questions, activities and aims of music education vary between individual teachers, students, policy makers, schools, and governments. As a teacher you perhaps expect, or you may be expected, to prepare students for a high degree of competence in performance, or it might be that your work environment prizes creativity, composition, improvisation, or multi-instrumental capability. Do you have national standards or a curriculum to which you will be held accountable, and if so, to what extent are these compatible with the expectations of your school's administrative leadership, governing boards, or the aspirations of students in your classes? Maybe you hope to foster in your students a love of music that leads to a life of music making that they enjoy, or perhaps you want them to win competitions in singing or instrumental performance for their school. The total of all of these possibilities (and many more not listed) connects music teachers worldwide regardless of individual circumstances. Assuming that there are universal expectations shared by everyone that teachers teach and students learn, this chapter is about the social fact that neither music education nor music as a school subject exists in a vacuum. The selves of music learners and teachers are both embedded in their own personal worlds and also in the context of compulsory schooling as a political mandate. It is in the plurality of those contexts that relationships are forged, either negative, positive, or indifferent.

For positive relationships to be formed—a likely goal of all educators—students must feel that what they bring to the (music) schooling process is being taking seriously and accepted by the teacher, classmates, and other school authorities as being authentic and important. When that happens, the teacher likely gains pedagogical authority in the eyes of the learner. In this chapter, we address how music pedagogy and pedagogic authority connect to what the learner brings to the schooling process as personal, that is, authentic, musical knowledge. We do this by beginning with music as a school subject in the social realities of compulsory education. From there, we connect those macro level educational concerns to individual students' authentic musical engagements and each teacher's desire to gain increased pedagogic authority by finding new pedagogic solutions to persistent challenges facing not only music educators but all educators. There is hardly any school teacher who does not look for better ways by which to reach her or his students. We call this search mode pedagogic re-orientation.

Music as a Subject in the Social Realities of School

Within the context of school music, music education is integrated into educational traditions and school policies that must be actively dealt with in any decisions of what and how to teach. However, Canadian Stephanie Horsley (2015, 63) lamented that music educators have often "demonstrated a historical avoidance of issues related to politics, citizenship, and social justice." American Canadian cultural critic Henry Giroux (2016) highlighted a similar reticence among educators more generally. He wrote of the militarized finance state of which teachers in industrialized nations are a part and describes a pervasive political ideology that dismantles public and higher education systems around the world, in particular the global north. Such ideology, he maintained, runs the risk of students, teachers, and parents—among other stakeholders in the system—becoming angered by or disillusioned with the system or its effects, but being unable to see or to understand why (Freire 1968/1970/2000; Giroux 2001, 2014; Hebert 2015; Illich 1971). Finding the current pervasive neoliberal capitalist order to be cruel, sociopathic, and destructive, Giroux urged educators anywhere to act against that order with "passion, courage, and conviction" (2016, 108) to engender a more compassionate and critically aware society. Such action, however, may not always be possible or advisable—given individual, politically controlled circumstances.

Canadians Roberta Lamb and Niyati Dhokai (2015, 124) suggested that, similar to music educators in general, music education scholarship, too, has exhibited a tendency to live in a historically unaware perpetual present. However, as Paul Woodford (2012) contended, it is essential for music teachers to be aware of the socio-political climate and context that frame and determine their work and how it is perceived and received by others. Diane Reay (2010) and other sociologists of education described how education systems, from schools through to universities, serve to create, reinforce, and institutionalize social boundaries, an issue that permeates any sociology of music education. When holding to and promoting sets of social values that a majority of people consider to be the lay of the land, Lucy Green (2008b, 19) described such promotion as "a historically-bound way of constructing the world . . . [that] arises in accordance with the nature of its society, but it also acts back upon that society and influences the ways that individuals perceive and understand things." The more rigorously certain values are emphasized over others, the easier it is to discount, disengage, and disenfranchise anyone whose values do not match up with those in the (frequently silent) majority.

French sociologist, anthropologist, and philosopher Pierre Bourdieu referred to the social and societal underpinning of a person's beliefs and value assumptions as "habitus," explaining:

> The individual, the subjective, is social and collective. The habitus is socialised subjectivity, a historical transcendental, whose schemes of perceptions and apperception (systems of appreciation, tastes, etc.) are the product of collective and individual history. Reason (or rationality) is "bounded" not only . . . because the human mind is generically bounded . . . but because it is socially structured and determined, and, as a consequence, limited.
>
> (Bourdieu 2005, 211)

In plain text, school (music) teachers should always keep in mind that they work with people whose experiences, culture, and upbringing are different from those of the teachers and that each person's socialization processes, therefore, result in the construction of differently perceived realities. Working in a democratic society demands from its teachers that they incorporate knowledge of differences in experiences and perceptions in their daily lessons. Music teachers are asked to turn classroom spaces into places of opportunity through music-learning for all students, not just a select few.

Hardly anyone easily understands or appreciates that which is unfamiliar to them. Applying this seeming truism to the kind of music repertoire often taught in school music, Ruth Wright (2010, 48) critically commented that it is not (or should not be) "to reject western art music [or] . . . claim the superiority of other, including popular, genres. And it is certainly not to deny the irremediable task of education to enable students to recognize and realize decontextualized knowledge processes." Instead, Wright suggested, choices in repertoire should be about "the necessity of doing what it takes to make the latter possible," referring here to fostering in students the ability to place musical knowledge of all kinds into their appropriate and original contexts.

Although students are nearly always interested in music, even an expressed interest does not necessarily equate to an interest in *music in school* or an interest in *school music* (which are frequently perceived as the same thing). Working with students using music that is central to their identities can enact a more democratic educational experience in the music classroom (Green 2002).

Conversely, the act of discounting students' music—when it is so central to students' lives and sense of self—can distance students from the teacher and the educational experience as a whole. Accepting and valuing the musical knowledge and skills all learners bring to the schooling process, therefore, is essential in turning school experiences into learning for life.

Compulsory Schooling as Transmitter of Societal Values

For many years, the international community as represented by UNESCO-affiliated organizations has publicly addressed goals and objectives of compulsory education and its purposes worldwide to be reached by 2030. Among the numerous reports published as the result of committee deliberations at various levels of political power, seventeen basic goals have been identified that range from ending poverty, hunger, and racial as well as gender discrimination, to reducing other inequalities wherever possible—aiming for availability of clean water and sanitation everywhere, protecting living organisms below and above water, striving for peace and justice among all nations, and achieving all of these goals through relevant international partnerships (UNESCO 2014a and b, 2015a, b and c). The sustainable development goal #4 reads: "to ensure inclusive and equitable quality education and promote lifelong learning opportunities for all" (UNESCO 2014b, 21). If and when the goals are shared as targets to be reached worldwide, numerous objectives are no less ambitious, among them:

> [F]ree, equitable and quality primary and secondary education for all boys and girls; access to quality early childhood development, care and pre-primary education; equal access for all women and men to affordable and quality technical, vocational and tertiary education, including university; [and] a substantial increase [in] the number of youth and adults who have relevant skills, including technical and vocational skills, for employment, decent jobs and entrepreneurship.
>
> (UNESCO 2015b, 21–22)

Other objectives follow, most of which speak more to goals of literacy and numeracy than morality, and they remain a summation of desired wishes among an international community of (mostly) education experts and politicians.

The goals raise fundamental questions about the place and function of compulsory education in particular nation-states. For example, the report titled *Rethinking Education: Towards a Global Common Good?* (UNESCO 2015c) speaks to the difficulties of working toward the goal of sustaining ecological, economic, cultural, and educational values to which each nation-state aspires. Because compulsory education is considered a major contributor to achieving this broad goal, answers are needed to the question of "what knowledge is acquired and why [and] where, when and how [is] it . . . used . . . [by] individuals and society alike?" (UNESCO 2015c, 17).

Although the questions may appear legitimate and timely, Bourdieu and Passeron (1977, 5) would counter that "all pedagogic action is, objectively, symbolic violence insofar as it is the imposition of a cultural arbitrary by an arbitrary power." However, many other sociologists (a few of whom will be introduced by name in Chapter 5) accept schools as institutions in which certain standards of behavior, set by those in power, are to be transmitted by teachers to students. Compulsory education is an expected "gesture" of society, one that is as binding as are voting and paying taxes. It is a requirement ("rite of passage") that modern societies have instituted as a vehicle for societal enculturation and acculturation. This model presupposes an agreed-upon value system shared by a particular group of people within the hierarchy of social groups composing society. Often referred to as "the ruling class," it is not always clear, however, who has membership in that class: are appointed or elected representatives among "the haves"? The educated? Individuals of a particular skin color, or the able bodied? Furthermore, how do those "in power" delegate their responsibilities to other decision makers and trendsetters in a particular society, those—for example—who become the policy makers for education and schooling?

Answers to the previous questions vary, depending upon the political system that defines a nation-state and on the theoretical model explaining that system. When schools serve as the official transmitters of agreed-upon knowledge and skills, schools become the "gatekeepers" for determining what that knowledge is and what an educated/schooled citizen should be. The previously cited UNESCO reports attempt to provide international guidelines in that regard (for a detailed account of other international models, see Spring 2016). The reports speak to how much agreement can be expected to exist (and actually does exist) not only among nation-states but also, by extension, in the regions of a given country.

Industrialized democracies and, increasingly, smaller, developing nation-states tend to name as core values of what makes a "good life": health, material prosperity, being free from oppression of many kinds, such as being able to worship freely and speak one's mind. Along with material prosperity goes industrial prosperity, a goal that requires a workforce to contribute actively to the goals of material wealth and physical and spiritual well-being. The purpose of schools in society lies on the acquisition of skills and knowledge that have the greatest potential for enabling society to reach these goals. Historically, therefore, mathematical and scientific literacy have topped other educational goals, a point repeatedly criticized by educators in the humanities and arts and by educators in countries that do not share in the core value of individual prosperity and happiness as a basic human right.

Numerous social critics past and present (among them Bourdieu, Freire, Giroux, and Illich), have questioned the validity of educational goals that foster—if not cement—a market-driven economy (see also Chapter 6). Such practice, they have asserted, legitimizes and widens the gulf between those who participate in material wealth and those who do not. The widening gulf means ever greater poverty, alienation, and aggression of the "have nots" from the rest of society. Therefore, values that are traditionally sanctioned and transmitted to children through schooling do not and cannot create a better society *for all*, regardless of how time-proven they seem to be to certain groups in society. Therefore, and in order to move forward as a democratic nation-state, citizens should be encouraged from childhood on to think about what benefits everyone in society in equal measure. Such thinking requires a broad range of learning options and creative freedoms beyond the boundaries of accepted school learning.

In the conviction that compulsory, state-regulated, formal schooling cannot offer a diverse range of options and deliver instruction in creativity and divergent thinking, alternative and new models of learning are being sought that place first the need of each individual learner to teach himself or herself. Transmission of knowledge should have the declared purpose of transforming individual learners into independent thinkers (Apple, Ball, and Gandin 2010; Giroux 1988). This, in turn, would have the potential of changing society into a better (that is, socially just and equitable) national community.

The call for transformation, rather than transmission of knowledge alone, as the ultimate purpose of schooling has obtained renewed momentum in recent years (e.g., Arum, Beattie, and Ford 2011; Dimitrova, Bender, and van de Vijver 2014; Downes 2014; Gaztambide-Fernández and Sears 2004; Gorski and Landsman 2013; Sensoy and DiAngelo 2012; Suša 2009). All learners, regardless of background and prior experiences, should be given equal opportunities to become creators and active users of knowledge that contributes to the betterment of society. However, shifting the learner from a more or less passive receiver of knowledge to a participating, active contributor to the creation of new knowledge also requires re-thinking the teacher's role as prescribed knowledge dispenser into that of a facilitator of learning and independent decision maker. The corresponding pedagogy in that regard is similar to what American educator Donald Schön (1930–1997) called reflection-*in-action*. He took the blueprint for the model from his experiences as an advanced student of piano and clarinet and the one-on-one coaching he experienced during that time of his studies (for more, see Schön 1983; Rudolph and Frankel 2009; Yanow and Tsoukas 2009). However, although a fruitful merging of pedagogy and music, the studio model envisioned by Schön and others for all types of learning contains challenges for both teacher and student.

The studio model presumes that the learner wants to learn what the teacher has to offer. It demands individualization in the privacy of either a one-on-one teaching situation or in small group settings. Classroom management and related disciplinary actions would not concern the "trouble(d) kid" alone but everyone. As facilitators of learning, teachers would be asked to help their students develop intellectually (and musically) at a rate appropriate to each student's individual interests and predispositions. Accountability measures would be determined less by test scores and more on observing students' actions in the learning process.

Observation becomes an integral part of the teaching process: First, the teacher assesses what each learner brings to the educational experience. Second, the teacher accepts and affirms that what the student brings to learning is legitimate and important. Third, all subsequent teaching steps (and musical engagements) build on what the teacher has affirmed as authentic and "real" in the mind of the student. By most accounts, curricula often do not provide enough room for the first two steps in the sequence. It is a prerequisite, however, for what is to follow in the name of transformational learning.

Authenticity of Musical Engagement and Pedagogic Authority

Not only music education scholars but also ethnomusicologists and cultural theorists discuss the issue of authenticity in reproducing musical styles and genres in many performance venues (for details, see Chapter 4). Invariably, these venues and styles include such contemporary styles as punk, hip-hop, and numerous other forms of musical expression. Acknowledged as the preferred means of musical expression for the current generation of learners in many parts of the world (Campbell 1998; Green 2008a; Kallio 2015; Parkinson and Smith 2015), their exclusion from music education in the classroom has become unthinkable to teachers who wish to reach their students where they are. This is a long-standing pedagogic principle, most famously argued for in the English language by American education reformer and philosopher John Dewey (1934) along with many who followed in his footsteps, including music educators. They accept to work with what has meaning for students, while helping them empathically and non-condescendingly toward finding beneficial pathways for living their lives. That goal, however, implies that the music performed and listened to in music class is contextually authentic and not "tampered with" by the teacher to where it becomes "school music."

Authenticity of Musical Engagement

As Green noted, "unless the musical instruments are authentic and the skill is adequate, it is useless to pretend that classroom music is in any style, other than a special classroom style" (2008b, 253). Heavy metal is only heavy metal, and reggae is only reggae, when played on the right instruments at the right volumes in a context that is appropriate for the style. The blues played on Orff instruments is likely perceived as an inauthentic classroom exercise. After all, Sister Rosetta Tharpe and Stevie Ray Vaughan did not become the iconic blues musicians they are by playing xylophones. Music makers and audiences want music to be authentic, or at least to seem authentic from particular cultural perspectives. Knowing about and understanding these perspectives give meaning of authenticity to experiencing music (Moore 2003). However, because there are so many different perspectives, the concept of authenticity is highly variable. It may, therefore, be asking for the impossible to ever be fully authentic in one's music making.

Instead, we follow Bradley's (2015) and Schippers' (2010) advice that it might be preferable to engage students in ways that are relevant and meaningful in their own minds rather than being trapped by worries about being "objectively" and measurably authentic.

Small Group Discussion 2.1

Discuss what high school students of today might call "authentic" music. What is authentic music in your own experience? How useful could this term be when, for instance, determining repertoire for music listening classes; appraising student compositions, songs, and production; and when selecting (or having students select) performance repertoire?

Pedagogic Authority

As relationships are forged in music classrooms on a daily basis, students—consciously or unconsciously—accord *pedagogic authority* (PAu) to people, music, and systems that shape their learning environments. It is a term coined by Bourdieu and Passeron (1977) to describe the influence that is ascribed by learners rather than assumed by teachers. Music learners might, for instance, attribute PAu to older peers in a local hip-hop community, to a revered studio piano teacher, an admired family member, to a choir director or orchestral conductor, or to the music leader in a place of worship. However, PAu can also be attributed to books, recordings, television shows, or similar media. For instance, someone preparing to become a producer might accord PAu to particular recordings produced using a classic analogue recording console and two-inch tape or a DAW (e.g., ProTools, Logic, or Digital Performer). Another example might be a songwriter/composer who accords PAu to *OK Computer* by Radiohead, Beethoven's *Symphony No. 3*, or *To Pimp a Butterfly* by Kendrick Lamar.

PAu may also be accorded to the system of graded examinations as it is made available through the Associated Board of the Royal Schools of Music. Similarly, local, state, and national brass band competitions and competitive school band festivals in the United States can have pedagogic authority, as can talent contests found the world over. Sometimes, the individuals, traditions, and practices to whom and to which your students ascribe pedagogic authority can be motivating, inspiring, and empowering. But they can also be harmful or unlawful. The connection between learning and identity construction is inextricable; it is "part of the narrative process of identity construction and construal" (Smith 2013a, 6). Worded slightly differently, learning is integral to the act of constructing and construing one's identity and inevitably changes people, implying a *de facto* alteration to what a person knows, understands, or can do.

As Colin Durrant (2003, 13) suggested, learning turns human capabilities into abilities. Such transformation occurs when the learners accept the teacher's pedagogic authority, a process that takes time, trust, and open-mindedness on everyone's part. One always hopes, of course, that the individuals, traditions, and practices to whom and to which students ascribe pedagogic authority motivate, inspire, and empower them to live up to their fullest (positive) potential. But pedagogic authority can also apply to gang leaders, hateful lyrics that entice violence, or lifestyles of musicians who abuse substances.

Not only students ascribe pedagogic authority when learning, but teachers do, too, when they uphold certain traditions and pedagogies over others or favor familiarity of repertoire over what is unfamiliar to them. Questions you might, therefore, answer for yourself as the teacher you are or want to become, include the following: to whom do you ascribe pedagogic authority in your own learning? Your own teachers? Your students? Your colleagues? Particular books you read? This book? How do you react to having to learn new repertoire or to seeing the world through your students' eyes?

When considering pedagogic authority, you might thank about what Lucy Green (2008b) referred to as *celebration*, *alienation*, and *ambiguity* through musical experiences can arise equally when pupils and teachers with diverse backgrounds, tastes, preferences, assumptions, and social conditioning come together in school music settings. We hasten to add, of course, that not all of your students will feel equally celebrated, alienated, or ambiguous in all music classes. After all, attempting to reach students with the same effects at all times would be a project doomed to certain failure. Also, it would be difficult to imagine that students learned anything if they remained perpetually in their respective cultural comfort zones.

The reason for exploring pedagogic authority as a concept lies in explaining to your students the differences in reaction and reception to music education in school settings. When embracing the phenomenon as real and embedding it firmly in your mind, you should be able to make authentic repertoire decisions. You may not always know exactly and right away the effects of those decisions on your students, but your awareness of how your choices and actions affect and impact students' perceptions will alter your own mind-set and, ultimately, earn pedagogic authority from your students. You might even become a curriculum expert who helps put in place curricula, materials, and teaching methods that empower students to become their own teachers (see Chapter 6).

Small Group Discussion 2.2

Think of the people, music, and institutions to which you, personally, ascribe pedagogic authority. Share these with your peers in a small group and consider how common or different ascriptions of PAu in your group could lead to (mis-)understandings. How would you as a teacher incorporate such knowledge into your own lessons?

Pedagogical (Re-)Orientations to Adolescents' Learning Needs

The processes of identity construction and construal (realization) are continuous throughout a person's life (Erikson 1950; Frith 1996; Hall 1996), but the age of adolescent youth has repeatedly been identified as a period of significant change in young people's sense of themselves. It is around this time that puberty occurs and that many teenagers (at least as far as the identification of a commercialized teenage subculture since the 1950s in the Western world is concerned) further explore changing identities in peer groups. No longer do young people rely solely on family relations (Coleman 1965) but form their own peer group support systems. For many teachers, the centrality of music to the lives of young people in this phase of identity realization is one of the most exciting features of working in a music classroom with adolescents. As Andy Bennett (2000, 195) observed, "in a very real sense, music not only informs the construction of the self, but also the social world in which the self operates" (see also Bennett 2006; DeNora 2000, 2006; Frith 1981, 1996).

Often, the music with which teenagers most readily identify is a form of popular music, and many music educators recognize the motivational and pedagogical value of incorporating popular musics into their lesson planning (Cremata et al. 2016; Kratus 2007; Krikun 2009; Powell and Burstein 2017; Vasil 2015; Wright 2010, 2014). At various levels of engagement, with different age groups, and in the name of all manner of educational goals, students are encouraged to perform, write, record, produce, listen to, discuss, and/or collaboratively create music in a variety of styles (Allsup 2008; Bell 2015; Dunbar-Hall and Wemyss 2000; Green 2008b; Gullberg 2010; Karlsen 2010; Knörzer, Stark, Park, and Rolle 2015; Randles 2012; Rolle 2013; Smith in press; Väkevä 2006, 2009, 2010; Wallbaum 2000; Westerlund 2006).

Popular music has been brought into school classrooms in a variety of ways, among them an approach called Modern Band that teaches the basics of instruments and songs germane to broadly popular styles (Powell and Burstein 2017). In some education systems, popular music is so well established as the norm in mainstream general school music education that it risks jeopardizing the transmission of a country's heritage in the Western classical tradition. An insufficient number of students comes through the system to perpetuate art music in its many forms and to populate opera houses and symphony orchestras on an ongoing basis (Hebert, Abramo, and Smith 2017; Tønsberg 2013). However, if focusing on students' music (whatever style this may be) as means to earn pedagogic authority (and to share that PAu through the use of music), it can be achieved through sensitive application of a particular pedagogical approach drawn from the way artists and performing musicians make music (Gouzouasis, Irwin, Miles, and Gordon 2013; Green 2008a, 2014). Musical Futures is one such popular music learning practice, imported into the classroom setting from outside of school. It is an internationally tried-and-tested pedagogical approach that enfolds non-formal and especially informal learning processes (D'Amore and Smith 2016).

Bringing Informal and Non-Formal Learning into the Classroom

Non-formal learning generally refers to teacher-directed learning where the teacher acts in a coach or mentor role and uses teacher-selected material. Informal learning is present when students engage in self- and peer-learning with the help of material of their own choosing and/or invention. Musical Futures' approach has been applied and its impact studied in the UK, Australia, Canada, Singapore, Hong Kong, and Brazil. It develops students' motivation, enjoyment, and skill acquisition in music lessons (Singapore Teachers' Academy for the aRts 2016) and can be a powerful means of engaging students' and teachers' creativities (Smith in press) (see Chapter 7 for further discussion of this and other pedagogical options).

Many music educators look for ways to build bridges between different cultures and subcultures of students, between students and families' perceptions of school and the education system, and between students and teachers. It is not always their call, however, to engage in new ways of pursuing shared aspirations; taking into account multiple competing and complementary pressures from schools, head teachers, parents, and other stakeholders, not everyone has the same opportunities for becoming a bridge builder. But the first step is always to decide for yourself what you want success to look like in terms of positive outcomes of and through music education: do you aspire to a high level of interpretive performance in an orchestra, marching band, or choir for a select 20 percent of high school students? Do you aim for a more inclusive, but less virtuosic, musicality for a greater proportion of students, seeking a musical life beyond school? Do you wish to engage students' creativities through composition, production, and songwriting? Dependent on context and circumstances, maybe you aspire to achieve each of these ends, others besides, and are open to changing your goals as those of your students evolve.

If you choose to use music in the classroom as a tool for exploring contemporary society—as a window on to contemporary culture and to build community in the class and the school—one way in which to do this can be to explore particular musics, musicians, their attitudes toward their work, and the cultures from which they emerge. This can take the form of discussion and critique of contemporary issues surrounding and impacting students' lives, and the society in which they live, and showing how those issues have been dealt with by various musicians throughout centuries. Two pedagogical approaches—or rather sets of approaches—are highlighted here by name as entry points to familiarize yourself with contemporary orientations to teaching music: punk pedagogies (Smith, Dines, and Parkinson in press) and hip-hop pedagogies (Snell and Söderman 2014). As their names suggest, these pedagogies draw on aspects of punk and hip-hop cultures, but it is important to bear in mind that the approaches are—quite intentionally—loosely structured and defined. Their adoption does not necessarily imply applying them at the exclusion of other approaches or requiring that everyone appreciate the associated musical styles. Both punk and hip-hop musics are part of bigger cultural phenomena that invite personal expression and creativity as the basis for democratizing schooling processes at all levels. A music teacher's role should always be to help bring students to the understanding that their particular social realities and commensurate assumptions are not necessarily those of their peers, classmates, or even their teacher.

Punk and Hip-Hop Pedagogies

Punk music, while notoriously tricky to delimit, tends to involve mostly people with guitars and drums and electric guitars (predominantly white in "Western" countries, although punk's diaspora is widespread), performing short, aggressive, often politically charged songs with a critical stance toward society at large. Estrella Torrez (2012, 135) asserted, "Punk pedagogy requires that individuals take on personal responsibility . . . by rejecting their privileged places in society and working in solidarity with those forced on the fringes. By doing so, we strive to undo hegemonic macrostructures." She suggests that if teachers lead by example and foster educated debate, they can engage in ethical actions through music. This approach—unrealistic in the mind of some music educators and eminently practicable in the experience of others—can carry a powerful message for teachers and students alike because punk pedagogies deliberately challenge the status quo by questioning transmitted wisdoms and standard methods and approaches. Students of all ages are encouraged to adopt an empowered, discursive stance toward their own environment and world. They are encouraged to do so by examining that world and critiquing their assumptions about it by means of self-directed study. Jessica Schwartz (2016) went even further in her advocacy of punk pedagogy, by asserting:

> Punk must be explored as cultivating literacies that are refuted as such by academia and K-12 music educators. The narrow prism of what has historically been authenticated by learned societies as musical literacy often prevents students from developing and cultivating their expressive talents in a methodological, respected way. Punk, and more broadly, DIY [do-it-yourself] musicality demands a more fruitful address of such creativity and the implications it has when contemplating humanistic enquiry.
>
> (Schwartz 2016, 149)

What Schwartz advocates embodies ideals and hopes of contemporary democratic societies that aspire to a more just world and greater individual agency

(DeLorenzo 2015a; Sormus 2016). By eschewing a clear, common set of core ethics, punk pedagogies afford and permit teachers a fresh approach to teaching in their individual contexts without providing constraints. As Tom Parkinson (2017a) and Mike Dines (2015) demonstrated, punk pedagogies build on the work of critical pedagogy (Freire 1968/1970/2000; Giroux 2007, 2014; for more, see Chapters 4 and 5) and anarchist pedagogies (Antliff 2012) that aim to celebrate, affirm, and empower marginalized students and communities, empower individuals, and oppose the global corporatization and marketization of education and the school classroom.

Hip-hop music tends to be more male dominated than punk, featuring performers who rap (speak) over "beats" (copied or originally produced backing tracks). Like punk, however, the lyrics are often politically charged and protest existing injustices, both personal and publicly acknowledged; this is overwhelmingly the case despite much of the most commercially successful hip-hop advocating and fueling excessive consumerism (Kruse 2016a). Adam Kruse asserted that there is tremendous value to incorporating and developing pedagogies of hip-hop into school music education contexts (2016a and b) and warned educators to be mindful of mainstream popular culture's fetishizing of white Westerners' views of black (African American) people and culture and demonization of perceived "otherness." As Karen Snell and Johan Söderman (2014, 165) observed, hip-hop "has too much potential for helping students develop their own identity through intellectually and musically stimulating experiences to be ignored by school music programs". They further urged that "hip-hop should hold a place of *central importance* in school music curricula" (2014, 167, emphasis in original) and that it can serve as a window onto multiple world cultures and perspectives because of its reliance on the practice of sampling.

Hip-hop music has frequently been associated with perpetuating and advocating overtly homophobic and misogynistic attitudes (Jarman-Ivens 2006), although it can also be socially conscious and emancipatory. The emphasis in hip-hop on lyrics helps position this style of music as particularly useful for highlighting and discussing important and complex social and political issues, helping to democratize music-learning spaces in ways that other musics (including other styles of popular music) cannot perhaps so easily do. From its beginnings among African Americans in 1970s New York City in the United States, hip-hop has been adopted and adapted by marginalized and oppressed peoples around the world (Fox 2016; Snell and Söderman 2014). Thus, as Johan Söderman and Ove Sernhede advised educators:

> It is dangerous if formal institutions, like the school, try to colonise this cultural expression by developing a kind of hip-hop pedagogy with the intention to create just another instrumental tool for formal learning [while] at the same time

> it is obvious that, for example the school, have a lot to learn from hip-hop and the way the activists develop their skills and knowledge raising practices in the creative processes of song writing, breakdancing and other types of aesthetic performances.
>
> (Söderman and Sernhede 2016, 12)

Writing that advocates for either hip-hop or punk pedagogies, along with that which focuses on characteristics of the associated musics and sub-cultures, can provide vital tools in empowering students through helping them see means of activism and resistance (Ladson-Billings 2015). Students who are already engaged in hip-hop and/or punk communities outside of school would find their musics and cultures validated in the school environment, thus affirming, celebrating, and validating the students' musical identities.

Some teachers and culture critics question the suitability of punk and hip-hop music for inclusion in schools, because subversive attitudes and confrontational, offensive lyrics are intrinsic to the musics' origins and sub-cultural value. Clearly, these aspects need to be managed with pedagogical care if and when the musics are brought into school settings. From a sociological point of view, however, the challenges around some popular musical styles are no greater than less frequently discussed (but nonetheless salient) issues that surround the teaching of Western classical music (see e.g., Baker 2014; McClary 1991). Indeed, the assumption that popular music as part of a music curriculum is inherently troublesome, mostly because of the messages delivered by the lyrics, is possibly based on a lack of knowledge about the causes and origins that led to the creation of many symphonies, operas, military marches, and chamber music. All refer either explicitly or implicitly to the social standing of a dominating culture over others in terms of social hierarchies created by education, social class, age, colonization, and race. But all have been subsumed into the fabric of mainstream culture in many societies. It would, therefore, be the task of a sociologically informed and pedagogically re-formed teacher to use examples from a broad range of musical styles in order to enable students to identify the phenomena that underpin artistic styles and societal divisions on the one hand, and their commonalities on the other.

To summarize this chapter, one of the many challenges facing music teachers in their work is to navigate, negotiate, and reconcile complex musical and personal worlds that must include popular musics and democratic pedagogical approaches in the classroom (Nyberg 2015). Your role as a music teacher does not necessarily entail embracing any one pedagogical approach exclusively, wholeheartedly, or in perpetuity. But the approaches you take should be rooted in shared characteristics of compassion, empathy, and empowering potential as these offer music teachers exciting opportunities to connect meaningfully with learners' lives, nurturing a community of learners and fostering strong bonds among them.

Interview Project 2.1

Interview teenagers in your family or community about their understanding of *music in school*. Direct the conversation toward issues about bringing music making outside of school into school.

Class Projects

1. In small groups, choose a challenging current social or political issue discussed in the media (this could be of significance at a local, national, or international level). Select musical compositions of the past and present that address a comparable issue. Explore how these different artists (performers, arrangers, writers, producers) have expressed themselves and develop some ideas for how you could structure lessons on the basis of what you find. Give a short presentation to the entire class about ideas from your group, inviting further suggestions from the class.
2. Select a hip-hop musician of your choice and examine the text of one of his or her raps. Write an essay explaining what in the text and delivery you find affirming or disconcerting and why.
3. How would you explain differences between punk and hip-hop to your grandparents?
4. Make a list of different kinds of music you would like to learn to perform and/or listen to and develop a manageable, realistic plan to engage in some of those activities on a regular basis.

Questions for Class Discussion

1. Think of the people, music, and institutions to which you, personally, ascribe pedagogic authority. Share these with your peers in a small group and consider how common or different ascriptions of PAu in your group could lead to (mis-)understandings. How would you as a teacher incorporate such knowledge in your own lessons?
2. Reflecting on your own music upbringing, what were your most favored activities and style(s) to perform? How did you grow musically, and what have you done to broaden your musical horizon beyond the musics with which you most readily identify?
3. Using the previous discussion points as a start discuss the pros and cons of incorporating hip-hop and punk musics and pedagogies into particular school classroom settings.

Key Sources (for full information, see References)

Freire, Paolo. 1968/1970/2000.
Giroux, Henry A. 2001.
Green, Lucy. 2008a.
Green, Lucy. 2008b.
Ladson-Billings, Gloria. 2015.
Nyberg, Johan. 2015.
Smith, Gareth Dylan, Mike Dines, and Tom Parkinson. (eds.). In press.
Snell, Karen, and Johan Söderman. 2014.
Wright, Ruth. 2010.

3

Teaching as Work

This chapter addresses what sociologists, past and present, have said about:

- Becoming Socialized to an Occupation
- Social Concerns across Geo-Political Boundaries
- Teaching as a Career on the Profession-Labor Continuum

Hildegard: In my preparation as a music educator, I was educated in a music conservatory (or academy as it may be called elsewhere), in a college of education within a large German university, and a school of music in a large university in Texas. I have also worked in some of those places and found that each had its own way of situating music education. In the conservatory, it provided the bread and butter for many professors even though they would much rather have taught performers. In the college of education, music as a curricular subject seemed to be little understood and valued, and in the music school affiliated with a university, education as a discipline was little understood and valued. Once I accepted my occupational "in-between-chairs" placement, I felt empowered to work with it as a strength: I was able to live comfortably in all of these places without forgetting that each had its own professional limitations and opportunities.

Gareth: As an undergraduate performance student at a conservatory of music in the UK, I found the faculty incredibly enthusiastic about training us "young bucks" as performers; those professional educators, though, were often less enthusiastic about encouraging students to go into teaching, viewing it as a less noble art than music making. When I later developed my craft as a teacher, however, I quickly discovered that I did need not be a musician *or* a teacher; I could apply myself to both disciplines in equal measure; indeed, they were far from mutually exclusive. I have frequently found it striking—and continue to do so—that many (although by no means all) of my educator colleagues have all but given up performing, and a majority of my performer associates resist teaching or, while doing it, feel that they must be seen to resent teaching, while often applying themselves to both lines of work with equal fervor. This says a lot, I believe, about how music and music teaching are perceived as work.

Introduction

Chapter 1 alluded to the fact that how you see yourself in comparison to those around you can be a matter of labeling, either in terms of labels you attach to yourself or those that others attach to you. However, regardless of who attaches them to whom, labels convey to others certain unspoken messages that impact all forms of communication, verbal and non-verbal. This chapter places your (current or future) identity as a musician-teacher into the context of what sociologists have said about teaching as work and how specific occupations bring with them distinctly different levels of perceived professional status, esteem, and publicly acknowledged worth.

American sociologist Howard S. Becker (1970/1977) suggested the term "professional" to be "an honorific title" (93), given to members in a particular occupational category and accepted as such by the lay public. Traditionally, therefore, doctors and lawyers (and, in former times, the clergy) were believed to be professionals because they came across as independent decision makers. Obviously, this observation dates back to times when doctors were free to choose whom they served and how much they charged for their services. As doctors in many countries now work in nationalized health systems or health maintenance organizations and lawyers become employees in ever-larger corporate firms, professional autonomy is arguably diminished. Clients are assigned rather than selected, and the supervisory control shifts from self-governed boards to more complex bureaucratic systems of hierarchically tiered power relationships. This type of work comes close to what Becker labeled as a semi-profession. He placed nurses and social workers under that term because both types of workers have specialized skills that are applied in relative freedom from supervision even if the clientele is assigned and the fee structure pre-determined. In contrast to professionals and semi-professionals as defined by Becker, a laborer's work allows little to no personal decision making. Tasks are assigned, "routinized," and under the control of a hierarchically tiered workforce. The lower the tier on which a laborer is positioned, the more easily she or he is replaceable; individual skills and knowledge matter less than the execution of particular tasks.

Becker's distinctions among occupational labels reflect (1) a certain degree of perceived decision-making autonomy in a paying job, (2) who your colleagues are and where you stand in the workforce, (3) perceived or actual career mobility and status in terms of pay, and (4) your commitment to specialized work tasks and skills. Where, then, does school teaching as an occupation fit in regard to decision-making power? Is it a profession akin to that of what doctors and lawyers do? A service as provided by skilled nurses and social workers? Or is it labor similar to that that undertaken by assembly line workers? Finally, is it a type of work unified enough across subject matters and locales that one category suffices to describe the work that teachers do in varied workplaces and different subject matter areas? Before you answer these questions for yourself, we introduce ways by which sociologists have answered them. We present the material under the headings of (1) becoming socialized to an occupation, (2) social concerns across geo-political boundaries, and (3) teaching as a career on the profession-labor continuum. Consequences for music teachers as subject matter experts and staff members, a topic already touched on in Chapter 1, may then illuminate more clearly the two worlds of which music educators are integral parts.

Becoming Socialized to an Occupation

In this section, we expand on describing Becker's (1970/1977) work and familiarize you with classic studies by Dan C. Lortie (1975/2002) and Ronald M. Pavalko (1971). The three men's inquiries have spearheaded numerous other studies both inside and outside of music education (for some representative examples outside of music education, see Beijaard, Meijer, and Verloop 2004; Bolton and Muzio 2008; Combe and Buchen 1996; Döring 1992; Ingersoll and Perda 2008; Michaelis-Jähnke 2006/2012; Moran and Abbott 2006; Terhart, Bennewitz, and Rothland 2014). Often, later findings confirmed what Becker, Pavalko, and Lortie reported first; where findings differed (from elsewhere in the world), they have helped provide a more comprehensive picture of a still under-researched, worldwide occupation.

We review what the aforementioned authors observed, respectively, about such issues as career mobility and status, teacher self-selection and retention, and other concerns connected to teaching as work as perceived in the United States. We then compare those findings to more recent data from other parts of the world that may serve as a backdrop for outlining what is known about the occupational socialization of music teachers as school employees. This, we hope, will assist you in considering your own work as a music teacher or what is on your mind as you prepare for music teaching as a career.

Becker's Research on Teachers' Career Mobility and Status

To capture the nature of work from a sociological perspective, Becker looked at teachers (1951/1980, 1952, 1970/1977), medical students (Becker, Geer, Hughes, and Strauss 1961/1977), dance musicians (Becker 1963a and b), and undergraduate students (Becker, Geer, and Hughes 1968/1995). His findings regarding teachers in the United States were based on sixty interviews about perceived prestige, influence, and income as indicators of upward mobility in the workforce. Unless a teacher chose to step into an administrative role as head of a school, the desire to teach at better schools (a lateral career move in sociological terminology) was perceived by most teachers as seeking an improvement in their teaching position. A better school, in the interviewed teachers' opinions, was determined by the social-class composition of the school population, that is, the "presence or absence of the 'right' kind of pupils, parents, principal, and colleagues" (Becker 1970/1977, 168). Next to looking for better schools, career patterns were also characterized by a teacher wanting "to adjust to a routine of work which [was] customary, congenial, and predictable" (171). This desire for maintaining routine was accompanied by a teacher's willingness to serve the cause of education more than his or her own career aspirations.

Longevity in a position meant increased authority and status with pupils, parents, and colleagues. Once a satisfactory position had been obtained, teachers perceived career dangers as coming only from the outside—for example, new school administrators took over, and/or socio-economic changes in the neighborhood led to an ethnically different student body. The latter change presented the greatest challenge because a changed student body meant a different relationship with the public, especially the parents, and thereby also a change of social status for the teacher. Furthermore, teachers perceived students from a lower-class economic background and of different ethnicities to be more difficult to teach, while those students' parents were perceived as being easier to deal with than parents of wealth and higher social standing.

In general, the teachers felt that parental interference in the educational process upset "an otherwise predictable and controllable institutional structure" (Becker 1951/1980, 243). The teachers believed that such interference from what usually were upper-middle-class parents questioned a teacher's professional authority. Becker interpreted this belief as "a chronic feature of service institutions." It signified to him an "indifference or ignorance of the client with regard to the authority system set up by the institutional functionaries" (Becker 1970/1977, 151). In today's language, the interpretation might be worded in more subtle terms, but Becker's findings suggested that teachers often seemed to be unaware of "the mechanics" behind the larger system that employed them.

Pavalko's Research on Teacher-Perceived Self-Selection and Retention

Interested in identifying patterns of retention and attrition in a particular type of labor force, Pavalko chose teaching because of the extensive training needed and the investment of resources that go with that training. But he also had noticed its less-than-desirable career continuity (high attrition rates) and wondered about the sociological implications for such discrepancies in training intensity and relatively short-lived work commitment. Placing teaching under the sociological categories of "industrial sociology, social stratification, and the study of complex organizations" (1971, 1), he sought to determine its place on what he called the occupation-profession continuum. Among the factors defining that continuum are (1) the occupational choices people make and the social significance behind such choices; (2) occupational socialization processes before, during, and after professional training; (3) vertical and horizontal career mobility; and (4) the impact of the work setting and its accompanying ideology on a person's perceived degree of work alienation.

The 1957 and 1964 surveys that Pavalko conducted in the United States were limited to women teachers because he considered elementary and secondary school teaching a female-dominated occupation. With socio-economic background functioning "as a selective factor in the recruitment of teachers" (1972, 243), the women who pursued teaching as a career but did not stay in it were generally from higher socio-economic backgrounds and measured higher on intelligence tests (1972, 247). As might be expected for the period during which the surveys were conducted, the strongest contributing factor to teacher attrition was marriage. Pavalko's data also suggested that teaching as an occupational choice attracted women from what Pavalko called the upper-lower classes and the lower-upper classes. He referred to these categories in a three-tiered system of upper, middle, and lower classes. These labels clearly require revision, or at least contextualization, in light of more recent categorizations (Fussell 1983/1992; Rose and Harrison 2014; Savage 2015).

Overall, Pavalko's data described a labor force in which a person does not stay permanently. He called the phenomenon a "discontinuous labor force participation" (1972, 239) and applied it to teachers who taught for fewer than five years. Of note here is that comparable statistics have since been reported for different countries and teaching specialties (e.g., Billingsley 1993; Chen-Hafteck 1997; Clandinin et al. 2012, 2015; Cooper and Alvarado 2006; Karsenti and Collin 2013; Ladd 2007; Lindqvist et al. 2014; Macdonald 1999). We should add, however, that Lindqvist et al. (2014, 94) found "teacher attrition [to be] a more non-linear and complex phenomenon than what . . . typically [has been] proposed." Observed drop-out cases often seemed temporary because "out-of-school experiences can in many cases be understood as individual initiatives to enhance teaching ability in the long run" (2014, 94). Furthermore, better pay and work conditions as reported in 2003 for many developed countries (among them France, Germany, Japan, Korea, Luxembourg, Mexico, New Zealand, and Portugal) may be contributing factors to teacher retention (Ladd 2007). It is noteworthy in this regard that the salaries grow proportional to an economy's Gross Domestic Product (GDP) and "how a country's salary structure for teachers compares with those in competing occupations" (Ladd 2007, 207). However, in countries where teacher attrition is relatively high, salary is not the only cited reason. In England, for example, where reportedly the rate of attrition rose from 8 percent to 10 percent between 1999–2000 and 2001–2002 (rising to 10.4 percent in 2014), salary was but one of the cited causes for quitting teaching (National Union of Teachers 2014). Government initiatives and increased stress levels were given as more important reasons, a finding that underscores what Pavalko had reported for the United States and what has been reiterated by teachers in more recent international surveys (Cooper and Alvarado 2006).

Lortie's Research on Teaching as Work

Like Becker and Pavalko, Dan C. Lortie engaged in a large project on occupations in general, of which his book *Schoolteacher: A Sociological Study* (1975/2002) was but one part. It serves here as a validation and summary of what Becker's and Pavalko's studies initiated. It also has become a classic reference in newer studies that often provide more global perspectives on teaching as work than the aforementioned American sociologists did. Based on ninety-four interviews with elementary school teachers as reported in 1975 and consistent with the responses of 2,316 teachers to a survey conducted by the National Education Association (NEA) for the 1965–1966 school year and reported in 1967, five factors attracted all responding teachers to their respective jobs:

1. "To work with (young) people" (1975/2002, 27).
2. "Opportunity for rendering important service" (28).
3. Wanting to stay in the school environment because "I liked school" (29).
4. Material benefits of financial security (30–31).
5. Work schedule/time compatibility (31–32).

Listed in order of importance as ranked by the interviewed teachers, Lortie discussed the issues throughout his book, which we summarize under four of his chapter headings: recruitment and reaffirmation; the limits of socialization; career and work rewards; and perspectives on purpose, uncertainties, teacher sentiments, and interpersonal preferences.

Recruitment and Reaffirmation

Across gender and racial divides and whether an interviewee held an inner-city teaching position or worked in the suburbs, teaching was considered a career choice of "valuable service" with "special moral worth" (Lortie 1975/2002, 28). This sentiment was coupled with "love for (the) students" and positive memories of one's own schooling. Lortie also noticed a conflict between wanting to be of service to others while also being upfront about issues of monetary rewards and benefits. He saw in that conflict "normative pressures" that made "it probable that material benefits influence[d] teachers' decisions more than their answers indicate[d]" (30). Incentives of higher salaries usually did not enter into alternative career choices, but Lortie observed that "a significant proportion" of the men whom he interviewed came "from homes marked by economic insecurity and low social status" (30).

The Limits of Socialization

Regarding the interviewees' responses to how they had become the professionals they perceived themselves to be, Lortie distinguished between such factors as (1) formal schooling (both general and specialized), (2) mediated entry (apprenticeship and mentoring), and (3) learning while doing (57). He found that relatively few hours were required in the United States for learning how to teach. The rather short "mediated entry" in the form of practice teaching (pre-service teaching) at the end of a student's educational studies did little to change the teachers' view that one learned how to teach "while doing."

When it came to the teachers' specialization in subject matter skills and knowledge, the teachers attached significance to the training they had received prior to teaching. In fact, their commitment to those skills and knowledge was strong. Unfortunately, though, Lortie, Becker, and Pavalko did not identify the subject matter each teacher had specialized.

As far as what caused the teachers to choose their work, imitative learning proved to be a powerful source of wanting to become a teacher—so powerful, in fact, that the profession did not come across as having an agreed-upon "common 'memory' or technical subculture" (70) to which everybody adhered in daily practice. One taught as one had been taught. This finding is similar to what Williams and Randles (2017) reported about American music teacher trainees, who found it difficult to imagine their futures other than replicating the concert band performance model with which they had grown up.

A regular apprenticeship—a sequenced "series of tasks of ascending difficulty" (Lortie 1975/2002, 72)—is practiced in many crafts and professions. Neither a student's experience during pre-service teaching (while still an undergraduate trainee teacher) nor the first teaching position came, in the interviewees' judgment, close to that model. Learning how to teach continued to be seen as an intuitive, individualistic approach of selecting what appeared to work for each individual rather than what the teaching profession has established as agreed-upon strategies and behaviors. Lortie drew these conclusions because he found that when it came to mentorship and guidance through supervisory leadership by the head teacher, head master, or some other designated person, teachers rarely heeded such advice. They relied on themselves and on colleagues closest to their own rank to know what was effective teaching.

Career and Work Rewards

Income profiles between members of different professions differ greatly. In some professions, a person may begin with very little income but, with success, will gain ever-higher earnings. Lortie called these staged income profiles. They usually go hand in hand with upward shifts in status. Unstaged profiles are those where "income gains may be steady but small" (1975/2002, 82) and status remains relatively unchanged. In comparing his findings on teaching with data on the legal profession (1959), Lortie found that the absence of career stages in teaching led to tentativeness of future commitments. The result was what he called a disjunction between involvement by time and money expenditures and "satisfaction as measured by readiness to teach again" (1975/2002, 91). The disjunction was smallest for married female teachers and highest for males. As a result, "few beginning teachers project[ed] long futures in the classroom; men expect[ed], in the main, to leave, and women [saw] their participation as contingent" (99) on personal circumstances.

Perspectives on Purpose, Uncertainties, Teacher Sentiments, and Interpersonal Preferences

Concerning teachers' personal views about issues they faced every day, teachers connected most closely with the students they taught. This observation supported Pavalko's findings according to which teachers took pride in their craft by describing successful moments of teaching even if those moments involved only one student. Teachers labeled their own interactions with the students according to how they saw themselves as moral agents, intellectual motivators/facilitators of learning, or "inclusive" teachers. Lortie suggested these differences in role perceptions also reflected "value differences [among the teachers] which retard[ed] occupational solidarity" with colleagues and other professionals (1975/2002, 115). However, among the occupational uncertainties listed by the teachers were roles as leaders on the one hand and, on the other, accepting and endorsing "the hegemony of the school system on which [they were] economically and functionally dependent" (186). These internally contradictory role perceptions seemed to shape the interactions with parents, colleagues, the principal, and the general public as much as the roles of moral agents, intellectual motivators, and inclusive teachers shaped their work with pupils.

International Perspectives on the Occupational Status of Teachers

Very few teachers appear to choose their profession for social status (e.g., Day et al. 2006; Hargreaves, Purves et al. 2007; Lortie 1975/2002), but the role of social status in teacher attrition has become a concern worldwide and has prompted numerous UNESCO-sponsored reports, national research projects, and journalistic reports providing international comparisons (e.g., Cooper and Alvarado 2006; Darling-Hammond, Berry, Haselkorn, and Fideler 1999; Dolton and Marcenaro-Gutierrez 2013; Greiner 2013; Hargreaves, Purves et al. 2007; Kelleher et al. 2011; Khadaroo 2013; Leavitt 1992, 2013; Ostinelli 2009; UNESCO 2014a and b, 2015a, b and c). From the many available reports, we have selected two as examples of what is being done worldwide to examine teaching as work and its status among other occupations. The first selection was jointly sponsored by two British universities and described teaching as work in England; the second, sponsored by UNESCO, focuses on five industrially developing countries, with emphasis on the feminization of teaching and related matters (Kelleher et al. 2011).

Teachers' Occupational Status in the United Kingdom

Conceptualized as an interim report, Linda Hargreaves, Mark Cunningham, Anders Hansen, Donald McIntyre, and Caroline Oliver (2007) wanted to "establish base line data and monitor changes in perceptions of the status of teachers and their profession, among teachers, associated groups, and the general public, between 2003 and 2006" (2). With those data in hand, the report's authors wanted then to "to understand the factors that might influence perceptions of status and teachers' attitudes [and] identify how perceptions of teacher status can be improved" (Hargreaves, Cunningham et al. 2007, 2–3). Through several survey and media studies, the authors were able to draw a comprehensive picture of "the attractiveness of a teaching career, the status of teachers compared with other occupations and what activities people associated with teaching" (Hargreaves, Cunningham et al. 2007, 3). They obtained this picture from:

- Public opinion (1,815 adults in 2003 and 1,252 in 2006).
- A random sample of teachers (2,350 in 2003 and 5,340 in 2006).
- Groups associated with teachers (teaching assistants, governors, and parents totaling 2,749 for both years).
- A total of 590 trainees (from 2003 to 2005).

Interestingly, but perhaps not surprisingly, the authors identified differences in opinion over the time span of nearly forty years (1967, 1979, 1988, 1997, and 2003), excluding years outside the interviewees' personal experience. Specifically, respondents ages fifty-five and over saw their occupational status as a negative, whereas younger teachers attached to it a more positive value. All respondents perceived a steady and significant decline in status, although the degrees differed between the groups surveyed. For example, experienced teachers had the greatest drop in perceived status and teaching assistants the least, whereas parents consistently rated teacher status higher than did teachers themselves. Overall, the authors reported "40 years of decline in the status of teachers" in the United Kingdom (Hargreaves, Cunningham et al. 2007, 31).

Despite the acknowledged factor of being externally controlled, "a coherent, stable and largely shared view of teacher professionalism was found" (41). At the same time, though, "teachers were unsure" whether a shared "professional" language was needed for "talking about learning and teaching" (42). Overall:

> When comparing the status of teachers with that of twelve other professionals, the public felt, consistently, that primary and secondary teachers were most similar in social status to social workers. Despite a decrease in the proportion of respondents feeling this way (40 percent in 2003 and 35 percent in 2006), the comparison of teachers and social workers remained the strongest, largely because they work with children or young people. Primary and secondary head teachers were likened most often in social status to management consultants, because of the level of responsibility associated with the job and head teachers' authority to make decisions at work.
>
> (Hargreaves, Cunningham et al. 2007, 4)

The authors concluded:

> Status was not a word that teachers used comfortably or frequently. For them their sense of vocation, deep commitment, and being able to help their pupils sustained them even in situations where their sense of status was under threat. That said, being trusted as professionals, being challenged and given responsibility, through democratic and distributed school leadership and collegial support, enhanced their sense of status.
>
> (Hargreaves, Cunningham et al. 2007, 9)

Women and the Teaching Profession in Developing Countries

Kelleher et al.'s (2011) extensive study, co-sponsored by the Commonwealth Secretariat and UNESCO, used five nation-states as its observation cases: the Commonwealth of Dominica, Lesotho, India, Samoa, and Sri Lanka. Providing detailed statistical, sociological, and educational explorations of feminization in said countries, the report also includes a thorough review of literature and a comparative analysis of available data from the United Kingdom and Canada. Trends long observed in Western industrialized nations also emerge in other parts of the world. Foremost among Kelleher's observations is that places where the teaching profession is fully feminized, illiteracy is close to being eliminated. Citing Cortina and San Román (2006), she observed, "In the context of countries that have achieved the goals of Universal Primary Education and gender parity in education, historical analysis indicates that an influx of women in the teaching profession has been central to these successes" (Kelleher et al. 2011, 4). From a *statistical* standpoint, feminization is expressed in benchmarks established by the Organisation for Economic Co-operation and Development (OECD). A *sociological* definition takes into consideration "causes, consequences and implications" of such statistical givens (Kelleher et al. 2011, 2). A comprehensive understanding of the data requires both types of analysis.

Statistically, an occupation is said to be highly feminized when more than 70 percent of the workforce are women. A 50–69 percent level of feminization would suggest a low to medium degree of feminization. Anything below 50 percent would be called a low level of feminization. With the data provided by UNESCO in 2010 for the time span of 1999 to 2007, the highest degree of feminization in the teaching profession for both primary and secondary grades can be found in Central and Eastern Europe. When it comes to primary school teachers alone, Central Asia is more feminized than North America, Western Europe, Latin America, and the Caribbean. Although an upward trend was observed between 1999 and 2007 for all of the regions named, Arab states and countries of Central and East, South, and West Asia as well as the Pacific have remained at a medium level of feminization for primary school teachers and a low level for secondary schools. Sub-Saharan African countries showed the lowest level of feminization across all levels of teaching, but data reported separately for each individual sub-Saharan country showed important differences in the degrees of feminization among those countries. Although Nigeria, Kenya, Ghana, and Uganda showed no appreciable change in the number of female teachers in compulsory schooling, countries including Botswana, Namibia, Lesotho, South Africa, and the Seychelles had a high majority in female teachers in primary schools and "a small majority of female teachers at the secondary school level" (Kelleher et al. 2011, 3).

Sociologically, Kelleher analyzed the statistical data for (1) goals articulated in the *United Nations Millennium Education Goals and Education for All* document, and (2) broader gender equity in all nation-states. In regard to the worldwide education goals, the feminization of the teaching profession should be considered a must in developing countries, so that "the dual challenge of expanding education and universal provision while ensuring quality and equity" (4) can be met. At the same time, a more nuanced understanding of teaching by gender is needed:

> From a purely human resourcing perspective, female human labour has been instrumental at fulfilling capacity needs, while from the perspective of educating women and girls the presence of women teachers has been a major contributing factor. . . . In countries where girl child education remains a challenge, a dearth in female teachers within the system has been identified as one of the core barriers to gender parity and equality in education, [. . .] most specifically where girl child retention in school is concerned.
>
> (Kelleher et al. 2011, 5)

In short, the documented feminization of primary school teaching in many parts of the world would suggest that it serves a much-needed dimension of equalizing access to education everywhere.

In her analysis, Kelleher acknowledged that in countries with high female participation in the teaching workforce, issues of boys' underachievement and under participation have become new realities. However, citing Drudy (2008), Kelleher also pointed out that "issues surrounding boys [being marginalized] appear prevalent in countries that have achieved universal primary education and gender parity education" (5) and that such trends are more attributable to specific subject matter areas than to a general trend of boys' marginalization in school. She concluded:

> These dualities of impact and consequence—women in teaching as instrumental in education provision generally (and female education in particular) on the one hand versus an entrenching of gender inequalities through the feminization of the profession on the other—makes the topic one of multi-layered issues and applicability in the developing context.
>
> (Kelleher et al. 2011, 6)

Social Concerns across Geo-Political Boundaries

Increasingly, what happens locally impacts events globally. Countries compete against one another in education while seeking to work collaboratively to produce highly qualified workers that are employable everywhere. As a result, government agencies, educational foundations, and related associations take a keen interest in what happens in teacher education institutions in terms of how teachers are prepared for work in their subject matter areas and as pedagogues. Often driven by efforts for quality control and economic efficiency, these large-scale interests purport to make schooling more affordable and available for all, thereby strengthening basic literacy skills across regions, if not countries.

Although teaching has become a truly worldwide occupation, it is also nonetheless marked and impacted by the social concerns prevalent in particular countries. For example, in the past, the study of teacher attrition and retention has universally focused on such issues as teacher salary, job security, mobility, and status. More recently, however, gender, (dis)ability, and race have been fully acknowledged as powerful influences on work-related issues.

Job mobility and status seem to be of greater concern for male secondary school teaching personnel than for primary school teachers. Subject matter expertise also plays a role in that regard but—as already stated—little information on this topic exists thus far. "What seems to be lacking," Cooper and Alvarado (2006) observed in their UNESCO report on the preparation, recruitment, and retention of teachers, is a framework for policy that creates what Darling-Hammond et al. (1999, 185) called a "coherent infrastructure of recruitment, preparation, and support programmes that connect all aspects of the teacher's career continuum into a teacher development system that is linked to national and local educational goals." Such an infrastructure would need to acknowledge macro concerns of social class, gender, (dis)ability, and race as being integral to a particular system of education, its prevailing policies, and local practices.

Feminization of Teaching, Feminism, Race, and Social Class

As Kelleher et al.'s (2011) report suggested, the feminization of teaching seems to have afforded access to primary education in more countries than was the case even thirty years ago. On the other hand, we concur with Lamb and Dhokai (2015) that "while some voices within music education declare feminism as divisive and irrelevant, [. . .] feminism [is] at the heart of struggles to ensure girls' education and women's rights worldwide" (125). Both feminist concerns and women's issues are all too often perceived as issues only for those whom they affect most directly. This perception is due to what Bourdieu (2001) referred to as *Masculine Domination*, the effects (and building blocks) of a social structure in which sexism and misogyny are so endemic and widespread that people do not see the actions, behaviors, and systems (e.g., language and economic standing in society) that perpetuate and uphold the structure.

Music teachers can play an important role in combating this systemic social "blindness." Feminism has a role to play in that regard when assuring vigilance and a socially clear vision. As American author bell hooks (2000, 1) wrote, "simply put, feminism is a movement to end sexism, sexist exploitation, and oppression." However, it may be that feminism has fallen short of reaching those goals because of its increased focus on, and diversion toward, a mainstream, white, middle-class feminism (McLaughlin, Casey, and Richardson 2006). In hooks's words:

> White women and black men have it both ways. They can act as oppressor or be oppressed. Black men may be victimized by racism, but sexism allows them to act as exploiters and oppressors of women. White women may be victimized by sexism, but racism enables them to act as exploiters and oppressors of black people. Both groups have led liberation movements that favor their interests and support the continued oppression of other groups. Black male sexism has undermined struggles to eradicate racism just as white female racism undermines feminist struggle. As long as these two groups or any group defines liberation as gaining social equality with ruling class white men, they have a vested interest in the continued exploitation and oppression of others.
>
> (hooks 1984, 16)

Indeed, hooks's words are powerful reminders about the complex connections between gender, race, ethnicity, capitalism, and other forms and means of societal division (McClintock 1995; see also Chapter 6).

It is a statistical fact that "[b]etween now and 2050, the vast majority of population growth will come from racial minorities. By 2050, the America that many on the right are so nostalgic about will be a thing of the past" (Talley 2010). Many classrooms in Western societies already show clearly the influx of different ethnic communities on learning content and methods of teaching. Children of political refugees and asylum seekers, immigrants, and undocumented workers sit side by side, struggling to fit into new homelands and become peers to those students to whom nothing seems to be new. Teachers are expected to help those who struggle to achieve success and those who succeed to excel in learning. Diverse perceptions and experiences among the student body make up the daily reality of teaching, which includes the teaching of music.

Small Group Discussion 3.1

Share with each other experiences as a worker in a job (teaching or otherwise). Where were you in the hierarchy of positions as you perceived them? How did you act in terms of commitment to your assigned tasks, your desire to move up on the ladder of positions, and your relationship to others around you? Did you feel discriminated against in terms of gender and race and how those two variables played out in your work day?

Teaching as a Career on the Profession-Labor Continuum

As we discussed earlier, Lortie used the term *status* within the stratification of hierarchically tiered occupations in society, whereas Pavalko considered the term as a place on a continuum ranging from an independent, decision-making worker (the professional) to a fully externally controlled worker (laborer). In the research by Hargreaves, Purves et al. (2007), the term *status* morphs into a psychological connotation of self-perceived pride, worth, honor, prestige, and professionalism—all terms that Becker called honorific. Such broadening of the term takes it out of a purely sociological realm. British sociologist Eric Hoyle (2001), therefore, suggested distinguishing among occupational prestige, status, and esteem.

Occupational *prestige* is the "public perception of the relative position of an occupation in a hierarchy of occupations" (Hoyle 2001, 139); it is closest to what Lortie examined. Similarly, occupational *status* "is the category to which knowledgeable groups allocate a particular occupation" (Hoyle 2001, 145) and occupational *esteem* "is the regard in which an occupation is held by the general public by virtue of the personal qualities which members are perceived as bringing to their core task" (147). We suggest that the three concepts together describe what in lay terms is thought of as professional status. Although most successful teachers consider themselves to demonstrate professionalism in their work, it is different from what Hoyle's three concepts suggest. Professionalism is a combination of self-assessed attitude and observable behavior (Tichenor and Tichenor 2004–2005) and can be observed among professionals and laborers alike. This is why the application of the term "professional" to one's own work seems to be such an important attribute when describing what it means to be fully committed to carrying out all work-related duties, be they self-chosen or imposed.

Teachers' Roles as Staff Members

It has been said that the notion of a doctor without a patient or a teacher without a pupil would be absurd. Likewise, professional conductors work with accomplished (paid) performers and report to symphony orchestra boards, not school administrators. Music teachers employed in schools work with less experienced, aspiring music learners and report to superiors who usually are musically less experienced and educated than the teachers. Whatever the job, a professional's roles are defined by the individuals with whom she or he comes directly and indirectly into contact. A teacher's occupational socialization plays as great a role in this regard as do the organizational structure of the institution and the resulting work conditions.

Personal choices are almost always embedded in larger (macro) issues of opportunities that families, communities, and other social groupings afford us. Known also as "status properties" (Picart 2013), they are connected to, if not determined by, the places and spaces that groups of individuals occupy in particular societies. Although the properties may differ significantly across nation-states and respective socio-political and economic circumstances, all of them impact how music teachers function in a wider society. As private citizens and working employees, teachers are embedded in the macro structures surrounding them. Therefore, how you see yourself in the place and space called "home" is as important as how place and space are seen by the world, and how that place is perceived as treating the rest of the world. It is about you in the interconnectedness of local economics in a certain socio-geographic region and the global standing of a specific nation-state in the world. It is also about your social standing in those particular contexts.

Acknowledging and mapping the aforementioned connections have long been the purview of all of the social sciences. Also referring to such "mapping" as "human geography" (e.g., Cloke, Crang, and Goodwin 2005; Norton 2014; Tuan 1977), sociologists become geographers of a special kind. They describe and analyze social structures of family, groups, and communities large and small in light of who controls or holds power over whom, who moves on and who stays behind, and how power structures allow or inhibit upward mobility in various fields and occupations. Issues of social class, race, ethnicity, (dis)ability, and gender become central to those analyses; so do all distinctions of social status, marginalization, deviance, and "otherness." Applied to music teaching as work, status properties are defined by the subject matter (music) just as much as they are by how school teachers are perceived by others in the school community.

A Case Study on School Organizational Structure and Work Control in the United States

To examine the relationship between school organizational structure and work control in the United States, Charles Bidwell, Kenneth Frank, and Pamela Quiroz (1997; see also Bidwell 2000) measured the effectiveness of schools by (1) the roles of faculty and students in particular instructional settings; (2) the emergence, consistency, and stability of experiences that shape those roles; and (3) key organizational attributes of schools with highly competitive outcome goals. *Work control* was the term used to describe teachers' thoughts about the purposes and methods of teaching and how those thoughts compared with actual teaching practices. The researchers hypothesized a direct link between certain types of teachers (*the rigorist*, *the moral agent*, *the pal*, and *the progressivist*) and the controls that schools exercise. At least three of the four teacher types (the progressivist, moral agent, and pal) were similar to Lortie's earlier (1975/2002) teacher categorizations.

The control mechanisms present in and defining a teacher's workplace were labeled (1) bureaucratic, (2) autocratic-oligarchic, (3) market, or (4) collegial. Relative to school size and client power, the latter refers to the influence and/or pressure parents and students, via their parents, can exert on what schools do. Of thirteen selected high schools in the Chicago metropolitan area, the larger schools enrolled 2,500 to 3,000 students and employed 200 to 300 teachers; the small schools enrolled 300 to 600 students and employed between 30 and 80 faculty. Regardless of school size, parents of higher socio-economic status (SES) had greater clientele power than parents with a lower SES, meaning that parents from different socio-economic backgrounds exercised different degrees of control over school issues. As confirmed by the principals in schools with higher SES clientele, such control even reached into curriculum issues, a domain usually believed to be controlled by the experts—the teaching staff. The connection between teachers and administrators appeared to be "soft" (if not weak)—an observation Lortie also made (1975/2002).

Small Group Discussion 3.2

If "roles are bundles of socially defined attributes and expectations associated with social positions" (Abercrombie, Hill, and Turner 2006, 332), how would you describe the roles you play in work-related situations (including being a student)? Identify for yourself and share with your classmates incidences of role "consonance" and "dissonance."

As you think about your own envisioned or existing teaching career in music, you might find it unnecessary to ponder where you are on the profession-labor continuum. After all, many a teacher's sense of what it means to be and act as a "professional" stems from a strong sense of self in relation to serving the students. But there is also the macro perspective to be considered, the fact that society at large has a view of what teachers do and are responsible for, that may not match with your own perception and understanding. Such a gap in perception can cause communication problems between you and your colleagues (including school administrators) and between you and your students' parents.

In Chapter 1, we suggested your greatest source of professional pride likely stems from your sense of self as a musician, a pride that cannot be, and usually is not, shared by most colleagues whose subject matter is not music. Whenever you communicate with any of them (including school administrators), remember to emphasize commonalities with others rather than differences. Where you are on your career ladder is one such important point of commonality; another might be your role as educator rather than musician, spoken to by Becker, Bidwell, Lortie, Pavalko, and Hoyle (and others) in different, but equally valid, ways.

Often it is the role of moral agent that connects the music teacher to his or her colleagues outside of music (including school administrators). Because, however, not all of them share the same musical expertise you have, they may interpret your role of moral agent differently from the way you perceive it. To engage in meaningful communication with others, therefore, it becomes important to take differences in perceptions seriously and work with them as representing multiple professional realities.

British music educator Keith Swanwick (1999/2012) once observed: "we all have an accent" (20); at times it is hard to understand a speaker's intent, at other times he or she may sound just like you. We consider it important in a person's professional life to work on understanding especially those accents that are least familiar. This is meant both literally and symbolically and a recurring theme throughout the remainder of this book. The metaphor applies equally to who you are as an educator, musician, private citizen, and citizen of the world.

Writing Project 3.1

Describe how your socialization as musician has impacted or is likely to impact your view of yourself (and others' views of you) as an educator. Consider possible conflicts you might encounter when molding those two roles into one in various possible workplaces (e.g., part-time music director in a place of worship, full-time music teacher in an ethnically integrated inner-city school, a rural high school, or in international or online contexts).

Questions for Class Discussion

1. In thinking back to schools you attended, how different did they seem to be from each other in administrative style and sense of school community? What factors do you believe contributed to those differences?
2. If you are a teacher already:
   a. How do you see your own role as a staff member in light of what this chapter addressed?
   b. How do you understand your place in the institutional hierarchy?
   c. How comfortable are you with your place in that hierarchy, and (how) do you negotiate possible conflicts that may arise from being a part of such a system?
3. If you are a student preparing to become a teacher:
   a. What experiences in prior contexts and during your teacher education program have provided you with insights into what it means to be a professional performer?
   b. What experiences in prior contexts and during your teacher education program have provided you with insights into what it means to be a professional music teacher?
   c. How do you (expect to) combine the respective socialization experiences as musician, teacher, or possibly other roles to inform your sense of self (or selves) as a music educator? What do you bring to the table of music education that is uniquely *you*?

Key Sources (for full information see References)

Becker, Howard S. 1951/1980, 1970/1977.
Darling-Hammond, Linda, Barnett T. Berry, David Haselkorn, and Elizabeth Fideler. 1999.
Day, Christopher et al. 2006.
Dolton, Peter and Oscar Marcenaro-Gutierrez. 2013.
Greiner, Lena. 2013.
Hargreaves, Linda et al. 2007.
Kelleher, Fatimah et al. 2011.
Khadaroo, Stacy T. 2013.
Lortie, Dan. 1975/2002.
Mantie, Roger and Gareth Dylan Smith. 2016.
Pavalko, Ronald M. 1971.
UNESCO. 2014a, 2014b, 2015a, 2015b, 2015c.

4

Music in Social Theories

Voices from Ethnomusicology, Music Sociology, Cultural Theory, and Music Education

This chapter provides a brief overview of:

- Early Sociological Scholarship of Relevance for Music Educators
- Thinking about the Value of Music as a Social Construct

Hildegard: Throughout my musical life, especially when I was younger, I always have had a very strong sense of what I thought was good music and not so good music. Growing up with church and concert music by what I considered the four Big Bs (Bach, Beethoven, Brahms, Bruckner) and reveling in the works of Haydn, Mozart, Schubert, Schumann, Wagner, Mahler, and Richard Strauss, I did not feel I needed much more than that to fulfill my musical appetite. I knew little about French classical music, about the Russian symphonic repertoire (with the exception of Tchaikovsky) and nothing about jazz or other American musical traditions. That changed, however, when I came to the United States, where the palette of musical works was much greater and more varied than what I had known before. And then I learned about ethnomusicology as a discipline all of its own. The first person to bring it to my attention was Gilbert Chase, who introduced students at the University of Texas at Austin to an incredibly rich repertoire of shape note singing and other musics from the pilgrims onward. The second person was Barbara Reeder Lundquist, who presented a talk at the 1984 national meeting of music educators in Chicago on the connection between ethnomusicology and sociology, and the third person was Charles Seeger, who, at that time close to 90 years old, impressed me with an insatiable appetite for furthering research on musics of everyday culture. Those early encounters opened my mind to musics "out there" that I still don't know. I have learned to see connections where I used not to see them and wait with my judgments until after I have learned all there is to learn about any kind of music. The moral: don't judge until after you get engaged doing it. The result: I now love dancing to country and western music!

Gareth: I, too, grew up with a very strong sense of what was "good" music, and what was "bad." This was almost entirely based on advice from my father: classical music, most hymns (apart from Charles Wesley's), jazz, folk, and rock were good (respectively, and in virtually any combination); anything that my mother or school friends liked or that was promoted on television was rubbish—music's heyday was long behind us. I developed friendships with others locally who shared musical tastes with my dad, and I began to play music that I felt was worthy of my time and my father's approval. What I utterly failed to grasp as a teenager, and even as a young adult, was how the value that I ascribed—and had been taught to ascribe—to music, at home, and later through advanced classical and jazz musical performance training, was intrinsically interwoven with and representative of socio-political structures, of which most of the occupants were largely unaware. When I came, as a master's degree candidate, to study psychology, philosophy, and sociology of music education, each class and reading felt like I was entering a parallel universe where none of my assumptions rang true and everything I had previously believed could be demonstrated to be built on shaky, if not downright false, suppositions. Sociology, for me, while persistently challenging (and, in equal measure, alluring), has been and continues to be nothing short of transformative. It enables and requires me to question the previously unquestionable and provides answers that provoke me to take meaningful action in and beyond the classroom.

Introduction

This chapter reviews music as a construct in the larger frame of social theories. To practically minded readers, such undertaking may seem superfluous. Why worry about theory if you are interested in practice? Why engage in gathering "book knowledge" when the doing of music is so much more important? Why worry about thoughts from the past when what matters is about living in the present and working for the future? Our response to these questions lies in the firm conviction that actions never occur in a vacuum. People think and act on the basis of past ideas and achievements, consciously and unconsciously. Being informed about the work of those who came before us can help us to understand where we, along with our ideas and actions, stand in the bigger picture about the learning and teaching of music in the society in which we live. This chapter, therefore, introduces you to what lies in the past and invites you to use current thought to develop further your own opinions as to how the place(s) and space(s) you call home have shaped your own beliefs—spoken or unarticulated—about music as a social and artistic phenomenon.

When Sociology of Music Began

French philosopher-sociologist Auguste Comte (1798–1857) is generally credited with having coined the term "sociology." Preceding him were the many philosophers since Plato and Aristotle, who had long argued about the nature of knowledge, the arts, society, and the ethical conduct of the individual in society. Philosophy, psychology, and the arts were often inseparable in those arguments. But even before the term sociology became a household name in music, musicologists, historians, and philosophers—independently of one other and in different parts of the world—discussed issues of music and society from various angles. Some focused on the origin of what contributes to what we refer to as musical styles. Others were more interested in the arts as being affirming powers in what makes us human. Musicologically informed sociologists wondered about social conventions governing art consumption, whereas sociologically informed musicologists looked at the social functions of music in the history of Western and—later—other musics.

Bringing sociology into the fold of academic discourse in music has caused some people to wonder where sociological thinking begins and psychological thought ends—a challenge reflected in sociology's close academic cousin, cultural psychology (Barrett 2011; Cole 1996). Similar questions arise around the boundaries between what music sociologists talk about as compared with what ethnomusicologists and cultural theorists have to say. The boundaries of these various disciplines are porous, shifting, and overlapping.

For instance, when Charles Seeger (1886–1979), together with his wife Ruth Crawford Seeger (1901–1953), studied the folk heritage of the United States, John Blacking (1928–1990) immersed himself in the culture of the Venda in Africa, and Eileen Southern (1920–2002) traced African American musical heritage from its beginnings, all three scholars called attention to socio-musical conventions outside the "legitimized" mainstream of Western classical music.

Providing important ethnomusicological micro views of music making in other parts of the world, these researcher-musicians paved the way for similar efforts by scholars of today to portray what goes on in the subcultures of the Western world. Case descriptions can be as specific as when Patricia Shehan Campbell (2010) found out what songs school children had "in their heads" or when sociologist Tia DeNora (2000) asked women in the United States and United Kingdom about their everyday music habits. Other cases homed in on the specific conduct common to particular sub-groups identifiable by age, gender, and ethnicity, and further stratified by purpose, income, musical style, and performance genre. The data thus obtained formed the material from which theories were constructed that distinguished an everyday culture (spelled with a lowercase letter "c") from high Culture (with a capital "C"). Although not stated in those terms by anthropologists, economists, philosophers, or social scientists, the conceptual distinction was present in those and other disciplines.

Socio-musical scenes and contexts comprising **c/C**ultures of society have been examined by scholars for many years: grooving jazz bands, an audience reacting to a rock concert in a sports stadium, symphony orchestra musicians, (drum kit) drummers, and songwriters at work. All of these snapshots and numerous others contribute to the mosaic of a macro cultural system. One scholar may separate musical and social contexts from each other while another might argue their interconnectedness. A third scholar may seek to determine the relative value of a piece of music almost exclusively by the purpose (musical or social) for which it was composed, performed, distributed, or consumed, and a fourth writer might rely on how performing musicians describe the meaning they derive from making music in specific contexts and for socially situated purposes. In short, many scholars from various parts of the world have contributed to perspectives about music as a social construct. All of these efforts have benefited music educators, who often share the examined perspectives and thereby advance knowledge about music learners and the latter's role in the educational process. For the purpose of this book, we are keen for you to consider where you stand on these issues and how your understandings could impact your actions as a music educator.

Early Sociological Scholarship of Relevance for Music Educators

Max Weber (1864–1920) and Theodor W. Adorno (1903–1969) are often considered two of the most influential scholars in the early days of music sociology, in general sociology, and in political and economic theory. Weber's landmark essay *The Rational and Social Foundations of Music* (1921/1958) laid the groundwork for sociology of music, although many of his other works dealt with the study of religion, economics, and law. Adorno's text on a sociology of music (*Introduction to the Sociology of Music*), first published in Germany in 1962, was one of the first to outline that dimension of academic discourse in and about music.

Originally written in German, the works of both authors benefited greatly from English translations because the translators re-organized and simplified sentence structures in both cases. Adorno's writing style was edited by the translator E. B. Ashton, who cut in half nearly all sentences and ordered them more sequentially. The translators of Weber's essay, Don Martindale, Johannes Riedel, and Gertrude Neuwirth, organized the text into chapters and provided an introduction. Johannes Riedel has a visible connection to music education and sociology in the United States through his very readable article "The Function of Sociability in the Sociology of Music and Music Education," published in 1964 in the *Journal of Research in Music Education*. Before further describing Weber's and Adorno's respective works in greater detail, mention must also be made of the 1965 founding of the "Institut für Musiksoziologie" (Institute for Music Sociology) by music sociologist Kurt Blaukopf in Vienna, Austria. Now under the leadership of Alfred Smudits, the institute is dedicated to interdisciplinary projects and research of musical, cultural, and socio-political relevance (IMS 2016).

Weber's "Theory of Rationalization"

Weber's overriding scholarly interest was proving to himself and others that at the root of Western economic theory lies the protestant work ethic. This is characterized by a drive for (1) rational efficiency, and (2) economic profit, both of which together drive Western societies' quest for material wealth and scientific discoveries. Rational efficiency is the result of a process Weber calls rationalization, one of the most general elements in Weber's theory (Elwell 1996). The process of rationalization is responsible for an increased division of labor, bureaucracy, and mechanization of all aspects of modern Western societies. The result, in Elwell's (1996) online wording, has been "depersonalization, oppressive routine, [and] rising secularism," leading to an increased loss of individual freedom (Elwell, 1996, see also Gerth and Mills 1946). To test the validity of this general economic theory, Weber sought support for the validity of his ideas by applying them to the arts, law, religion, and, especially, music.

Weber looked for the construct of rationality in music by theorizing about the acoustic properties of Western classical music alone. In doing so, he articulated his thoughts as a philosophical treatise, in which one thought led to another without headings, subheadings, or other guidelines for the reader. Two of the translators, Don Martindale and Johannes Riedel, provided a substantive foreword and labeled Weber's basic points about the rationality of music and its social structure as follows: (1) the relationship of harmony to melody; (2) prediatonic scales in relationship to Western scale systems; (3) the impact of the rationalization of scale systems on the role of the musician as magician, virtuoso, and professional; (4) poly-vocality and poly-sonority in relation to music rationalization; and (5) instruments and the rationalization of non-harmonic tones through equalization and tempering (Martindale, Riedel, and Neuwirth 1958, xi–lii). Using his knowledge of physics and acoustic properties of sound, Weber argued that the harmonic relationships between pitches due to the invention of equal temperament made Western classical sounds and sonorities superior to non-Western pitch systems. This superiority, he maintained, was not due to aesthetic qualities inherent in a given musical piece but to the process of rationalization inherent in the Pythagorean theory of sound. Weber declared it the most efficient tonal system of sound among all other systems. We should note, of course, that Weber's argument is somewhat circular in that it celebrates the efficiency of a system that prizes efficiency! In making this case, he was arguably privileging a particularly Western-oriented worldview that prioritizes the rational and efficient; musics from other cultures may well celebrate different musical attributes over rationalization and efficiency, and thus would, in those other contexts and according to those other criteria, count as "superior." Pitting musics and/or aesthetic systems against one another to determine their relative worth, however, is arguably less useful than seeking to understand the nature of musics and those who are engaged in them across social and cultural contexts.

Theodor W. Adorno's *Introduction to the Sociology of Music* (1962)

A founding member of the so-called "Frankfurt School of Critical Theory," Adorno helped develop Critical Theory as a post–World War II offshoot of Marxist social philosophy. Formerly a composer, Adorno was particularly interested in examining from a neo-Marxist philosophical perspective the place and function of music in society. Here one should distinguish Marxism as a philosophy from its economic application in autocratic political systems, a distinction that is at the core of the Frankfurt School of Critical Theory.

Like Marxist theory, the method of reasoning in Critical Theory lies in the use of what is called dialectic reasoning (or logic), a method of argumentation historically rooted in the German philosophical scholarship of G.W.F. Hegel (1770–1831). It involves both a thesis (a statement of what is) and its antithesis (a statement posed as the thesis's opposite). This juxtaposition leads to a dynamic tension in the argument that is never resolved. The argument is propelled forward only by means of a synthesis that, in turn, becomes the next thesis. The process is open-ended and without a pre-established conclusion. Truth lies in the *process* of developing the argument, not, as is the case in propositional logic, in its conclusion.

The application of dialectic reasoning to social issues in society is called critical theory because, following Marxism, it asks about the economic and political constellations that cause human behavior to be what it is. Adorno used dialectic logic in his examination of the methods by which empirical realities can and, as he maintained, should be researched. Such an examination would include the study of music and music behavior.

Adorno's Application of Critical Theory to Music

Throughout his career, Adorno wrote about "the changing role of (art) music in contemporary mass society, as compared with the past" (Etzkorn 1973, 19). He contrasted art music and its origin to how popular music is created and distributed through the mass media and technology, which at the time the book was written consisted primarily of radio and television; the Internet would not begin to impact music consumption for another 35 years. Adorno's analyses of radio and television music focused on the "disconnect" between what he believed to be an individual's real musical needs and media-created, media-fed musical needs for "the masses." Individuals as members of large groups become prey to the free market system and are controlled by laws of supply and demand ("laws of the marketplace") rather than by their own free will. Access to bourgeois Western art music was, of course, also beyond the control of most people's free will, unless they were relatively wealthy and well educated.

In Adorno's view, collective musical needs created by the media are artificial, as they do not correspond to the actual musical values an individual holds. He called this phenomenon the social alienation of music, a characteristic he saw present in all media-created music. Adorno argued that what classical music lovers call serious or art music is characterized by a somewhat greater autonomy from commercial pressures and manipulations than is the case with mass-produced popular music. Thus, while he saw some need for sociological analyses of art music, he did not engage in it. He did acknowledge, however, that classical music can also become socially alienated music when, for instance, it is used in shopping malls, hotels, or elevators as background music. In other words, whenever music is used for commercial rather than aesthetic purposes, it ceases to be art music because it loses its authentic purpose of art for art's sake. He called this type of music "consumer music."

Alongside his philosophical position on the nature of popular and classical music and their historical and economical positions in society, Adorno proposed a hierarchically tiered typology of listeners, musical styles, and genres. It was based upon his analytical insights into the compositional complexity of different musical works as correlated to listeners' degrees of musically informed responses. The more complex a composition is and the more a listener hears that complexity, the more authentic the listening experience. In Adorno's view, popular music, manipulated for purposes of market-control, could not lead to an authentic listening experience. Adorno's position on popular and classical music as being either fully market-controlled or free of those pressures was adopted by a number of music scholars. It also led to the rather widespread, but recently contested, view that sociology (of music) is to the study of (Western) popular music what musicology is to the study of art music.

Today, critical theorists interested in the study of music hold that good music exists in all categories of musical style, from jazz to rock to reggae to salsa. What qualifies a piece as good lies in the way it is produced, composed, and brought to the audience's attention. Again, the primary criterion for "quality" remains authenticity of purpose. For example, if a recording artist has an active part in the artistic/creative process, the music is authentic and, therefore, valuable. Once principles of market research and consumer behavior govern the production of a piece of music for the purpose of mass distribution, then the music must be considered alienated from the artistic process. The music is non-authentic and, thus, of little worth and value. Another school of thought holds that the notion of "works" is antithetical to understanding value and meaning in many musics and forms of music making. The scholar who probably best epitomizes this view is U.S. socio-musicologist Charles Keil, who maintained, "Participation [in music making] gives us the best answers to the oldest questions about the meaning of life" (2002, 40).

The work of Weber, Adorno, Keil, and others has impacted academic discourse on sociology of music and music education as well as teaching practices. However, as time goes on, theories take on new forms linguistically and conceptually; this is why ideas about society and its constructs (or aspects of them) are never stagnant. Thoughts and theories are altered and/or amended through the ongoing exchange of beliefs and emerging empirical observations. Thus, while early textbooks in the English language on sociology of music maintained Weber's and Adorno's basic premises, later efforts moved in new directions.

Early Textbooks Following in the Footsteps of Weber and Adorno

Several publications in the English language comprise fairly comprehensive early texts on what a sociology of music might be or look like. The earliest authors in this regard were German-Australian Alphons Silbermann (1909–2002), Croatian Ivo Supičić (pronounced "soo-*pee*-tsh-itsh"), and German Americans Paul Honigsheim (1885–1963) and his former student Peter Etzkorn (1932–2000). Then followed *Whose Music?* (1980) by Canadian cultural theorist and sociologist John Shepherd and his British co-authors Graham Vulliamy and Trevor Wishart. The *Sociology of Music* (1983) by Americans Fabio Dasilva, Anthony Blasi, and David Dees then preceded British sociologist Peter J. Martin's *Sounds in Society* (1995). Prior to any of those works, two American sociologists, John Mueller (1895–1965) and Max Kaplan (1911–1999), had urged music educators in the United States to view their work and art in sociological terms (Kaplan 1966; Mueller 1958).

In 1958, Mueller in particular saw the following topics to have practical relevance for music teaching practices in the United States:

- The aesthetic systems of thought expressed by musicians and lay people.
- The nature of music as perceived by different groups of individuals.
- The notion of the arts as "naturally" interrelated.
- The social nature of musical taste.
- The functions of music and education in (any) society.

Kaplan suggested a schematic for music educators that showed how social roles, institutional and subject matter loyalties, and other obligations of the music educator are always interconnected (Kaplan 1966, 69). The schematic speaks to:

- The relationship between macroanalyses and microanalyses that illuminate how a music teacher is connected to the institution he or she serves.
- The community of which the school is a part.
- The roles that are connected to any of those places regionally, nationally, and internationally.

All the previously named contributors to sociological thought in music and music education provided the beginning of a body of knowledge and a way of knowing—an epistemology—that continues to grow. Viewing music as a social science, Silbermann described the structure of socio-musical groups (e.g., professional orchestras, community music groups) as functionally embedded in the cultural fabric of society. Like Mueller, Silbermann (1957/1963) argued that a sociology of music needed factual observations about how music functions in society prior to interpreting the meaning people attach to such functions. Only with data in hand, Silbermann argued, would it be possible proactively to plan and structure activities for musicians, non-musicians, and audiences alike.

Supičić first published his book in 1964 in the Serbo-Croatian language. The text focused on two interrelated purposes: setting subject matter and methods for a sociology of music apart from musicology on the one hand, and for general sociology on the other. Both objectives together—"the study *on* the sociology of music as an autonomous and specialized discipline, and that of research *within* the sociology of music itself" (Supičić 1987, xi)—were the focus of his work, replete with references to German and French scholars from musicology, ethnomusicology, aesthetics, sociology, and philosophy. The book provided a much-needed historical background for what then followed in Anglo-American scholarship on music sociology. The author also introduced the concept of what the French call *milieu*, an important term comparable to *social context* in the English language and to what Bourdieu (1984) later called *habitus*. The second part of the book covers the many empirical manifestations and functions of music in society, including the roles and functions of professional musicians.

Peter Etzkorn (1973) published *Music and Society: The Later Writings of Paul Honigsheim* based on a manuscript that Honigsheim had intended as a sociology of music for an English-speaking readership. However, struggling to understand the American popular music culture at the time (a trait connecting him with Adorno), Honigsheim never completed his envisioned text. It was left to Etzkorn to select which papers to use in finalizing the manuscript. However, he organized them according to the chapter titles Honigsheim had conceptualized:

- The Intended Meanings of Music.
- The Cultural Evaluation of Music.
- The Socio-Economic Position of the Musician.
- The Social Structure of the Audience.
- The Social Forms and Musical Forms (Etzkorn 1973, 32).

Of the various theories outlined by Etzkorn, he detailed several Eastern European (Marxist) approaches toward thinking about music in sociological terms. In addition to addressing music sociology and Marxism in some detail, Etzkorn outlined how the two disciplines of musicology and sociology interacted with each other in the early days of sociological thinking about music. It is a theme most recently reiterated and traced by Shepherd and Devine (2015). A *musicological sociology*, Etzkorn maintained, can be as useful as a *sociological musicology*. Perspectives from both approaches should inform each other.

John Shepherd, Phil Virden, Graham Vulliamy, and Trevor Wishart (1977/1980) tackled the formidable question of what school music curricula in democratic societies should look like. Acknowledging the presence of multiple musical languages in society and in the classroom, the authors used a perspective derived from Critical Theory to argue for valuing popular music for its own socio-musical sake. At the time that the publication made its mark in the United States, popular music in the repertoire of school music was becoming more commonly accepted in Europe, especially in the United Kingdom and Scandinavian countries (see Vulliamy and Lee 1976, 1982/2016; Vulliamy and Shepherd 1984). In *Music as Social Text* (1991), Shepherd articulated further how those who claim to value art music seemingly only for its musical sake actually do so for its socio-musical value. A listener or music maker reacts to a particular piece of music not only because of the sounds themselves but also because of the situation in which the listening and performing take place. Meaning is made—that is, constructed within the context familiar to the listener—at the moment the sounds are heard. Meaning derives from the interconnection between:

- What knowledge and experiences the listener/music(k)er brings to the social situation in which the music is heard.
- What knowledge and experiences the listener/music(k)er associates with the piece itself.
- How both types of knowledge and experiences relate to each other, positively or negatively, at the moment the music is heard.

Because all three conditions together contribute to how meaning is constructed for any one given piece of music, Shepherd suggested for music teachers to make these three points part of their curricular content. From within a neo-Marxist educational philosophy, the complexity of a composition would be of lesser consequence than the complexity of the social situation that creates a person's need or desire to play or listen to it (see also Shepherd and Wicke 1997).

The Sociology of Music (1984) by Dasilva, Blasi, and Dees grounds music in a broad-based, interpretive social theory that has interesting implications for curriculum discussions in music education. The theory is interpretive because it follows what philosophers call the hermeneutic method—an approach toward scholarship that combines descriptive and qualitative investigative techniques. It is a useful method also for music educators who engage in critical self-reflections for the purpose of improving their own thinking processes and teaching strategies. Like the other sociology of music scholars before them, the authors touched on (1) the social nature of all music making, (2) the relativity of social contexts and musical meaning, (3) the dialectic nature of such realities as well as the diverse roles of musicians and audiences in today's society, and (4) the social inequality of musicians' work. A wide range of case studies illustrate the numerous relationships that exist between music performance and attire, organizational structure of an ensemble, and social symbolism in dramaturgical works. The cases, as eclectic as they were, illustrate human behavior as indicators, or symbols, of social self-image: who one wants to be or how one believes one needs to act under certain circumstances and in different musical contexts. Performers who make a living by playing in different venues know about these codes of conduct as indicated by dress codes, language, and audience expectations.

Conceptualizing his work as a critically reflective response to the works by Silbermann, Adorno, and Supičić, British sociologist Peter Martin (1995) took the position of a social interactionist while maintaining pivotal constructs of Marxism and Critical Theory (for details regarding these theories in application to education, see Chapter 5), in support of the idea that musical meaning is socially constructed, that is, dependent on the space and place of the musical experience. Language is the most direct reflector of such space and place and, therefore, impacts, and is impacted by, musical form, socialization, and previously attained knowledge. Martin, therefore, critiqued his music sociological forerunners for the almost exclusive focus on European art music. Any sociology of music, he suggested, needed to be inclusive of music "created, performed, and heard" all over the world (x).

Subscribing to Adorno's concept of music as representing the society within which it is created, Martin then discussed (1) the relationship between social and musical structures, and (2) music as social action. He concluded with what he called the music business in a capitalist society, focusing on "the production of music in industrialized societies as a business rather than an art" (1995, 217). This conclusion connects him to Max Weber's theory of the rational and social foundations of music and allows him to place issues of music business, technology, and consumer conduct into the framework of bureaucratization and rationalization. He accepted the commercialization of music, conceding that all music in a capitalistic society falls under the rules that govern that society. The so-called serious music scene of the classical tradition is part and parcel of commercial pressures as much as it is art. Likewise, the so-called commercial music (as defined by Adorno) has artistic merit when the songwriters and performers view themselves as artists. A sociology of music should address both worlds with equal rigor and attention.

Building on these arguments, Martin later published *Music and the Sociological Gaze: Art Worlds and Cultural Production* (2006), carrying further the connection between musicological and sociological approaches to the analysis and study of music. In doing so, he showed how differences in musicological and sociological discourse can make it difficult to do justice to the protocols adhered to in either of the disciplines. An analysis of music as a socio-musical artifact differs from a sociological analysis of musicians' conduct in various cultural and institutional settings. Accordingly, answers to how music is used in society differ from how and why a particular composition is constructed the way it is or why performances or other musical activities take place in the ways they do. Ultimately, though, both types of analysis are likely essential in a sociology of music that fully accounts for the complexities of music making and listening.

Sociological Texts with New Footprints

There is hardly any better way to show how following in someone's footsteps can create altogether new footprints than by looking at music education and sociological thought from the middle of the twentieth century on. The physically most visible proof in that regard is perhaps the founding of several centers or institutes in Europe and the United States dedicated to the sociological study of music and/or the arts. In Europe, for instance, there are the aforementioned Institut für Musiksoziologie (Institute for Music Sociology; IMS) in Vienna, the Centre for Contemporary Cultural Studies at the University of Birmingham, and the Centre de Sociologie de l'Innovation, Mines Paris Tech. In the United States, possibly best known is the Center of Cultural Sociology at Yale University. The relevance of the named centers for music educators has not always been immediately apparent, but the centers have made and continue to make available important documents about the socio-aesthetic and political meanings of music, culture, the media, and youth culture, often impacting in subtle ways curricula for music teacher training and development in several countries.

Significant footprints for thinking in sociological terms about music education practices were left also by Christopher Small (1927–2011), who—as a native New Zealander with later roots in the United Kingdom and, eventually, Spain—had

> started to chafe at what he perceived as the elitism and inhumaneness of the ideologies surrounding the Western canon. He had already bailed from the world of avant-garde composition for which he had left his native New Zealand . . . [He] preferred teaching in colleges, in which context he began to piece together the critical narratives about Western classical music that burst into the scene in his *Music—Society—Education.*
>
> (McClary 2016, 231)

Small's second book, *Music of the Common Tongue* (1987/1998), by his own accounts his best-liked work, paved the way to his final work, *Musicking* (1998), whose title made Small a household name among music educators. The term asserts that "doing" music is a social activity, whether an individual player engages in music making in the privacy of her own room or a symphony orchestra presents a subscription concert (Small 1998; see also 2010, 2011). To music means "to take part, in any capacity, in a musical performance, whether by performing, by listening, by rehearsing or practicing, by providing material for the performance (what is called composing), or by dancing" (1998, 9). Musicking is the "doing," the ritual by which musickers explore, affirm, and celebrate the relationships they consider to be ideal.

Undoubtedly, Small's vision of what it means to engage in music also informed Froehlich's first edition of *Sociology for Music Teachers*, directed primarily at those facing teaching realities in the United States, and Ruth Wright's (2010) *Sociology and Music Education*, a "reader" volume of themes integral to sociology of music education. Through sixteen voices coming from Europe (Greece, Norway, and the United Kingdom), Australia, Canada, and the United States the following themes are articulated in Wright's book:

- Relevant research and theoretical concepts.
- The place of class, power, and prevailing cultures in school music.
- Ethnicity and gender identity.
- Contrasting formal and informal learning and teaching modalities.
- Listening and school musicking.

In addition, an approach referred to in some non-English speaking countries as *Musikdidaktik* is problematized as one that justifies non-performance routes to music learning. Situated in the German-language concept of *Bildung*, the term speaks to a general learnedness (or literacy) among a citizenry (for more, see Chapter 7). Furthermore, Wright's book also includes a chapter on systems theory as espoused by German system theorist Niklas Luhmann and his associates. Proposing to look at music education as a system unto itself, the field takes on its own identity (Johansen 2010). An "Afterword" by Christopher Small challenges music educators to become serious about the building of human relationships as the foremost purpose of all of music making and listening. Because in his view the institution or school cannot foster those relationships, de-schooling music education (that is, removing music education from school curricula) should be the answer. It is a radical response by a radical thinker.

Froehlich's and Wright's efforts to put into perspective the broad field of sociology in its application to music education are joined by many scholars from around the world, among them numerous psychologists, philosophers, and historians. Music educators are indebted to all of them, but here we can only highlight a very few. We do so under the heading of thinking about the value of music as a social construct.

Small Group Discussion 4.1

Following up on what you have read so far, consider with your classmates where you stand on the notion of music as a social construct. Do you see a divide between musical and social purposes, or do you find them entirely linked together? In what ways? What are the implications of your views for both teacher and student actions in the studio, rehearsal, or a range of different classroom settings?

Thinking about the Value of Music as a Social Construct

The usefulness of sociological lenses in the study of music has been no secret to ethnomusicologists examining such constructs as musicianship, musical ability, and "the musical work." Charles Seeger, for example, suggested that "true" musicianship becomes manifest by a thorough understanding of all musics in the culture of which one is a part, not just that of the European classical tradition. Unlike some other ethnomusicologists of his time, he advised his readers to consider the commonalities rather than the differences between musics of varying geographical regions and sub-cultures (Seeger 1977, 1994). Similarly, John Blacking formulated what he called the cultural analysis of music, distinguishing it from its stylistic analysis. He thus pointed out that musical skills and social skills are acquired simultaneously. In *How Musical Is Man?* (1973) Blacking made clear his understanding that musical ability is a defining characteristic of being human, not a special trait reserved for talented, gifted, or highly educated individuals. On the basis of this understanding, he advocated forms of informal music learning by cultural immersion. By this he meant learning instruments by rote, whether these were, for example, Caribbean steel drums, Celtic harps, Irish fiddles, or American dulcimers.

Acquiring musical skills through immersion and imitation rather than through music reading and sequential instruction speaks to the difference between learning through living and learning through schooling (see also Green 2002, 2008a, in Chapter 2). The first type of learning deals with a musical literacy that comes from a person's involvement in social situations (DeNora's [2000] cultural traditions with a lowercase "c"). High Cultural literacy would be the ability to read, write, and perform the notated score of a musical composition regardless of the social context in which such skills might be required. For many school music teachers, the challenge lies in combining both types of literacy in their pedagogies. This applies to the teaching of all kinds and styles of music.

Among musics of the United States, for instance, African-American musicians are equally situated in all cultural and Cultural landscapes. Eileen Southern first articulated this somewhat neglected empirical fact by portraying and chronicling through ethnographic essays, articles, iconographies, and discographies the legacy of classical and popular musics as they have defined Afro-American musical **c/C**ulture from the seventeenth century onward all the way to the late twentieth century (Southern 1971/1983/1997). Several additional resources have since extended that story (e.g., Banfield 2010; O'Loughlin and Charles 2015; Peretti 2009), notably among them also Small's aforementioned *Music of the Common Tongue: Survival and Celebration in African American Music* (1987/1998).

In their 1987 publication, *Music and Society: The Politics of Composition, Performance and Reception*, (ethno)musicologists and cultural theorists Richard Leppert and Susan McClary outlined important macro constructs for understanding music as conduct—socio-musical as well as political acts in very particular contexts. However, the creative act of conceptualizing a piece of art is but one dimension of understanding the ultimate work. Equally important is the analysis of how performer(s) and recipient(s) of the performance (or work of art) are socially engaged in the performance itself.

Jacques Attali, a French economist, argued similarly that the political-economic power of music should be central to considering music's significance and use in society. He contended that music creates a socio-political environment, and can be understood as a tool for creating or consolidating a community that "links a power center to its subjects" (1985, 6). Key to understanding the relationship of individuals and communities with their milieus (Bourdieu might say, their habitus) is to consider how noise, silence, music, and the evolving political places and uses of all of these factors converge in communities of music makers and listeners.

For Adorno and his immediate followers, the distinction between popular and art music lies in the degree of authenticity attributed by a listener to the music she or he hears or performs. Authentic repertoire, according to this point of view, must not have been adulterated by mass media influences and technological manipulations. This, then, becomes the justification for including classical music and "world" ethnic musics in the curriculum, but not popular music. As pointed out in Chapter 2, many contemporary critical pedagogues reject Adorno's position. They maintain that all music making and listening are socially situated and integrally linked to today's means of communication (Frith 1996; Gracyk 2007; Green 2008a; Moore 2001). Even if those means are mass-media controlled and technologically driven, they are no less authentic than a live symphonic concert performance or a quartet of string players gathered in the privacy of someone's home. To attach such terms as authentic or inauthentic, good or bad, desirable or undesirable, beautiful or ugly is to ascribe value judgments outside the realm of sociological observation. More important would be to examine the reasons that cause someone to attach those value judgments to a musical experience.

Despite a general resistance by most sociologists to attach value judgments to music, Weber's sociological framework declared the Western musical "language" superior to musics of other cultures because of its acoustic properties. Although he conceded that poly-rhythms and poly-tonalities have the potential of becoming integrated into the Western musical vocabulary, Weber also believed that the Western tonal and harmonic language provides the greatest and most efficient vocabulary for musical expressions of all kinds. In his view, the vocabulary is so malleable and pliable that it has become the basis for pop, rock, fusion, rap, salsa, and other musics of the world. Authenticity, then, lies outside the properties of music itself. The question arises: if (high) Culture is as media-controlled as (everyday) culture, is authenticity a sufficient standard by which to judge what to include in or exclude from a curriculum?

Writing Project 4.1

On the basis of your knowledge of history, develop some ideas of how music making in different performance venues of the past was accompanied by what Dasilva et al. (1984) called behavior codes. Determine relevant behavior codes of today's many different performance venues and compare them with what you know about past musical conduct and contexts. How might these comparisons impact your understandings and work as a music teacher?

Musical Authenticity as a Curricular Standard

If the individual rather than the community were the exclusive standard of judging what is moral, right, and ethical in a society, the community as the societal core would vanish. This is the position that Briton Roger Scruton articulated in defense of "culture in its higher and more critical form" (Scruton 2000, x). He stated what other functionalists might say as well: "it is impossible to give a convincing defense of high culture to a person who has none" (2000, x). As elitist as such as position may appear, Scruton pointed to the importance of high culture as the core of a curriculum threatened by an ill-informed preference for popular communication over a subject matter-based, historical understanding.

In a historically grown, social-political body that is bonded together by symbols of knowledge shared over generations, Scruton saw religion as one such symbol, music another. Both symbols, along with the other arts and literature, form the social capital of society. This capital unites a nation and educates its citizens. Formal education provides "connectivity" between generations, and the rites and customs "legitimize not only the actions but the feelings that advance through them. It is easier to feel serious emotions when this is what society expects; easier still when provided with a repertoire of accepted gestures" (2000, 14). Feeling exists only "when it finds objective form, in words, gestures, plans and projects. A feeling involves a picture of the world and a stance towards it; it is predicated on understanding" (Scruton 2000, 16). The purpose of any formal education should be to provide that understanding (see also Gebesmair 2006, 2009).

High culture "teaches us to live *as if* our lives mattered eternally" (Scruton 2000, 16). Like religion, it "addresses the question which science leaves unanswered: the question what to feel. The knowledge that it bestows on us is not that of facts or of means, but that of ends, the most precious knowledge we have" (17). Shared value judgments are essential in holding a society together. But to be shared, they have to be taught. Music in the realm of high culture, along with the other arts and literature, stands for more than a social document of its time. As a symbol of collective thought and meaning, it represents aspects of a humanity that transcends any one composer's life. This is a position also held by German Marxist and critical theorist Herbert Marcuse, who made the case—to some extent like Adorno—that any art work, although situated in a social context, also critically examines that very context (Marcuse 1978). Thus questioning Karl Marx's interpretation of art as representing "the interest and world outlook of particular social classes in a more or less accurate manner" (Marcuse 1978, ix), Marcuse found the greatest level of authenticity in the work of art that questions reality in such a way that content and form become one. In Chapter 6, you can find more on authenticity as a criterion for making aesthetic judgments in the music classroom.

Small Group Discussion 4.2

1. How useful is it (and how might it be useful) to distinguish between commercial and aesthetic purposes of music? How would such a distinction be beneficial in setting curricular goals and objectives?
2. Where would you be, musically and socially, if not for your school music experiences?
3. Plan teaching strategies for a classroom setting of your choice that highlight how "**C**ulture" and "**c**ulture" interact in your own life and your students' lives.

Questions for Class Discussion

1. What benefits, if any, lie in distinguishing between process and product when setting music educational goals?
2. Which of the books described in this chapter appeal to you the most and why?
3. What does it mean to be culturally and musically educated? Do you agree with this distinction, or do you believe both terms describe similar processes and outcomes? If so, what are these?
4. As you compare publications from the middle of the last century to how writers present their ideas now, where do you see the greatest differences in present-day and past writing styles, pedagogies, and concerns?

Key Sources (for full information, see References)

Adorno, Theodor W. 1962/1976.
Attali, Jacques. 1985.
Dasilva, Fabio, Anthony Blasi, and David Dees. 1984.
Etzkorn, Peter. 1973, 1989.
Frith, Simon. 1996/2011.
Kaplan, Max. 1966, 1990.
Marcuse, Herbert. 1978.
Martin, Peter J. 1995, 2006.
O'Loughlin, Michael and Marilyn Charles, 2015.
Scruton, Roger. 2000.
Small, Christopher. 1987/1998, 1998.
Weber, Max. 1921/1958.

5

Sociology of Education

Social Constructs with Relevance for Music Teachers

This chapter speaks to:

- Selected Sociological Theories in Education—Past and Present
- Achievement and Opportunity Gaps among Learners
- The Hidden Curriculum in Education and Schooling

Gareth: Hildegard, what impact have sociologists of education had in your professional training and work?

Hildegard: A great deal! Not only was the first university reading I ever took at the University of Hamburg "Sociology of Schools" but the first research course I elected to take was taught by a sociologist with education as his specialization. Prior to enrolling at the university I had done some volunteer teaching and always assumed that teaching meant to share what *I* knew. The "sociology of things" alerted me to a different idea: take the students' knowledge and broaden it to where they can work with it constructively. Later, I heard the same concept talked about in my teaching method classes and in psychology courses, but approaching it from a sociological perspective was an eye-opening experience with consequences for the rest of my work as a teacher. This kind of thinking impacted my lesson plans and gave me a better insight into what it means to make curricular decisions at all levels. Curiously, though, my friends and family were always quite surprised that a music teacher would be involved in sociology. In fact, they still are wondering.

Gareth: I began my doctoral studies thinking I wanted to study psychology, but my advisor said she thought that what I really wanted was to be a sociologist. Although I was initially unconvinced, I tested her idea by attending relevant conferences and reading pertinent texts. I soon discovered that the ways in which sociologists view the world around them and seek to understand values informing and underpinning society really spoke to me. I frequently felt like a veil was being lifted as my assumptions were challenged or destroyed, time and again. My teaching changed virtually overnight, when, as you, Hildegard, I experienced the epiphany that teaching need not, and should not, be about trying to make sure everyone in the room learn what I'd learned and thought was important. Sociologists of education help keep me in check by revealing to us more of the bigger picture: there are values, worldviews, meanings, and realities for people beyond my day-to-day experience. While some of these have a bigger or more visible impact on learning than others, none should be overlooked or can be dismissed as unimportant.

Introduction

This chapter is about current sociological thought on schooling for the twenty-first century. Specifically, the chapter covers thoughts and theories concerning (1) the place of schooling in a particular society (the macro view), (2) what such schooling should or might look like in the context of a particular classroom (the micro view), and (3) how such variables as "income, age, gender, race, ethnicity, organizations, and geographically circumscribed communities" (Turner 2006, xi) create that very context (the meso view). In practical terms, some of the questions sociologists of education ask are also those that teachers and parents ask: is each child safe and looked after in school, and does each child get the resources to learn what there is to learn? Jeanne Ballantine and Floyd Hammack (2009, 6–7) called these and similar questions worries about school safety, parental and teacher control in school learning and funding, the acquisition of basic and advanced competencies, the place of testing and other measures of learning progress and achievement, opportunities for advancement into well-paying jobs, and fairness in the classroom environment.

Many of the issues mentioned by Ballantine and Hammack connect personal worries about an individual child to the larger picture of societal and institutional decision making. In sociological terminology, the personal level of experiences is subject to what sociologists call microanalyses, and the study of societal structures and constellations is referred to as macroanalysis. In between falls the analysis of what connects macro with microanalyses: the meso—or mid-level—analysis. It speaks to the settings in which the personal and the societal are acted out. In the case of education, those settings may be schools, educational agencies, and committee structures that bear on local decision making, or similar places in which personal concerns are turned into official action.

Sociologists of education strive to show the interrelatedness of everyday pedagogical classroom realities to the macro, meso, and micro structures that define what education as a discipline is about (e.g., Ball 2004; Ballantine and Spade 2014; Böhnisch 2003; Brooks, McCormack, and Bhopal 2013; Hallinan 2000; Michaelis-Jähnke 2006/2012). All three analytic sets are needed to portray fully what takes place in the world of education. All analyses must be tied together by a particular vantage point or perspective consistently applied to all actual observations. Each such vantage point is a theory, a set of principles that holds the observations together.

Over the years, sociological theories have flooded the field of education and continue to trigger new ones when existing theories are found to be insufficient or even invalid for fully explaining school realities. All theories work in response to each other and should be read and discussed accordingly (Lemert 2005). This is one of the reasons why Michael Apple called the resultant diversity of extant theories "messy, dynamic, somewhat elusive and invariably disputatious" (Apple, Ball, and Gandin 2010, 1). He also reminded his readers to follow Patti Lather's (1988) caution to "always think of any one 'ism' in the plural" (Apple, Ball, and Gandin 2010, 1). This advice clearly reflects what many feminist scholars of various philosophical persuasions imply when they question the validity of existing categorizations, their assumptions, and definitions, and painstakingly trace differences in beliefs among feminists of different persuasions and geographies (e.g., Acker 1987; Crenshaw, Gotanda, Peller, and Thomas 1995; Haraway 2004; Hartsock 1998; Hill Collins 2000/2002; Hines 2013; Roberts and Connell 2016).

Within the acknowledged messiness and diversity of theories, there is nonetheless agreement on the labels used to describe an individual's primary and secondary socialization phases—as discussed in Chapter 1. The years of primary socialization are those most influenced by direct caregivers, be they parents, grandparents, or guardians, as these provide the first model of conduct for young and, to some extent, older children. Secondary socialization is referred to as the time during which increasingly greater influences from outside the nuclear family change a young person's perceptions about the world "out there." This phase includes formal schooling, media influences, and the growing influences of peers. It is also the phase that likely speaks most directly to working (music) teachers because they are aware of how transitions from one phase to the next can bring with them new challenges in the classroom.

As important as agreements are about the first two socialization phases in a child's growth and development, even more important is to understand the nature and quality of influences each phase brings with it. Teachers work with those influences, fully aware that some of them can be productive for the learning process, whereas others may need to be controlled and/or manipulated for the good of the child and society. In this regard, however, national, cultural, and ethnic differences in traditions, including their histories, may lead to disparate interpretations of what "good" or "productive" means. Consequently, who receives what kind of education and for what (and whose) purpose differs among nation-states around the globe. Such goals as literacy and morality, for example, may be agreed on and shared in concept by many peoples of the world, but the assumptions behind the terms and the practices and behaviors that they inform, frequently differ (Leyshon 2011).

In this chapter, we place the plurality of theories on the betterment of society through education into a framework that reflects how sets of theories (or "isms") feed into one another and how, through that process, new theories may emerge. Illustrated in Figure 5.1, the grouping follows in large part what Ballantine and Hammack (2009) suggested as their first three major categorizations, namely functionalism, critical pedagogy, and interactionism. But following Apple's suggestion, we name those categories in the plural. We then add another category of theories, which we call topical theories. It serves as the umbrella for feminist, race, gender, and related theories. This choice emphasizes Ballantine and Hammack's observation of the "ongoingness" of articulated thought processes in the sociology of education. Figure 5.1 depicts these processes as moving, related cog wheels, in which each wheel stands for what might be considered a "a family of theories," with each wheel's teeth representing a plethora of viewpoints, foci, and emphases within a particular family. All teeth are responsible, however, for keeping the discourse going, always providing new avenues for explaining realities.

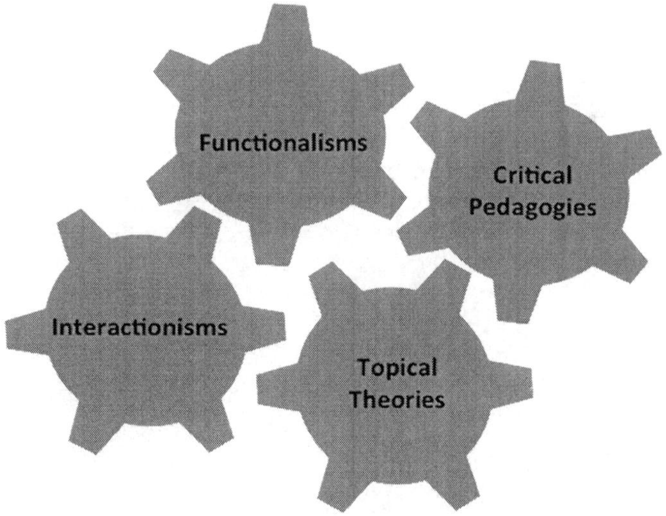

Figure 5.1 Visualizing the Connectedness among Various Theoretical Frameworks

Small Group Discussion 5.1

How would you explain to a twelve-year-old what sociologists do? Support your answer with examples that have a bearing on learning about music in society.

Selected Sociological Theories in Education—Past and Present

No theoretical model remains stagnant; theories are the result of thinking about practical matters in ways that explain lived observations and lived experiences. This is the case also for what functionalists, critical pedagogues, interactionists, and topical theorists do when they examine and reflect on one another's insights into pivotal constructs used to explain schooling realities at all levels of analysis. Ultimately, it is for you to decide whether a theory helps to explain or shed light on your realities as a teacher. Where it does, embrace the model; where it does not, find ways to articulate your disagreements, determine their reasons, and find ways to communicate those thought processes to your peers. This virtual and real discourse is the driving force behind what all educators strive for: the improvement of daily classroom practices in terms of goals, affordability, and equal access.

Early functionalists following in Émile Durkheim's (1858–1917) and Max Weber's footsteps accepted that the purpose of compulsory education was to meet the demands of society for an educated and productive (national) populace that served society as a whole. However, early critical pedagogues, also referred to as conflict theorists, questioned to varying degrees the value, place, and function of schooling as it existed in particular societies. Ever since those earlier days, many variations of beliefs in the purpose of compulsory schooling have arisen. Structural functionalists differ from technological and social functionalists, critical interactionists from systems analysts, critical feminists from other feminists, and critical race theorists from cultural nationalists.

Selected Functionalists in Education

Durkheim's work on moral education as the basis for developing a societal identity and Weber's belief in literacy as the basis for social control continue to be at the center of discussions on compulsory education. This demonstrates that both functional and critical theory have been part of the educational discourse in Western societies for a long time. For Durkheim, pedagogical matters required a sociological framework because it made visible "the relationship between society and its institutions, all of which he believed were interdependent and therefore resulted in social cohesion" (Ballantine and Hammack 2009, 14). All parts within the educational process—the family, the school, the community, and society at large—function dependently on each, hence the term functionalism.

Building on Durkheim's thinking, Talcott Parsons (1902–1979) was one of functionalism's best-known early representatives in the United States. Like Durkheim, he considered a country's education system central to maintaining a national culture—in his view, the glue holding a people together. Although much of his work focused on examining a society's social stratification from a macro perspective (e.g., 1937, 1951), one of his landmark essays for education was the analysis of the classroom "as a social system" (2015), the location where "'the business' of formal education actually takes place" (298). Considering compulsory schooling as a major tool of enculturation and, to some extent, even acculturation is shared by many current-day functionalists.

Enculturation processes are those that socialize an individual to the norms and values defining a society's social, cultural, and ethical fabric. Acculturation "describes the process by which an outsider, immigrant, or subordinate group becomes indistinguishably integrated into the dominant host society" (Scott and Marshall 2009, 27). In either of the processes, a person's socio-economic status, class, gender, and ethnicity are vital in understanding how all socialization agents interact with each other through formal schooling and informal learning (Ball 2004; see also Chapters 2 and 6).

Belonging to a particular social group is a matter of a person's willingness to submit to somewhat "prescribed and static expectations of behavior" (Abercrombie et al. 2006, 333). To belong one must conform. An example of this truism can be seen in young adolescents. Although many factors can complicate the transitional and ambivalent adolescent socialization phase, what may come across to outsiders as erratic, subversive, and defiant behavior, full of risk taking and certainly not static, signifies to the adolescent belonging and conformity and, thus, stability. For many young adults, therefore, experimental drug and alcohol use, gendered stereotyping, and non-conformist conduct toward authorities of all kinds signify conformity with peers (Ball and Tyson 2011; Morgan 2005; Sensoy and DiAngelo 2012; Smith and Hart 2010).

Of particular note among (functional) systems analysts of today continues to be the distinction Parsons made between ascribed and achieved social status (e.g., Luhmann 2006, 2012; for a brief English description of Luhmann's work in application to music education, see Johansen 2010). An ascribed social status is determined at birth by virtue of the race, ethnicity, and social-economic class into which one is born. Achieved social status is the result of how one is raised to assume certain roles throughout life in interactions with others. That these binary categorizations are insufficient when explaining socialization processes becomes clear when considering not only issues of transgender and bisexuality but also what many people refer to as inborn abilities over learned achievements.

For example, the world of music knows about conflicts between ascribed and achieved status in matters of what often are referred to by lay musicians and the general public as artistic talent and musical ability. Popular opinion, somewhat simplistic, tends to view musical ability as an inborn (ascribed) trait rather than an achieved one (Hallam 2001; Sloboda and Davidson 1996; Smith and Durrant 2006; Welch 2001). Similarly, but outside of music, inequities in learning opportunities may well be caused by misinterpreting ascribed and achieved status among learners of different social classes, gender, and ethnicities. Consequently, what is inborn and what is acquired through work and opportunity are central questions in education. In recent years, these questions have taken on renewed urgency because of the relocation of immigrant and refugee families in parts of the world beyond their homelands. The concepts of ascribed and achieved status alone become insufficient to deal with and address in a constructive manner differences in religious and other social expectations.

Although contemporary sociological thought tends to reject starkly binary terminology, most early functionalists considered gender and race to be ascribed statuses and transgender and bisexuality achieved statuses. It was less clear how intelligence and achievement were to be categorized. In that regard, the work of American James Coleman (1926–1995) provided first, groundbreaking empirical data (Coleman 1961, 1965). His large-scale empirical study offered insights into the relationship between specific young adolescent subcultures in a racially divided educational system, showing statistically significant differences in measures of intelligence and learning achievement between black and white adolescents, although not between Asian and white students. The findings, as politically controversial as they were in the eyes of the study's critics, carried forward scholarship and teaching practices in education and national education policies in and beyond the United States.

The strongest connection between earlier and more recent functionalists in the sociology of education is a shared belief in the power of systematic observation and data gathering, as major tools for guiding policy makers and curriculum experts in their decision making (Arum et al. 2011; Carter 2005; Downes 2014; Gorski and Landsman 2013; Hanson 2001; Holland, Skinner, Lachicotte, and Cain 2001; Holz and Grimus 2013; Kincheloe and Horn 2007; Kozol 1991, 2012; Lareau 2011; Plößer 2005; Richards and Zenkov 2016; Vohs and Baumeister 2011). The classroom is considered the laboratory in which new ways of democratized learning are tried out and tested. Such ways include focusing on individualized instruction that is based on informal learning models, and re-thinking and re-designing testing content and procedures that control an entire school curriculum (Fryer and Levitt 2004; Lee and Ready 2009; Seidman 2012). Furthermore, alternative pedagogies are tried out and documented as solutions to racial and gendered inequalities in the classroom (Milner 2004; Plößer 2005; Richards and Zenkov 2016; Trumbull, Rothstein-Fisch, Greenfield, and Quiroz 2001). Often in connection with scholars in the field of comparative education, functionalists propose numerous managerial and curricular changes in the form of vocational schools (as are common in many European, South American, and Asian countries), learning tracks (as in Australia, Canada, and the United States), or both (as in the United Kingdom). In countries with several official languages, schools offer bi- or multi-lingual education, but even countries with only one official language have begun to provide instruction in several languages and offer remedial programs for various student nationalities and levels of learning.

Functionalists in education also pay close attention to the politically and economically advocated globalization of education (e.g., Downes 2014; Goldstein 2004; Suša 2009; Suša and Vodopivec 2011; Vohs and Baumeister 2011). They advocate for working toward accepting student and teacher diversity, providing ethical care, and embracing inclusionary practices that promote social justice (Gilligan 1982; Gorard and Smith 2004a; Gorski and Landsman 2013; Noddings 1984; Prengel 2006; Reich 2012). If implemented systematically, these efforts are believed to turn skills of reading, writing, and doing basic mathematics into functional tools for living a productive, useful life for the individual and society.

Small Group Discussion 5.2

Thinking about your family, how you would describe your own ascribed and achieved social status? How might, or how did, your own perceived status hinder or assist you in becoming a music teacher who is comfortable with communicating with learners from backgrounds different from yours?

Selected Critical Pedagogies

Critical pedagogies are the result of applying major constructs of critical theory to issues concerning education. Forerunners of critical theory, Marx and Weber are generally credited as important contributors to critical pedagogy. To explain the term "conflict," Weber made the observation that there was "a tension in society and its parts created by the competing interests of individuals and groups" (Ballantine and Hammack 2009, 17). This tension in part shapes the everyday realities of all teachers. When viewed from a Marxist perspective, the tension causes alienation between those who hold power and those who do not (the distinction between the "haves" and "have nots"). As long as the prevailing class system contributes to organizational hierarchies that cement the status quo of societies rather than advocate or permit change, the tension, or experience of conflict, remains. Once the tension becomes too strong, change in the power structures occurs by force. Applying major constructs from conflict theory to the field of education, then, has resulted in critical pedagogies as a major branch in the sociology of education.

To connect particular critical theories with human faces, we single out just a few of the most influential thinkers who applied conflict theory to education; in order of birth: Americans Charlotte Perkins Gilman (1860–1935) and W.E.B. Du Bois (1868–1963), Brazilian Paulo Freire (1921–1997), Briton Basil Bernstein (1924–2000), Austrian Ivan Illich (1926–2002), Frenchman Pierre Bourdieu (1930–2002), American Randall Collins (born in 1941), and American/Canadian Henry Giroux (born in 1943). Each of them focus(ed) on particular issues confronting their respective cultures, but all speak or spoke to basic socio-political inequalities and resultant achievement gaps present in their countries, perpetuated by each society's educational institutions.

Charlotte Perkins Gilman earned her position among early feminist critical pedagogues in the United States because of her contributions that examined the place of a child's home environment as the first site for socialization and, thus, education. The home environment is the place where the unequal distribution of rights between man and woman, girls and boys, and husband and wife begins and becomes reality (Gilman 1898, 1903/1910). In economic terms, those gender and role realities (and inequalities) cause what Karl Marx called the unequal production of material goods. Unlike Karl Marx, however, Gilman emphasized the gender component as "the moment when the species begins to control its food supply" (Lengermann and Niebrugge 1998, 125). Therefore, "class stratification arises out of gender stratification" (125) and a child's primary socialization, including access to education, is first and foremost shaped by gender inequalities. Although she was in her time a well-known and respected sociological theorist, Gilman was until quite recently excluded from the canon of "official" contributors to sociological theories, itself a matter of sociological significance.

W.E.B. Du Bois experienced the same exclusion from the canon of critical pedagogues most likely because of racial discrimination. His early writings were guided by strictly empiricist methods (e.g., Du Bois 1899, 1910), but in his later works on race Du Bois became a vocal advocate for equality and schooling equities in the United States. Those works made him a central figure also among early critical race theorists who found empiricist methods rooted in functionalism ineffective in calls for social justice. In Du Bois's studies, monographs, and essays, of which several were published posthumously, education always played a pivotal role because he considered it an important tool in shaping social consciousness about race as a socially (achieved) rather than biologically constructed (ascribed) reality (Du Bois 1945, 2014).

Basil Bernstein began his lifelong work as a socio-linguist by examining how the power structures within an individual's life are determined by the linguistic discourse present during primary socialization (Bernstein 1971–1975/2003, 1990/2003, 1996/2000). Because individuals from different social classes engage in everyday conventions in disparate ways, their modes of accessing knowledge differ as well. For example, not all social classes and cultures permit a child to argue with a parent as to why certain family or cultural rules are necessary. Similarly, not all students are comfortable with engaging in teacher-initiated (and expected) class discussion, whereas others expect a dialogue. Such conventions, specific to particular places of schooling and subject to societal traditions and expectations, are symbols of power; language, therefore, signifies who controls (or dominates) whom, and who is controlled or dominated by whom. Consequently, the ways in which children acquire their primary linguistic skills say a great deal about their abilities with, as well as attitudes toward, the spoken word as a communicative tool.

Pierre Bourdieu questioned altogether the validity of formal schooling in any institutionalized form and pointed out how unequal distribution of social status is connected to unequal possession of what he termed *cultural capital*. He used the term in conjunction with two related forms of capital—economic and social—to outline a comprehensive critique of capital as power (Bourdieu 1986). Just as financial wealth is distributed unequally in capitalist societies, so is cultural capital. In his view, therefore, schools sustain and affirm the cultural "haves" and their power in society (Bourdieu 1977, 1993; Bourdieu and Passeron 1977; Bourdieu and Wacquant 1992). Cultural capital, as reflected in what schools teach, is neither equally accessible nor shared by everyone in society because of [illegible] in the workforce and corresponding career paths. Like Bernstein, he [illegible] probed the socio-political and economic roots of any type of knowledge, and [illegible] that formal education in schools serves the purpose of solidifying [illegible] relationships rather than eradicating them. Consequently, he [illegible] knowledge of publicly sanctioned art, music, theater, and literature was for the purpose of reflecting hierarchical tiers of social status, rather than a means of dismantling that hierarchy.

Like Bourdieu, Paulo Freire and Ivan Illich argued against a sole reliance on schools as major socializing agents. Unequal access to learning resources creates an ever-deepening gulf between what members of society can constructively contribute with or without school knowledge and what they are allowed to contribute once given permission to do so by those who control the workforce. Originally directing their writings at societies in Latin America, Freire and Illich also included industrialized nations in their criticism of schools becoming controlling social forces far beyond the mere acquisition of basic reading and writing skills.

Following Bourdieu's footsteps in the critique of educational thinking as cementing a collective societal status quo, Randall Collins (1979, 1999a, 1999b, 2004) gave this phenomenon the name "credentialism." The label holds that socio-economically advantaged individuals reach higher level positions because they gain credit (credentials) for where and who they are prior to having actually proven themselves. Culture critic Henry Giroux (1983, 1988, 2001; Giroux and Penna 1983) saw in such credentialism the cause for the apparent inability or unwillingness of those in power to bring about fundamental change in schooling processes. Compulsory education tends to stifle, and often render impossible, a learner's self-perceived need to obtain knowledge for particular purposes and self-set goals. For learning to be effective, it should transform the learner, not simply lead to memorization of facts. Because the structure of most schools makes it difficult (at best) to reach such a goal, Giroux and other critical pedagogues like him have continued to critique the inequities embedded in school learning as part of a planned systems design. It is the design itself that is believed to cause systemic gaps in achievement and opportunity common to nearly all forms of schooling. We address both aspects in greater detail later in this chapter.

The prevailing sentiment among current-day critical pedagogues is opposition to an emphasis on formal schooling in nearly all industrialized nations that appears to de-value informally gained, experiential knowledge. The latter is a much-needed form of learning in all societies as it tends to be forward looking, entrepreneurial, and empowering. Critical pedagogues would, therefore, argue for a type of learning in which many useful and relevant skills can be and are obtained outside of formal schooling and are valued culturally and monetarily. Officially sanctioned school knowledge is insufficient in determining what an educated society is or should be (e.g., Bernstein 1996/2000; Denzin and Giardina 2007; Diversi and Moreira 2009; Schugurensky 2015). Most critical pedagogues emphasize the power of informal learning and education in all its forms as a step toward reducing poverty along with other racial and social injustices and inequalities.

Current discourse among critical pedagogues continues to address fundamental questions about the feasibility of collective goals in schooling for all as a means to benefit culturally and economically the well-being of each individual in society. The issues are about formal schooling as the key to building a socially just and economically equitable community or as a hindrance to realizing those very goals. The often-cited educational goal of instilling patriotism and national pride in all school-age children, too, is examined critically because both goals, presumably as symbols for love of and service to country, can be and have been misused, if not abused, throughout history (see the topic of nationalism and militarism discussed briefly in Chapter 2). Critical pedagogues are equally critical of the general educational goal of maintaining a country's workforce for the common good of a nation's citizenry and/or the aim of providing a certain level of cultural learnedness (what the Germans and Scandinavians call *Bildung*; e.g., Blaut 1993; Carlsburg 2009; Davies 2004; Holz and Grimus 2013; Hornberg 2010; see also Chapter 7). No goal is ever good in and of itself. It always needs to be re-examined in light of what is good for the individual rather than the community as a whole. Critical pedagogues aim to ensure that educators remain vigilant of this perspective.

Small Group Discussion 5.3

Share with each other your own experiences of what from compulsory schooling really stuck with you. Consider the subject matter areas where such learning took place and reflect on how "school" learning turned into "life" learning, if at all.

Selected Interactionists in Education

Americans Charles Horton Cooley (1864–1929) and George Herbert Mead (1863–1947) are key figures in what has become known as the *Chicago School of Sociology* and in what later emerged as the theory of interactionism. It is a scientific theory that grew out of empiricism and morphed into pragmatism as a philosophical position, first articulated by Americans Charles Sanders Peirce (1839–1914), William James (1842–1910), and John Dewey (1859–1952). Unlike Dewey, however, neither Cooley nor Mead spoke directly to matters concerning the nature of schools and formal learning. Others around them, in particular some of Mead's female colleagues, did so in a variety of ways (Deegan 1991; Lengermann and Niebrugge 1998; Morgan 1980; Morgan 1983). Sharing in the belief that the human organism is best understood in relationship to its environment, women in particular broadened the concept of learning to include social interactions on playgrounds, in shelters, in settlements, and in other places where learning of all forms takes place (e.g., Addams 1902, 1912; Talbot 1910).

Reviewing symbolic interactionism as it has been used in different academic disciplines since the late twentieth century, the constructs of context and perspective have remained dominant (Charon 1998; Reynolds and Herman-Kinney 2003). Interactionism is the vantage point not only of a particular discipline but also of those who work under its label. For example, the answers an interactionist in education gives to questions about schooling would, by necessity, differ from those formulated by a functionalist or critical pedagogue. The object dealt with in each discipline shapes how those in that discipline describe the world. Each perspective is a social construct rather than an absolute, objective phenomenon. This belief is a social philosophy known as social constructivism or, simply, constructivism. Also sometimes referred to as constructionism, its basic constructs have been most famously described by Peter Berger and Thomas Luckmann in their 1967 landmark book *The Social Construction of Reality*.

Most interactionists writing about education use the term constructionism rather than constructivism to denote a socio-cultural approach that connects the psychology of learning to sociology and philosophy (Abercrombie et al. 2006, 320), although both terms seem to be equally understood as referring to a perspective informed by pragmatism. For example, when examining schooling from an interactionist point of view, not any one disciplinary vantage point is considered sufficient to answer the question of what schooling *really* is. It would require sociologists, educationists, psychologists, and representatives from other disciplines to put together a composite construct to get close to defining schooling as a social phenomenon.

Two important offshoots of interactionism are *reference group theory* and *labeling theory*. They have impacted music education scholarship, especially in the United States and Canada, since the mid- to late twentieth century. Two of the founders of *reference group theory* were Robert K. Merton (1911–2003) and Tamotsu Shibutani (1920–2004). Both men (functionalists in many ways) contributed significantly to answering the question of how individuals interact with the many different groups of which they are a part (Merton 1957, 1967; Shibutani 1987). This inquiry includes how, at the micro level, each person functions as a family member, classmate, spouse, colleague, peer, or friend. On the macro level, reference group theory addresses how the individual aligns his or her own expectations with those of larger social groups, among them those deriving from one's socio-economic class, chosen occupation, and the racial, political, and religious affiliations with which one identifies.

Labeling theory extends reference group theory and is based on Cooley's notion of people's habit of wanting to label what they perceive to be different from themselves (see, among others, Becker 1951/1980, 1982/1984/2008; Hudak and Kihn 2001; Roberts 2004). Originally connected to studying what sociologists call deviance (otherness from what is considered a norm; see Chapter 3), labeling theory deals with individuals internalizing the meaning of a term in a particular way and the consequences of such an internalization for behaviors, performances, and educational outcomes. As Abercrombie et al. (2006, 210) observed, "The theory has proven a fruitful development of sociological understanding of the relationships between deviance, self-conceptions, social reaction and control."

Selected Topical Sociological Theories in Education

What thoughts have emerged from theories of functionalism, critical pedagogy, and interactionism—each with their respective sub-categorizations—that have carried into or inform contemporary sociological theories in education? The evidence suggests that especially critical pedagogues have included among them from early on theorists who singled out feminist, race, gender, and (dis)ability perspectives as sharpened (new) vantage points for addressing topics of systemic prejudice across societal institutions. Many music education scholars have since embraced those theories and search for ways to implement them in the practice of everyday teaching.

Feminists in particular (men included) remind pedagogues to be cognizant of each learner's equal rights on the one hand and each learner's uniqueness on the other (Prengel 2006). Feminists point to plenty of evidence that rights are not equally distributed. Children of undocumented workers and illegal immigrants in numerous countries continue to lack the kind of formal education children from families with documented residences have come to expect (Algan, Dustmann, Glitz, and Manning 2010; Bowles and Gintis 1976; Heath, Rothon, and Kilpi 2008; Kozol 1991, 2012; Manning 2010; Pinson, Arnot, and Candappa 2010). Child labor and differential access to schooling between urban and rural areas remain pertinent issues in many countries (e.g., Gunnarsson, Orazem, and Sánchez 2006; King, Orazem, and Paterno 1999), as do teacher preparation programs within individual nation-states. This means that teacher preparedness for different forms of schooling, too, continues to be a source of concern among feminists and other critical pedagogues as well as among educationists, parents, and policy makers.

Prevailing discourse among critical race theorists is as much a response to functionalists' claims of "color-blindness" as the response calls for broadening issues of race, law, and power to include issues of cultural mistrust, dissonance, and systemic conflict in schooling and other educational opportunities (e.g., Auslander 2008; Chinn 1997; Delgado and Stefancic 2012, 2013; DeLorenzo 2015a; Gillborn and Ladson-Billings 2010; Liu, Ahn, Baek, and Han 2004; Lynn and Dixson 2013; Museus 2014; Robinson 2006; Trumbull et al. 2001; Tyson 2014). Personal stories and counter-narratives are used as data to radically question prevailing civil rights laws as proof against equality under the law. A similar criticism motivates post-colonial scholars, who extend critical race theory to curricula and pedagogies in compulsory schooling as remaining bastions of what once were politically dominated and controlled Euro-American colonial powers around the world (e.g., Rizvi, Lingard, and Lavia 2006; Rodríguez-Silva 2012; Rosabal-Coto 2016). At the other end of the spectrum of topical theories are international functionalists who advocate for schooling as a global responsibility (e.g., Bourn 2008; Dimitrova et al. 2014; Pike 2000; Suša 2009; Suša and Vodopivec 2011; UNESCO 2015a, b, and c).

The multitude of perspectives that demonstrate and emphasize diversity should serve to remind readers of this book that, from a sociological point of view, one cannot easily use the word "normal" to describe that with which one may be familiar. Increased awareness of contexts and circumstances that you may not have considered in the past—from the macro of post-colonial and critical race theorists, to the micro of individuals' situations—sheds new light on the meso contexts of schools and music classrooms. Derived from critical pedagogues' healthy dose of skepticism toward prevailing hierarchies of power and accepted beliefs (official knowledge), the learning objective of "critical thinking" is now hailed as a power-affirming, educational mandate in many curricula. What once was a philosophical approach that questioned the economic and social distribution of "what is" in compulsory education has now been appropriated into a normative educational mandate and learning objective that invites students to:

- Test ideas based on prior knowledge and personal experiences.
- Apply what has been tested to new learning situations.
- Integrate such newly gained insight into already formed thoughts and familiar concepts.

It is also noteworthy that the basic skepticism articulated by critical pedagogues toward schooling can be observed in some countries among citizens who wish to place the responsibility for a child's educational needs (back) under greater parental supervision (as seems to be a trend in the United States, where it is referred to as home-schooling). Placing the responsibility of compulsory schooling under greater parental control would require decisions regarding what, in the eyes of a people and its political representatives, is or is not considered officially sanctioned school knowledge and what might constitute the skills required to lead a productive life. Once those standards become scrutinized because of varying belief systems and the uneven distribution of resources available to schools, new forms of schooling may have to be created that account for what functionalists, critical pedagogues, and interactionists alike agree are concerns and challenges in this still-young millennium. Among those concerns shared by many are the consequences of achievement and opportunity gaps in schooling on individual learners as well as how the latter may experience the hidden curriculum as it is potentially present in all pedagogies.

Small Group Discussion 5.4

Achievement gap
and Helix
(teachers like me
stats)
RP

Of [illegible] ideas do you take mo[illegible]ts yourself? Have you [illegible] your group; if not, beg[illegible] topics addressed eith[illegible] what extent do you share the concerns of thinkers discussed in this section?

Achievement and Opportunity Gaps among Learners

The Glossary of Education Reform (Abbott, Guisbond, Levy, and Sommerfeld 2014) defines achievement gaps as "the unequal or inequitable distribution of educational results and benefits" and opportunity gaps as "the unequal or inequitable distribution of resources and opportunities." In technical, that is, statistical terms, Ferreira and Gignoux (2014, 210) described both gaps as follows:

> [An achievement gap] is the simple variance (or standard deviation) of test scores. Its selection is informed by consideration of two measurement issues that have typically been overlooked in the literature: the implications of the standardization of test scores for inequality indices, and the possible sample selection biases arising from the Program of International Student Assessment (PISA) sampling frame. The measure of inequality of educational opportunity is given by the share of the variance in test scores that is explained by pre-determined circumstances.

By computing "both measures . . . for . . . 57 countries in which PISA surveys were conducted in 2006," Ferreira and Gignoux found that "inequality of opportunity account[ed] for up to 35 percent of all disparities in educational achievement" (210). The inequality was reportedly "greater in (most of) continental Europe and Latin America than in Asia, Scandinavia, and North America" and was found to be "uncorrelated with average educational achievement and only weakly negatively correlated with per capita gross domestic product. It correlates negatively with the share of spending in primary schooling, and positively with tracking in secondary schools" (Ferreira and Gignoux 2014, 210).

The "predetermined causes" of which Ferreira and Gignoux spoke generally refer to such realities as disenfranchisement among social classes, differences in home environments, minority status, gender discrimination, and cultural mistrust between socio-economic classes (to name a few). Many proposals exist for ways to eliminate or at least minimize these causes and others, and their impact on classroom learning, ranging from more instructional time and better tests to home schooling, private tutoring, and more vocational tracking options. As outlined earlier, critics of such functionalist measures might argue, however, that the hierarchy of socio-economic classes, prevalent in many societies around the world, prevents a fair and equitable re-distribution of resources and social capital (e.g., Anyon 1980; Apple 1995, 2000; Au 2009; Bernstein 1996; Giroux 2001). In other words, what is known about achievement and opportunity gaps among learners worldwide opens a universe of issues concerning access to schooling, opportunities for learning in general, and comparisons between quantifiable and qualitative learning outcomes.

Achievement Gaps

Similar to Ferreira and Gignoux, the U.S. National Education Association (NEA) defines *achievement gap* as "the differences between the test scores of minority and/or low-income students and the test scores of their White and Asian peers," but also adds that "achievement gaps in test scores affect many different groups," among them "boys in the early years and girls in high school math and science":

> Differences between the scores of students with different backgrounds (ethnic, racial, gender, disability, and income) are evident on large-scale standardized tests. Test score gaps often lead to longer-term gaps, including high school and college completion and the kinds of jobs students secure as adults.
>
> (NEA 2015)

Although this description is specific to the United States, international assessment efforts, similarly defined, have become common in seventy state/national economies (Beller and Gafni 1991/1996; Ferreira and Gignoux 2014; OECD 2015; Teddlie and Reynolds 2000). Consistent with the philosophical persuasion of the researchers involved, comparisons across nation-states are undertaken for various reasons: they may assess educational productivity per country (e.g., Lavy and Yadin 2010), question past approaches to such research (Goldstein 2004), or examine particular causes for observed and documented achievement gaps (e.g., Fryer and Levitt 2004; Gorard and Smith 2004b).

Opportunity Gaps

Opportunity gaps, clearly connected to achievement gaps, gain increasing attention from researchers who believe that test scores are the result, not the source, of inequality among diverse student bodies (e.g., Emmer and Sabornie 2015; Milner 2010; Scarlett 2015). Feminists in particular have brought attention to the social and economic conditions that create gaps of opportunity for learners of all ages. Those conditions are created when certain knowledge is held to be cultural capital (what Bernstein referred to as official knowledge) and other knowledge is considered superfluous (Hamilton and Weiner 2000). Once that happens, success in formal learning relies on high degrees of competitiveness in grades and test scores as indicators of attained knowledge. Such reliance, critics argue, is rooted in *economic* macro models that benefit society as a whole (e.g., Peragine, Palmisano, and Brunori 2014) rather than in *pedagogical* micro models that benefit each individual learner (e.g., Aerni and McGoldrick 1999; Arum et al. 2015; Au 2009; Dornbusch and Strober 1988; Kincheloe and Horn 2007). The well-being of the system itself, either its economic structure or the educational set-up, is of greater importance than the needs of individual learners. The question arises, therefore, as to how the increasingly multi-cultural and multi-racial democracies of today can do justice to the schooling needs of an ever more diverse student body, concerning issues of ethnicity, race, socio-economic status, (dis)ability, and gendered experiences affecting learning. After all, as education sociologist Roger Slee noted, "Exclusion is ubiquitous" (99).

Inequities and Inequalities Impacting Opportunity and Achievement

Several scholars (e.g., Butler 1990; Douglas 2010; Gilman 1898; Green 1997; McClary 1991; Smith 2005) have contended that one of the fundamental ways in which social inequality can be recognized, obscured, permitted, and dismissed is through the mechanisms of gender and gendering. Bourdieu (2001) called this process "masculine domination." The construct becomes visible in sexist language that shapes and expresses behavioral norms embedded in gendered practices. The established, normative male/female binary means that anyone outside the binary either self-perceives as, or is perceived to be, a non-identified (and not-valued) "other." By being sensitive to such gendered practices, including in all kinds of musics, teachers can control their students' classroom experiences and help students to see how gendering can impact individuals' experiences of schooling.

Most readily, masculine domination helps ensure that many products (various musics included) are directed toward consumers' assumed normative adoption of the heterosexual "male gaze," about which Bourdieu wrote. In popular music, for example, there is a great deal of pressure for gay and (especially) lesbian stars to conform to binary gendered societal expectations (Diamond 2005; Lieb

2015). Producers and marketers deploy strategies that Kristin Lieb (2015, 65) called the "fauxmosexualizing" of performers, whose sexualities are disguised as bisexuality in order to appeal to a heterosexual audience. The results of such market-driven conduct, although expected by most professional performers, can portray false realities that young adolescents seek to emulate but may find confusing (if not devastating) if they do not identify personally with presented gender norms. Similarly, music educators might want to think carefully about the impact of musical traditions in the curriculum that portray stereotypical labels for gender and sexuality: girls typically choosing the flute, clarinet, piano, or singing in a choir and avoiding technology; boys typically opting for playing brass instruments, electric guitars, or drums, and choosing to be DJs (Abeles 1979, 2009; Green 1997; Smith 2013a).

Although "male" and "female" tend to refer to sex (or biological characteristics) and "masculine" and "feminine" tend to denote gender (as learned traits and behaviors), both terms are societal constructs instead of clearly distinct categories (Butler 1990). Or, as sociologist Titus Hjelm (2014, 64) pointed out, "the differentiation between sex and gender continues to reproduce the idea that there are two and *only two sexes*" (emphasis in original), a binary terminology that can turn accepted gender conventions into heteronormative ideology (Warner 1991). They cement the notion that men and women—as "opposing" sexes—are meant for each other, an idea perpetuated in various musics.

Mora (2008) cautioned not to view gender issues as existing outside of or apart from specific cultural contexts that necessarily intersect with and impact upon gender as a principal force guiding personal conduct. Similarly, Valdez and Halley (1996, 148) pointed to Mexican American conjunto music as showing "a complex intersection of patriarchy with class and ethnicity." Parkinson (2017b) identified potential conflicts in that regard when teaching popular music in faith school settings. Song lyrics and other elements of popular culture in particular can clash with the competing moral and normative values of students, parents, teachers, and other community members.

Similar to being aware of the stereotypes embedded in concepts of sex and gender, "race" is a similarly ambiguous, yet vitally important, concept with bearing on music repertoire as carrying symbolic meaning (Roediger 2007). Who and what seems to matter in society at large are reflected by who among performing musicians and composers is known beyond local insider circles and what styles they represent. "Racial" identities are as integral to that reflection as are gender or nationality. Music education scholar Deborah Bradley explained:

> By employing the social construct of race, humans designate Otherness through labels they attach. The concept of race may categorize people according to physical characteristics (including skin color), by ethnic heritage, by shared language, by religion, by geographic location—it is a long and fluid list of factors determining who currently makes up society's others.
>
> (Bradley 2015, 191)

Notions of race alter with shifts in economic and political agendas and other changes in society. Students who already feel left out socially, economically, and/or because of disability, are likely to read symbols of exclusion through race faster than social insiders in school contexts.

Racial "othering" leads inevitably to racism, and although the term often tends to evoke the worst atrocities of genocide from history, it is as invisible and normalized throughout human society as is sexism (Bonilla-Silva 2003). Education sociologists David Gillborn and Gloria Ladson-Billings explained how, "for example, racism is figured in the distribution of material and educational resources and even in teachers' notions of 'ability' and motivation" (2010, 41). Racism is thus perpetrated through and ingrained in educational systems by what political sociologist Eduardo Bonilla-Silva called the "new racism" (2003, 25). White people claim color-blindness and thereby proclaim themselves non-racist while not acknowledging that racism is present in lack of opportunities in, for instance, language development, access to housing, or eligibility for financial loans and credits.

Like race, social class—or social stratification—is often a related factor in discrimination, including in music education. It impacts how students and teachers differentiate themselves (and thus are differentiated) from one another and on how both groups experience and describe their everyday cultural realities. For example, a teacher socialized into a middle-class set of values, teaching in a school with children from predominantly rich households, faces very different challenges from those the same teacher would encounter with children from a low-income background. Affluence allows for music lessons outside of school and other **c/C**ultural enrichment activities that for most low-income students are unattainable if not unthinkable. Socio-economic standing provides and maintains access to **c/C**ultural opportunities for some while it prevents others from even entering what Wright (2010) called a very uneven playing field.

In a similar way to that in which other more powerful groups can come to perpetuate social stratification, in a predominantly able-bodied society it is easy for a majority to adopt an "ableist" stance that that fails to accommodate or to account for disabled individuals and groups. There has been a shift in recent scholarship toward recognizing disability as one among forms of human diversity, instead of considering it as a deviation from a societal norm. However, music educator Alice-Ann Darrow (2015) noted that disability and ability are frequently neglected as part of discussions around inequity and equality, unlike other social categories mentioned earlier. Failing sufficiently to acknowledge and face up to issues of mental and physical disability result in what Thomas Hehir (2002) identified as "ableism." Mauriane Adams, Lee Anne Bell, and Pat Griffin (2007, 335) explained that "ableism operates at individual, institutional, and cultural levels to privilege 'temporarily able-bodied' people and disadvantage people with disabilities"; the notion of being temporarily able-bodied refers to the inescapable fact that nearly everyone will at some point in their lives experience deterioration of their mental and/or physical faculties, because of aging or other circumstances.

Identifying social inequities and inequalities among a nation-state's (and the world's) citizenry is ultimately concerned with addressing what in music education discourse is increasingly referred to as "social justice" (Benedict, Schmidt, Spruce, and Woodford 2015; DeLorenzo 2015b). Although the social justice agenda does not come from an exclusively or even mostly sociological perspective, it deals with concerns focused on music education as a social agent. That is, social justice in music education is concerned with how students are perceived and attended to in their human rights as learners. Thus, when educational objectives speak to equal access for all learners, those objectives should be specific enough to address what each objective means for the realities experienced by each and every learner in the classroom. Students of religious and ethnic minority groups, students of varying physical and mental abilities, students identifying with other than the narrow heterosexual norm discussed earlier, and others who do not know where they fit, should not feel that music education is not for them. On the basis of this premise, Barbara Coeyman (1996, 78) proposed a "feminist pedagogy," built on four principles of "diversity, opportunities for all voices, shared responsibility, and orientation to action." Her pedagogy reads as democratic and inclusive, addressing far more than the learning needs of women alone. Although directed at college-age students, she aimed for empowering and celebrating learning for all, rather than disenfranchising or alienating learners from the benefits of schooling at any level. The consequences of considering or adopting such a pedagogical approach clearly pose challenges for the field of music education.

All musics carry values that are celebrated by one group of listeners and performers, alienate another, and remain ambiguous to a third group as individuals respond to music's "inherent" and "delineated" meanings (Green 2008b, 246; see Figure 5.2; see also Chapter 2). Cemented or questioned stereotypes about

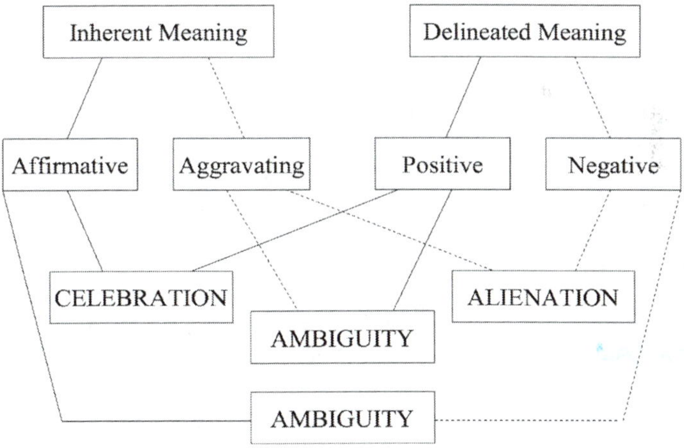

Figure 5.2 Experiences of Inherent and Delineated Musical Meaning

Source: Green, Lucy. 2008b. *Music on Deaf Ears: Musical Meaning, Ideology, Education*, p. 246. London: Abramis.

what might be considered "normal" conduct or attributes among students attending a particular school can also play important parts in that regard. Teachers who understand and are sensitive to these stereotypes can bring them to the attention of their students in a much more effective way than teachers who only focus on their own musical preferences as criteria for what music to include in curricula. Students can learn to articulate their reactions to songs and selections in an informed manner rather than simply talking about likes and dislikes. It is a teacher's task to see that stereotypical thinking (musical and social) is confronted, curtailed, and critically examined; it must be challenged, limited, or liberated (Abramo 2011a and b; Tobias 2014).

Formal Debates 5.1

In small groups, split into three teams of two or three discussants to debate one of the following:

- **a.** The role of testing in addressing achievement gaps.
- **b.** Pros and cons of streaming by ability.
- **c.** State-funded or alternative schooling.

While debating these points, take into account diversity in terms of "race," gender, class, (dis)ability, and assumptions of normalness in schools.

Reconvene your groups to share the main points identified by the teams and propose a system that would likely minimize both opportunity and achievement gaps in the best possible way.

Take note of three points advocated by the opposing team, and consider as a group how your school or national educational policy reinforces or challenges these. Does policy mostly sustain or disrupt the status quo?

Discuss the ways in and extent to which these two issues impact each other.

The Hidden Curriculum in Education and Schooling

If achievement and opportunity gaps are schooling realities, so is "the hidden curriculum"—that which is learned but not intentionally taught. It might be best described by what peace educator John McDonnell Tierney (2003) once called "be careful what you teach; it may be learned" (np). In academic language, *The Glossary of Education Reform* (Abbott et al. 2014) defined the hidden curriculum as:

> The unwritten, unofficial, and often unintended lessons, values, and perspectives that students learn in school. While the formal curriculum consists of the courses, lessons, and learning activities students participate in, as well as the knowledge

> and skills educators intentionally teach to students, the hidden curriculum consists of the unspoken or implicit academic, social, and cultural messages that are communicated to students while they are in school.
>
> (Abbott et al. 2014)

The hidden curriculum is also described through the passive learning realization (not to be confused with passive learning) function of the Snowball Self (Chapter 1). The cultural messages are present at all levels of formal schooling, from kindergarten to university-level studies and in all fields and specializations.

Functionalists might argue that the hidden curriculum can have both negative and positive consequences. They are negative when caused by learning gaps among students (e.g., Abbott et al. 2014; Fryer and Levitt 2004; Gatto 2005); they are viewed positively by educators who consider opportunities for character education, motivation, advancement, and personal refinement as necessary parts of schooling (e.g., Carlsburg 2009; Çubukçu 2012; Dreeben 2002; Eggleston 2000; Jerald 2006; Konieczka 2013). Critical pedagogues, of course, view the hidden curriculum as the consequence of the unequal distribution of economic and cultural capital in society and the resultant inequities that go with gender and race discrimination (e.g., Anyon 1980; Bowles and Gintis 1976; Dickerson 2007; Giroux 2001, 2014; Giroux and Penna 1983; Howard 2014; Jay 2003; Milner 2010). Interactionists are likely to argue that the cultural messages a learner receives are the inevitable side effects of all learning (Ballantine and Hammack 2009; Kentli 2009; Vallance 1973/1974). The best way to ensure that attributes of the hidden curriculum are interpreted as positive influences for a learner is to give him or her undivided, individual attention, an approach strongly supported by home schoolers.

Kentli (2009, 88) summarily concluded that the essence of the hidden curriculum is "a process [of social interactions] at all times [in which] tacit messages to students about values, attitudes, and principles" are being transmitted on an ongoing basis. It might even be possible to observe most of those interactions as parts of multiple micro level analyses. Observable interactions, however, also reflect institutional and societal macro structures and their respective sociocultural and political conditions. These macro structures and contexts determine the boundaries of what a teacher can or cannot do in the classroom. Working within these boundaries, and in full awareness of how they can cause or maintain learning gaps among the learners, requires teachers to play a large number of different roles in the pedagogical process.

There are, for example, the roles of knowledge dispenser, disciplinarian, and testing expert, alongside and overlapping with those of student advocate, motivator, learning facilitator, counselor, "pastoral carer," conflict mediator, and even substitute parent (Kentli 2009, 88). As these roles and more shift in response to students' needs and curricular demands placed on the teacher, the teaching-learning process turns into a complex and unpredictable array of role changes and reversals. The "do's and don'ts," integral to tacit assumptions about teacher and student roles in the classroom, can lead to a sense of message ambiguity, uncertainty, and confusion on the part of learners.

If role ambiguities between teacher and students contribute to the power of the hidden curriculum in the classroom, so do differences in styles of communication between, for instance, male and female or younger and older teachers, as well as teachers with social backgrounds much different from those of their students. Regarding the somewhat simplistic, but nonetheless important, binary of male and female teachers in the classroom, we described earlier what have become known as gendered occupations in teaching, nursing, and social work (see Chapter 3). Education experts worry that female teachers' dominance creates gendered learning inequities and further social inequalities (e.g., Beller and Gafni 1991/1996; Carrington and McPhee 2008; Cortina and Román 2006; Kelleher et al. 2011; Majzub and Rais 2010). As simplistic as any binaries are, the topic speaks to broader societal values than educational ones alone (Bartel 2004; Gould 1992; Gould 2004; Jorgensen 2008; Koza 1991; Lamb 2014; Rhein and Müller 2006; Rieger 1981; Siedenburg 2016).

Small Group Discussion 5.5

1. In thinking back to your own high school experiences (not necessarily in music), can you recall moments where "the hidden curriculum" became observable to you? How did it make you feel or behave? Try to describe those emotions and responses to your peers.
2. Identify and examine the origin and practices of up to three time-honored traditions that govern listening habits in concert halls, clubs, arenas, or other venues.
3. What are other time-honored unspoken assumptions about particular musics and associated practices that might be intimidating to "outsiders"?
4. *In your experience as a student*:

   Have you been taught by teachers who were primarily dispensers of knowledge, facilitators of learning, or both? Discuss these experiences and how they impacted the ways in which you valued and acquired knowledge and skills.

   In your experiences as a teacher:

   In what contexts and to what extent do you see your own role as a dispenser of knowledge or facilitator of learning? Have you experienced moments in which these roles conflicted with each other?

Class Projects

1. Divide the class into debating teams and discuss the Status Quo of Public School Music Education: How Functionalists, Conflict, Interaction, and Topical Theorists Propose Systemic Curricular Reform.
2. Put together a seven-minute presentation on "valuing" a Person In or Through Music.
3. Write a five-page essay on Interactionism as a Tool for Examining Music Education Practices As You Know Them.

Key Sources (for full information, see References)

Apple, Michael W., Stephen J. Ball, and Luis Armando Gandin. 2010.
Ballantine, Jeanne H. and Floyd Hammack. 2009.
Bernstein, Basil. 1971–1975/2003, 1977, 1996.
Blumer, Herbert. 1969/1986, 2004.
Böhnisch, Lothar and Karl Lenz. 2014.
Bourdieu, Pierre. 1977, 1986, 1993.
Bourdieu, Pierre and Jean-Claude Passeron. 1977.
Bourdieu, Pierre and Loïc J. Wacquant. 1992.
Collins, Randall. 1979, 1999b, 2004.
Freire, Paulo. 1968/1970/2000.
Giroux, Henry A. 1983, 1988, 2001, 2014.
Illich, Ivan. 1971.
Mead, George H. 1938.
Parsons, Talcott. 1937, 1951.
Schugurensky, Daniel. 2015.

6

The Music Teacher as Value Educator

This chapter is about:

- Living and Teaching Musically in and with **c/C**ulture
- A Brief Sociologically Informed Excursion into Aesthetic Education
- Challenges in Dialoguing with Students

Gareth: Having immersed myself to differing extents in learning to perform and appreciate rock, jazz, punk, Irish folk, and (Western) classical musics, along with hybrids of these in musical theatre contexts, I ought perhaps to feel at home as a performer and audience member in them all. Although I usually do feel welcomed by the various communities and cultures, I also experience anxiety regarding how fellow musicians—including those whom I teach—perceive me, and I wonder where I really belong. In an ideal world, one would (to quote rock band Aerosmith) just "let the music do the talking," but it seems like it's rarely that easy. On a good day, when I can just relax behind the drums and rock out, my world all seems to make sense. A big part of being a music teacher is to find and appreciate what makes my students tick. What's your experience, Hildegard?

Hildegard: Yes, I agree that teaching music should always begin with "what makes my students tick." Although that is hard enough, even harder is perhaps to enable them from there on to explore and discover what is unfamiliar and new to them—something they can sink their teeth into and become increasingly better at doing. A former doctoral student of mine once told me of a college professor who maintained that if you did not come out of graduate school a changed person, he had not done his job. I would carry this statement further by applying it to all schooling, from kindergarten on. The question, of course, is what I mean by "change." Change into what—into a more knowledgeable person, or even a better person? Better than what, or who? In turning my answers to these and similar questions into "teacherly" actions, I found these to be less guided by my beliefs than by what the institution in which I worked seemed to expect from me. Although trying to be socially responsible to each individual student, I also felt a responsibility to comply musically and academically with set standards of performance. Therefore, I nearly always found myself torn between roles of gatekeeper and gate opener (Froehlich 2007b)—a role ambiguity that troubles me still and, I believe, other (music) educators just as much.

Introduction

The distinction we have made in this book between music schooling as social and as musical acts—all of them embedded in the aesthetics of listening to, composing, and performing musical works—brings us now to addressing how you might make choices concerning the "why" and "what" of music teaching. Because social and aesthetic values go hand in hand, the question is whether there is a set of *valued knowledge* in school music on which all music educators can and do agree. If there is, what is it?

Your immediate answer might be that you want both high performance standards for the best of your students and a broad exposure to different kinds of music for as many of your learners as possible. You may even wish to see compulsory music schooling reformed into entirely new ways, while maintaining what you consider to be positive experiences from your own musical learning. In other words, your decisions as a musician-educator probably reflect the two worlds you know best: the musical realities that have shaped you and the musical realities you believe are closest to your students' experiences.

If you trained as a musician-performer, you likely learned to establish practice routines that allow you to perform different styles of music with relative confidence. You have learned to groove and have drilled difficult passages and know of the importance to repeatedly listen to other performers' interpretations of a particular piece of music or song. You know when you are "in tune" or "out-of-tune," stylistically correct, or rhythmically "out." Right and wrong may be "either/or" terms that have propelled you forward in your skills as a performer who aspired to satisfy your own expectations and those of your teacher, your peers, and your (future) audiences. In short, you may well know how to focus on the discipline of music as the medium by which to teach self-discipline, patience, and determination, not to mention developing a fine "musical ear," great performance skills, and being able to discern acceptable from unacceptable performances. There are but a few grey areas when you approach the teaching of music from this angle; not so, however, when it comes to the social dimension of music schooling.

Always remember that your students are neither your peers nor your audience; they are active participants in the learning process you design for their benefit, not yours. The decisions you make, therefore, should not be primarily about you and your musical strengths but about your students as learners, young people who need help in discovering and mastering skills that lie beyond those they already possess. Your own understanding of professional "rights and wrongs" may need to be modified so as not to lose the majority of your students to frustration about, disappointment in, and alienation from formal music learning. However, while you have the individual benefit of each student in mind, you continue to be held accountable to fulfilling overall objectives set by educational authorities and school communities. After all, as a school employee you are an agent of local, federal, or national institutions and thus a preserver of a particular cultural order, even hegemony.

Furthermore, you may experience that teaching environments are marked by "unpredictability, slowability, irregularity, immeasurability, anticipation, serendipity, and surprise" (Lapidaki 2016, 67). With the exception of the made-up "slowability," most of these terms may be familiar in various degrees to all teachers; but even the made-up term makes sense when you think of the time it takes to modify goals, objectives, and lesson plans for the benefit of as many individual learners as possible. All curriculum work is slow work and a difficult task even under the best of circumstances. In the meantime, you rely on the skills you acquired as a musician to provide the best and most expedient approaches to teaching your students the music you know and you hope they will come to like. However, each selection you make as a teacher also sends a signal of what, in your mind, has the most value musically, pedagogically, and culturally. You, therefore, take on, knowingly or unknowingly, the role of *value educator*—musically and socially. This chapter addresses how that role may bear on the articulation of educational objectives and other pedagogical decisions.

After first reviewing the meaning of living and teaching musically in the grand traditions of **C**ulture as well as the routines of everyday **c**ulture, we then speak to the basic question that illuminates what philosophers in music education call aesthetic education. In oversimplified terms, it is about the question of who engages in what kind of music making and listening where, when, why, how, and with what effect. Third, the chapter addresses challenges in learning to see yourself as a value educator dedicated to accepting diversity of values among your students and the wider school community.

Living and Teaching Musically in and with c/Culture

Next to the development of specific performance, composition, and collaborative skills, and the discipline associated with their acquisition, important music learning objectives in many countries include the study of an instrument of a learner's choice, individual creativity, imagination, and sensitivity to musical performance nuances. Although adhered to in varying degrees of specificity, the objectives may further include the advancement of aesthetic sensibilities in those being taught, often with emphasis on an introductory knowledge of basic music concepts, styles, and genres. The place of classical music in such objectives is often neither questioned nor that music considered automatically superior to popular music because renditions of both can and do become part of the performance and listening repertoire in many schools. Mariachis, fiddle groups, guitar ensembles, jazz combos, and other specialized music groups germane to a particular geographic and cultural locale can also be, but are not necessarily, basic components of a comprehensive school music program. Where such a more-rounded program exists, however, it is generally dependent on individual music teachers' initiatives and administrators' good will and support.

Despite the great variety of curricular options in compulsory music education programs, it seems safe to say that musics of "the grand tradition" (what has sometimes also been referred to as "music composed by [or attributed to] dead, white men") are still considered by some the "bread and butter" of what music teachers' work is about. There is less agreement among many music educators, however, on how musics representing everyday cultural traditions (what are commonly referred to as vernacular and popular musics) are included in curricular decisions.

Key factors in all aesthetic inquiries are usually who and what determine that certain traditions and artifacts are worth preserving over others and placing them into a canon of musical works said to have passed the test of time. Once a particular piece of music, a composer, or a songwriter ends up in that canon, what may once have been intended for everyday usage can turn into **C**ulture, that somewhat unspoken canon of works considered part of a society's valued knowledge. Those musics or artifacts that have not (yet) entered the Cultural canon, but surround people's daily lives in multiple ways, make up the "little traditions." These might be perceived as being in opposition to the grand traditions, running parallel to them, or interacting with them by feeding on each other. All musics, therefore, contribute to the **c/C**ultural makeup of a society in numerous forms of occupational obligations, self-fulfillment, and "serious leisure" (Elkington and Stebbins 2014; Mantie and Smith 2016; Stebbins 1992, 2001, 2007, 2006/2011, 2014). Each can add to someone's music knowledge and the desire to learn or be entertained; all can provide ceremonial and/or religious services; they can serve as tools for therapeutic or commercial reasons, or can act as carriers of, components in, and enhancers of personal moods, social engagements, and theatrical productions. All functions and traditions of music provide the tapestry that aestheticians examine and analyze and that comprises the social realities of which teachers and students alike are each a part. Mindful of this tapestry, **c/C**ulturally aware music teachers seek to incorporate it into the planning and delivery of their lessons.

It is impossible to account for all of music's social and aesthetic functions in any one curriculum, but teachers can invite their students to engage in and reflect on the diversity of musics explored, and encourage awareness of and respect for musics that are necessarily, if unfortunately, excluded. After all, the purpose of educating students musically in schools also hinges on what is possible in a particular school setting. In some cases, music is integral to the broader curriculum; in other cases, it is not. Trained musicians with a teaching license or its equivalent may be employed by large urban schools, whereas rural or smaller schools may rely on non-specialist classroom teachers to engage their students in music learning. Curricular priorities and agendas set by school boards and other governmental authorities add to the mix of what school music may or may not look like.

Last, but certainly not least, the implementation of educational goals depends on budgetary and scheduling issues not necessarily under the control of either teachers or school administrators. More often than not, both issues—budget and schedule—can impact (or are impacted by) teacher-student ratios, access to technological resources necessary to participate in **c/C**ultural events in the community, and availability of instruments and other musical materials. Almost always, however, those material matters are related also to the racial, socioeconomic, ability, and gendered makeup of the school population as a whole as well as to the musics with which everyone in the community is familiar outside of school. Thus, material matters and social issues are integral to any form of aesthetic education a teacher might choose to pursue.

Small Group Discussion 6.1

As a group, plan several lessons for a classroom setting of your choice that highlight how "**c**ulture" and "**C**ulture" interact in your students' lives.

Toward a Socially Inclusive Model of School Music Pedagogy

The value each person attaches to a musical experience, whether in the grand tradition, the little traditions, or both, denotes a particular "taste," a subject of considerable sociological interest since the field's inception and central to the work of aestheticians. Sociologically, however, taste might primarily be interpreted as a personal response to acquired cultural, class-based, and/or social values rather than as an agreed-upon set of pre-established values that are aesthetically "right" for everybody across time and place. This is why Charles Seeger saw value in all musical traditions and defined "true" musicianship as a thorough understanding of all musics in the culture of which one was a part. This is also the reason John Blacking advocated forms of informal music learning over the formality of schooling. It is all about the difference between learning through living and learning through schooling, a conceptualization similar to what American socio-musicologist and political activist Charles Keil (1979, 2002) advocated when he pursued throughout his life what Roger Mantie, describing Keil's life work, called the "goal of getting participatory musical practices into daily life" (2016, 624).

A comparable goal was advocated by Christopher Small (1987/1998, 1977/1996, 1998, 2010, 2011), whose work we first mentioned in Chapter 4. To denote the ongoingness of music making as "doing" throughout life, he proposed the term *musicking* as a verb rather than as a noun. In the doing, he insisted, social relationships are formed that define the musicking experience. He expressed doubts, however, that such experience could take place in school music at all (Small 2010). Unlike Small, American music education philosopher and praxialist David Elliott (1995; see also Elliott and Silverman 2015) used the term *musicing* to describe those moments during performance when both musical and self-growth correlate fully with sensations of enjoyment and satisfaction. To signify when the musical and social functions of music making are fully realized in the ways conceptualized by Small and Elliot/Silverman, Froehlich (2015) suggested to use the spelling of *music(k)ing* for such moments. This spelling would suggest that music(k)ers' actions are about valuing socio-musical relationships in music making while, at the same time, valuing the experience of self-growth and learning. Both types of music(k)ing goals are not always fulfilled at the same time, or even at all. In fact, as asserted by Philipp Ahner (2011) in his empirical study about a particular group of high school students in Germany, for students to achieve a symbiosis between both goals remained an unfulfilled challenge for their teacher. This challenge is familiar to many teachers and curriculum experts, perhaps especially in the large ensemble, performance-driven schooling models common in North America.

A cursory glance at thriving band, choral, and orchestra programs still prevalent in many secondary schools in the North America would seem to suggest that music educators are successful in providing opportunities for school music(k)-ing. In particular, students who participate for several years in those programs seem happy with (and thereby affirm and even celebrate) what they experience. They form relationships with mostly like-minded fellow musicians, acquire tangible skills in specific instruments (including voice), and develop the discipline to practice and excel in performing on those instruments. However, only a small proportion of students benefits from that experience or seek it past graduation, a point made by Shepherd and other critical theorists (see Gould 2007; Keil and Feld 1994; Regelski 1998, 2016; Shepherd and Devine 2015). Skeptical of the system, these authors question the educational and socio-political wisdom in promoting the large group performance model. Its "top-down," teacher-centered mode of decision making generally allows little time for critical reflection, personal or collaborative creativity, or transformative thinking in a community of learners in classroom or rehearsal hall settings.

Where large ensemble programs are successful, parents and local citizens tend to value the results because of entertainment the public performances provide at halftime school sports events and seasonal concerts. School administrators favor those events for the same reasons and also value the positive public relationship factor. Critics of this model note, however, that this top-down pedagogy has its roots in a (largely unconscious) militarism (Hansen 2005; Hebert 2015; Rhodes 2007). Anyone (students, teachers, parents, and other educational and societal stakeholders) who is unfamiliar with such a one-directional approach to learning, discipline, and group compliance, may find this form of schooling difficult or uncomfortable. It can induce disillusionment and anger with the system and its effects on the individual learner (Freire 1968/1970/2000; Giroux 2001, 2014; Illich 1971). The experience is opposite to what others celebrate as pleasurable and may continue to seek as adults when, after ending compulsory schooling, they perform in leisure and community music contexts of diverse kinds (Mantie and Smith 2016).

External to the school environment, lifelong commitment to music(k)ing is often instilled and maintained in music experiences germane to particular geo-cultural locales and individual backgrounds, such as community choirs (Durrant 2003; Partti 2012), rock bands (Kirschner 1998; Smith 2016), collegiate glee clubs (Mantie 2015), traditional folk music sessions in pubs and bars (O'Flynn 2009), and many other types of ensemble. Recreational music making occurs in numerous ways, including beat-making alone at home on a laptop computer (Rambarran 2016), composing for and in computer games (O'Leary and Tobias 2016), participation in online communities of diverse musics, and in, for example, choral ensembles, community orchestras, jazz bands, or clarinet choirs (Mantie and Smith 2016; Stebbins 2014; Waldron and Veblen 2008). Although recreational or avocational music making as described is present in many societies, increasingly higher levels of professionalization and commercialization of musics in many industrialized nations cause an ever-larger number of citizens to call themselves non-musical (or non-musicians). This is a trend that has prompted some curricular experts to call for and implement school music programs specifically aimed at encouraging lifelong participation in and enjoyment of music making (D'Amore and Smith 2016; Green 2008a; Pitts 2012). School music, these and others believe, could help strengthen the social, emotional, educational, and "neuropsychobiological" (Welch 2001) benefits of lifelong involvement with music(k)ing.

Community music activities outside of school settings stem from and respond to different socio-political imperatives and, therefore, are allowed to make use of a greater variety of forms of musical engagement than is possible in school music. In community music, the social experience is often at least as important for participants as is the desire for acquiring performance skills on one or more musical instruments. A key tenet for music education beyond music schooling alone is, therefore, a social responsibility to provide opportunities for musical engagement as acts of what Lee Higgins (2012, 43) called "unconditional hospitality." It is a demand that presents new challenges not only for normative, institutionalized school music education programs but also for providing young people of all backgrounds and means with broad musical experiences in safe and socially just learning environments. Assurances of unconditional hospitality—regardless of ability and disposition—would lead to doing away with graded learning and standardization of accountability measures. Instead, such an approach would place individual progress over group success, value what everyone in the classroom brings to the table, and prioritize helping socio-economically less advantaged learners succeed in and through music.

Small Group Discussion 6.2

1. Share with each other moments in your own music making **outside of formal schooling**:
   a. When you really felt fully immersed musically with the task at hand.
   b. When you felt alienated from the process of music making.

   What were your responses in either situation?
2. Think of similar moments **inside formal schooling** when your music teacher created either of those moments. How did you and how did your classmates respond?

A Brief Sociologically Informed Excursion into Aesthetic Education

In Chapter 4, we referred to Roger Scruton and Herbert Marcuse as two writers in favor of viewing musics of the grand traditions through different lenses than those through which to appreciate popular musics. These authors, along with many musicians trained in the Classical traditions of their respective cultures, object to the idea that all musics are "created equal." It is a sentiment whose validity has been debated ever since German philosopher Alexander Gottlieb Baumgarten's (1714–1762) *Aesthetica* (1750/1758/1961).

The term *aesthetics* derives from the Greek term for "sense perception." As a philosophical concept, aesthetics is part of a philosophical branch called axiology, which means the study of values. Studies in aesthetics are generally devoted to the conceptual and theoretical study of artistic products and their properties, thereby focusing on the maker of the art, its users, and the artwork itself. Of particular prominence in that regard have also been efforts to define and understand what has become known as aesthetic experience (see Levinson 1996, 2006; Reimer 1970, 1989, 2003; Shusterman 2000, 2008). Only more recently has the dimension of "everyday" aesthetics been added to what aestheticians address among their concerns (DeNora 2000; Dowling 2010; Kaiser, Nolte, and Roske 1993; Kivy 2004, 2009; Leddy 2012; Melchionne 2013; Nielsen 2009; Vogt 2003).

It is in the cross-over of everyday aesthetics with the aesthetics of "high art" that sociological analysis has its place. Kaplan (1990) listed four tenets central to understanding music and music(k)ing in society. Like Leppert and McClary (1987) suggested specifically for music, Kaplan argued that when considering all of the arts in a social theory, both their aesthetics and their social functions would need to be fully accounted for; second, the theory should contain the perspectives of those who created the arts, distributed, and listened to or viewed them; third, the model should address the role of education in any artistic development; and fourth, all aspects ought to be connected in the form of multiple relationships.

Next to Max Kaplan's work, one of the earliest journals to bring together under one academic roof sociological, musicological, and educational issues was the *International Review of the Aesthetics and Sociology of Music*, published by the Croatian Musicological Society since 1971. Located at the Zagreb Academy of Music and Musicology, the journal is multi-lingual and reflects numerous topics of interest to artists, educators, and performers alike. It speaks to multiple "art worlds" (Becker 1982), of which school music is but one among many dimensions. However, the diversity of perceptions, tastes, and predilections embedded in school music goes beyond questions about musicianship; music educators must also speak to the question of what it means to be a good citizen. This question is about ethical and moral conduct as integral to the study of value (axiology).

Many well-known advocates for early music schooling have asked how music education can contribute to the larger goals of value education as a societal goal. Among the long list of best known advocates in that regard are the Japanese music educator Shinichi Suzuki, the German composer Carl Orff, and the Hungarian composer/music educator Zoltán Kodály, all concerned about the relationship between good citizenship and the development of well-honed aesthetic sensibilities. Similarly, Venezuelan conductor José Abreu, founder of a music and social program known as *El Sistema* (Baker 2014), capitalized on his knowledge about the close connection between social and aesthetic awarenesses. Based in this case exclusively on performing Western classical music, the program benefited from full governmental (financial) support and provided free, regular breakfasts for the children and a safe place for them to spend their free time. Many similar programs worldwide have sprung up, although the question remains as to whether the social and aesthetic goals are always reached in equal strength and shared by all participants (e.g., Allan 2010; Allan, Moran, Duffy, and Loening 2008; Baker 2014; Cohen, Silber, Sangiorgio, and Iadeluca 2012; Majno 2012; Uy 2012; Winner, Goldstein, and Vincent-Lancrin 2013).

Answers to what it means to be a good citizen in a particular society, how music can or does help in that regard, and whether social and aesthetic values can be and are merged in school music, require empirical data. These data would have the purpose of describing what goes on in classrooms worldwide, showing whether the aims of school music in different societies are comparable, and what school music can do and has done to contribute to a person's life lived well. Evidence would be required on what takes place in schools worldwide in terms of citizen education, aesthetic education, socio-musical literacies, and immersive music(k)ing.

Efforts at canvassing school music practices globally do exist and are greatly encouraged by the various commissions of the International Society of Music Education as well as by individual scholars whose interest in the internationalization of music teaching practices are renowned (see Bontinck 1974; Cox and Stevens 2012; Elliott and Silverman 2016; Green 2011; Hebert et al. 2017; Hebert and Kertz-Welzel 2012; Kertz-Welzel 2004, 2013a and b; McCarthy 2004; McPherson and Welch 2012; Schippers 2009; Campbell 2004; Vogt, Heß, and Brenk 2014). From a sociological perspective, however, aesthetic and social purposes intertwine, a philosophical premise long elaborated on by many music educators (especially in the United States), who call themselves praxialists (Elliott 1995; Elliott and Silverman 2015; Regelski 1998, 2004, 2016; Regelski and Gates 2009), as mentioned earlier in this chapter.

At the beginning of this chapter we suggested that, regardless of geographical and socio-political context, even the most complex questions about the aesthetic aspects of a musical work, activity, or experience may be reduced to the question: who engages in music making and listening where, when, how, why, with what effect, and according to whose judgment? As simple as this form of questioning may be, each part of it serves as the basis for finding common ground amid the many different functions, purposes, and aesthetic meanings of the musics present in various societies and **c/C**ultures. Never rhetorical, the question can guide you, the teacher, in understanding the music under study, and can likewise aid your students in understanding their experience with it. Finding an answer to each part of the question allows for probing of diverse socio-musical and schooling realities of different times and places. Calling that approach aesthetic education would be as appropriate as calling it the teaching of socio-cultural or socio-musical literacy.

In the vast literature exploring particular subject matter goals in relationship to the purpose of education in general, the term *literacy* crops up frequently. For example, science educators refer to the connection between scientific literacy and social contexts as socio-scientific literacy (e.g., Levinson 2006; Lewis and Leach 2006; Ratcliffe and Grace 2003; Sadler 2009, 2011). They point to ways in which such literacy has to speak to the social contexts of those being taught (Sadler 2011, 1). It might not be far-fetched, therefore, similarly to call for socio-musical literacy as a goal in music teaching. But just as there are many "musics," it might become necessary to talk about socio-musical "literacies," acknowledging that multiple socio-musical issues shape each **c/C**ultural world.

A consequence of teaching toward socio-musical/cultural literacies lies unarguably in the teacher's role as a conveyor and transmitter of values that can last a lifetime. These values would include, and go beyond, aesthetic sensibilities alone. Students and teachers would be challenged to examine their own musical conduct in comparison with that of those around them and to examine alternative values—both present and past—as being equally valid. These examinations call for new approaches toward a time-proven pedagogical tool: the teacher asking non-rhetorical questions and the students finding answers relevant to their own understanding of themselves and the world around them.

Small Group Discussion 6.3

Think about the idea of "unconditional hospitality" and in what ways and to what extent you feel prepared to embrace this concept or approach in your music classroom.

Challenges in Dialoguing with Students

The professional education of many teachers tends to focus on their subject matter knowledge, pedagogical skills, and—in some countries—awareness of legal matters concerning teacher-student-parent responsibilities, classroom conduct, and a school's authority in the larger societal system of education. The teacher's individual role as a moral guide and important transmitter of accepted sociocultural values is usually assumed as long as everything goes smoothly in the classroom and with individual students. Only when problems become public is it likely that the teacher's function as role model and transmitter of values is highlighted rather than silently taken for granted. From a sociological vantage point, however, the role of teacher as value educator should be considered central to the preparation of educators anywhere (e.g., Harecker 2012; Hawkins 2015; Willemse, Lunenberg, and Korthagen 2005). The role requires an expansion of ways in which teachers engage students in seeking answers that are not necessarily self-evident or rhetorical and that may remain open for further debate. In short, teachers—in their role as value educators—face new challenges in the time-proven tasks of (1) asking questions, and (2) accepting student's answers as reflections of diverse realities.

Challenges in Asking Questions

Most teachers are familiar with asking direct questions to which they already know the answer. It is part of a method based on a teacher-initiated dialogue. Long known as discovery method, its roots can be traced to Socrates' reported way of engaging his listeners in stating what the questioner had in mind. Control over the dialogue stays with the person who asks the questions and thus steers the discourse in a pre-determined direction.

Envision an alternative situation in which the teacher poses questions, to which he or she is uncertain of the answers. This uncertainty initiates a conversation allowing for a variety of responses. All should be treated as having equal value when pursuing their implied consequences for action. For example, when students express what they like or do not like about a particular piece of music, their opinions form only the beginning of the questioning process. A dialogue should follow in which personal tastes are explored and the purposes and functions of different musics compared with each other; each song/composition—performed, listened or danced to, copied, or developed in composition—is being placed in its own context, time, and place. The dialogue that evolves can take place during a rehearsal or form the nucleus of a non-performance music class, guided by such questions as:

- For whom was the music written? Who listened then, and who listens to it now?
- Who performed it first? Who performs it now?
- From where (culturally and geographically) does the music originate?
- What were and/or are the market and cultural forces responsible for bringing the music to society's attention?
- Who were or are celebrated "stars" then of this music? Does or did the genre have "superstars" as some musics do now?
- What were and/or are prevailing audience/spectator/other musicker (e.g., dancer) protocols?

The logic behind asking such empirically based, socio-musical questions is to turn the music classroom into a place where multiple music-cultural frameworks can be explored in the context of a particular piece of music. You may also consider personalizing the above questions by canvassing your students' attitudes toward different types of music: does the music connect to their lives and experiences? If so, how? If not, why? Do the sounds (and/or texts) convey images with which learners are familiar? If so or if not, what other musics could enhance their involvement with the issues to which a particular text refers? These and similar questions give students the opportunity to explore their own relationships to various musics in comparison with those of others, present and past. Students search for (and thus research) their answers from multiple sources, similar to the work music scholars.

The format of dialogic questioning advocated here does have challenges, especially for teachers who, for example, first and foremost view their work as that of a conductor or studio teacher with very specific performance goals in mind. The type of questioning we suggest also moves away from relying on textbook knowledge as a principal gauge of learning because it allows learners to reach different learning goals at variable rates of skill and knowledge acquisition. In adult learning, the same approach is called dialogic pedagogy and has been proposed as a major tool for achieving transformational learning (e.g., Aukerman 2013; Lysaker and Furuness 2011; Ward 1994). We believe that it is a pedagogy applicable and appropriate at all levels of teaching.

Any documentation of learning progress occurs through other means than standardized testing alone. Observation and individual record keeping of learner participation, engagement, and contributions to the end result of a performance become the mainstay of measuring learning success. Furthermore, peer teaching by students can turn into a new form of knowledge assessment as well. In these and other alternatives to learning assessments, the teacher has to be flexible in regard to expectations of each learner and allow for different end results for particular groups of learners. Such flexibility may appear to put into question the teacher's authority as the musician she or he has been trained to be. However, acknowledging the validity of and valuing others' perspectives as equal to one's own, teachers can earn the respect of more students, who—in turn—may be more likely to ascribe pedagogic authority to the educator (see Chapter 2).

Accepting Students' Answers as Reflections of Diverse Realities

Questioning the origin of one's own values as a teacher may well be the beginning of transformative education for students. It requires working on oneself before seeking to change others. You are asked to engage in a new mode of meaning-making in the confines of schooling. Dilin Liu et al. (2004) referred to this new mode of learning and communication among teachers and students as "code switching." Although referring to language instruction, the term is appropriate also for turning knowledge transmission to knowledge transformation in other subject matter areas (Butler, Suh, and Scott 2015; Nieto 2000, 2004; Shulman 1987). Although by no means an easy goal to reach, code switching should, indeed, be considered essential for engaging students and teachers in transformative educational practices also in music (Abrahams 2004; Jorgensen 2003; Partti 2012).

Once music educational goals articulate code switching as an attainable communication skill in music, new explorations can take place even within performance classes. For example, familiar tunes—such as those heard in television commercials, films, and popular songs—could be rearranged by students and compared with the originals. Students could then conduct research (e.g., via the Internet) into similar topics and concerns discussed by poets, writers, and composers from former times. Following this, students might compose their own tunes to existing lyrics or write original songs and contrast them to what was common knowledge in prior eras. Needless to say, the teacher serves as facilitator in those searches, making suggestions and helping out along the way. This role can provide new pedagogic and musical challenges, especially for an ensemble conductor who is used to being the central decision maker in the music classroom.

Code switching in music means to value diversity of musical styles, genres, and pedagogical approaches. *Valuing diversity* is an achievable skill that involves both verbal and non-verbal forms of communication rather than merely being "the new cliché for the 21st century" (Benjamin 2002, np). We say this in light of researched expert opinion as well as on the basis of what many school music teachers already strive for. By no means unique to music education, valuing diversity involves the ability to step outside of one's own comfort zone, an essential requirement for teachers in countries that lay claim to being pluralistic/democratic societies. Although possibly seen by some as a cliché, the call for valuing diversity is rooted in the ever greater urgency of acknowledging "otherness" as a necessary part of "getting along." Intercultural understanding and admitting one's own shortcomings go hand in hand in this regard. Understanding otherness acknowledges realities of exclusion, marginalization, and elitism at the same time that it hopes for inclusion, acceptance, and full equality under the law and in day-to-day life (see also Chapter 2 and Chapter 5). It requires self-critique before one engages in critiquing others; examining your own values before questioning those held by others.

Teachers in many classrooms work hard to fulfill hopes of inclusion for themselves and their students when they make use of song texts written in language(s) spoken by first-generation immigrant and refugee students, welcome musics of all sorts being written and performed by their students, or invite artists into the classroom who connect the in-school world with what goes on outside. However, the evidence suggests also that more needs to be done to free music curricula from traditions that assume shared values when there may be none or only very few (e.g., Bowman 2007; Bradley 2007, 2012; Davis 2005; Dyndahl 2008; Gould 2004; Gould 2008; Lamb 1994; Reimer 2009; Rosabal-Coto 2016).

Your role as a global thinker in a local world can be uncomfortable when you are being asked to embrace diversity within your own, always limited musical and cultural "universe." Because each such personal universe is, by definition, confined, it renders all the more urgent the need for teachers and students alike to acquaint themselves with music(k)ing traditions and cultures less well known. Examples from symphonic and operatic literature could be as much a part of that unknown repertoire as students' personal favorites. When diversity becomes the driving force in planning such lessons, the familiar should precede the unfamiliar. However, what is or is not (un)familiar to different students gathered in one classroom is important to ascertain.

For example, hip-hop, gospel, EDM, and country music, often conveniently lumped together as "popular," represent values not all teenagers share equally. To them—as to many others—each style portrays and symbolizes different communities with distinct experiences in time and place. Once the origins of those perceived differences are understood, musical styles of the more distant past may take on new meaning as well. Verbal discourse may be one tool to use for exploring such differences, but more engaging for everyone could be if the students planned and produced concerts that took into consideration *valued differences* between performers and audience, and articulated those personally held values in program notes and introductory remarks to each performed song, composition, or production.

Ultimately, understanding the socio-political and musical origins behind diverse musics and your and your students' involvement in, experiences with, and appreciation of them becomes an important pedagogical objective across geographical and cultural boundaries. Furthermore, as you think about your own relationships to music *inside* and *outside* of school, how closely are these worlds connected in *your* life? Your answers, which will likely evolve over time, may determine in large part how you plan to involve your students in becoming broad-minded, culturally aware citizens with an understanding that appreciating and acknowledging diversity are not tantamount to having actually to like what one hears. Most important, however, is that you develop this sense of acceptance in yourself before you instill it in others.

Interview Project and Reality Check 6.1

After identifying three musician-teachers with whom you are familiar, ask them for about thirty minutes of their time to talk with you about their own views on what it means to them to be a (music) teacher. Ask them about their main goals and objectives as educators and as musicians in the environment in which they teach, their greatest challenges, and the choices they and/or their students make in repertoire selection. Document and reflect in writing on what you hear in comparison with what you have read in this chapter.

Class Project

Consider the following questions:

- What musical styles and traditions do you value? Which feel unfamiliar to you, or even threatening? How much do you know about the cultures surrounding these musics? Why and how would you go about incorporating unfamiliar music(k)ing practices in your classroom?
- With these questions in mind, prepare a five- to ten-minute presentation for your peers, including short audio and/or video examples.

Key Sources (for full information, see References)

Benedict, Cathy, Patrick Schmidt, Gary Spruce, and Paul Woodford (eds.). 2015.
Coeyman, Barbara. 1996.
DeLorenzo, Lisa C. 2015b.
Gould, Elizabeth. 2008.
Hebert, David G., Joseph P. Abramo, and Gareth Dylan Smith. 2017.
Hodges, Donald A. 2017.
Keil, Charles and Steven Feld. 1994.
Parkinson, Tom and Gareth Dylan Smith. 2015.
Regelski, Thomas A. 1998, 2016.

7

The Sociologically Savvy Music Educator

This chapter is about putting theory into practice by:

- Unlocking Students' Musical Sense of Self
- Students Discovering and Exploring Musical Traditions
- Affirming Students' Musical Skills and Knowledge as Cultural Assets

Hildegard: Gareth, we started this book with "What in the world does sociology have to do with music teaching?" Have we answered the question to your satisfaction?

Gareth: As the adage goes, "Projects are never finished, just abandoned." That, in a way, is how I feel about this book, always mindful that there is more that could have been added (or subtracted). But in the main and despite juggling professionalism, deadlines, and the desire to be timely and relevant, I feel we abandoned this book in the best condition possible. Moreover, writing this book was like giving a performance—we prepared hard, gave of our best, and ultimately our work captures a moment in time (plus, we have a little energy saved in case of encores). We have placed sociological inquiry into the midst of music teaching practices and have demonstrated its importance as a tool for practitioners in music classrooms the world over. With the caveat that each school music teacher deals with realities only known to him or her and that one can never account for all particularities of each individual teacher's situation in one book, I believe we have opened gates for other books to follow that will take angles we either missed or chose to leave for other authors to explore.

Hildegard: To my mind, the close connections between sociology, philosophy, psychology, and education make for a powerful group of disciplines. Situated either in the social sciences or the humanities, each is strong by itself but stronger still in conjunction with any of the others. Add to that mix music as a discipline, as well as something people *do*, and music educators find themselves with compelling arguments for the value of their work as school music teachers. Of all the disciplines mentioned, I believe that sociological thinking affords perhaps the most practical approach toward understanding the worlds of music. I hope our book has described this everyday applicability clearly and overtly enough that music teachers anywhere find it useful in carving out what works for them, always negotiating macro pressure points that impact micro worlds. I further hope that, in doing so, music educators would find enough commonalities across cultures and education systems that they could be united as an international team of "**c/C**ulture workers."

Introduction

This chapter draws together and summarizes core points and aims of the book. It is about how to consciously and deliberately apply knowledge of multiple identities and roles to classroom instruction, including what it takes for teachers to be socially fair decision makers in the classroom. Perceptions are always limited by a person's own socialization processes that bear directly on, and are in turn impacted by, each individual's musical and social identities—including the teacher's. As emphasized in previous chapters, thinking about formal music schooling in sociological terms lies in understanding why "one size does not fit all" and that, in order to be effective communicators, music teachers should have many different "hats" at their disposal. Both requirements are of equal importance in building and maintaining a successful music program. Fully recognizing the socio-musical gestures that define the individuals and groups with which music teachers come into contact determines when to put on what hat. This is not hiding who you are or speaking out of two sides of your mouth. Rather, the hats remind you about the language you should use when approaching particular topics or issues. For example, it is somewhat useless to choose highly technical, musical terminology when talking with musically untrained parents. Similarly, if speaking as an arts advocate to teaching and administrative colleagues, you may want to refer to experiences they themselves have or had with music inside and outside of school and ways their own music making may have enriched their lives.

In the mid-1960s, Max Kaplan illustrated the role complexities inherent in the work undertaken by school music teachers as interconnecting, ever larger spheres, with the music educator in the center. These spheres were labeled primary group roles, secondary group roles, school roles, community roles, and regional-national-world roles (Kaplan 1966, 69). Building on this functionalist model and casting a more specific theoretical net than Kaplan had done, the first edition of this book adopted George Herbert Mead's interactionist conceptualizations, to illustrate the multiple connections between each person's empirical selves and selves that are part of the larger, macro world. Applied to music education, the model depicted the roles of musician-educator and socio-cultural agent in their interactions with the specific groups that shape a music educator's workplace. The more musician-educators know about the values held by those groups with which they come into contact—be they students, administrative leaders, or colleagues (music and non-music colleagues alike)—the easier it is likely to be to find strategies through which to communicate constructively with individuals in the groups. Froehlich (2007) illustrated this communicative back-and-forth of musical and social selves in a classroom or rehearsal space as musicianship and educatorship intertwined at all times within the learning contexts students provide. Missing from that illustration was the important reminder that those contexts are created by each student's musical self, which is always integrally linked to the social self.

In Chapter 1 of this edition, we presented a more refined visualization of how the teacher's self grows into many different roles as the need arises. That model is the Snowball Self, dealing with what Smith (2013a) called the realization of learning and identity at three levels: (1) a person's overall concept of self; (2) overlapping, intersecting identities attached to particular roles; and (3) contextual identities that people realize (as in understand, and "turn into reality") according to where they are and what they are doing.

This perpetual movement of identities and snowball selves is happening all the time with you, your students, and colleagues. How students see themselves—who they see themselves to be—impacts on classroom behavior and relationships and influences what kind of musicians they perceive themselves to be. The ways in which a teacher manages the complex dynamism of identity and learning realization can impact directly on students' senses of celebration, alienation, or ambiguity (Green 2008b; see also Chapter 2). Each individual's sense of self as a musician as well as human being is impacted for the rest of his or her life—either positively or negatively. To be a positive force in a student's life, a teacher has to unlock a student's musicality and sense of himself or herself as a valued human being. This requires the teacher's ability to interpret students' conduct and its origins, as a springboard for students to discover and explore musical traditions and put into practice musical skills and knowledge as cultural assets.

Unlocking Students' Musical Sense of Self

Aside from genetic differences, not discussed in this book but a factor among learners of all ages, differences in socialization processes become apparent in all sorts of ways, most immediately however in daily verbal, non-verbal, and physical interactions with others. Sociologists use these differences to examine sociological theories, but teachers experience them as classroom discourse—when it goes smoothly and when it does not. In both cases, and whether you are a beginning teacher or more experienced, you know firsthand the consequences of those differences. You know why certain students display signs of boredom, lack of interest, or outright aggression toward what's going on in class. Similarly, you understand why others comply with teacher expectations or show enthusiasm for what the lesson has to offer. The sociologically savvy music teacher capitalizes on that knowledge by using the positive and the negative to improve on his or her teaching and to self-critically examine curricular choices, classroom management procedures, and daily classroom discourse. Sociologically, "bad" behavior becomes as important a signifier of meaning as does "good" behavior.

For you to interpret students' actions as social signifiers, your observer role is equally important as that of dispenser of knowledge and/or facilitator of learning. You look for signals in your students' conduct as to what expectations each of them brings from outside—their life experiences and identities—to the classroom experience. You also examine your own conduct as it triggers and responds to your students' actions. In short, the role (and contextual identity) of observer in you helps you gauge your students' relationship with the subject matter inside and outside of school. In the role of constant observer, you listen carefully to "sideways" remarks by your students, watch body language and facial expressions during the course of a lesson, embrace occasional outright criticism as constructive, and even ask your students for advice (Griffin 2011). It means watching out for moments in your communication with students (and/or others) that teach you about how they think. The moments usually trigger "aha" and/or "oops" moments on your part, alerting you to finding new ways of responding to your students. The technical term used by social scientists for describing such moments is "critical incidents" (e.g., Brookfield 1990; Gray 2007; Mezirow 2003; Tripp 1993/2012). Although an incident itself does not have to be monumental, the consequences for action triggered by it can be.

Critical Incidents as Teaching Tools

The second edition of the *Oxford Dictionary of Education* (Wallace 2015) refers to critical incidents as "situations or events of particular professional significance." The wording implies a certain degree of subjectivity as to what "significant" means. It can be a momentous situation (as, for instance, a fight between two or more students in class) or a minor event triggering new awareness (at times, momentous) in the teacher. Here is one such example that, as is often the case in such stories, requires some contextual explanation. The story is about what in English language idiomatic in the United States is referred to as "dress rehearsal." The term refers to the last rehearsal before a first (or only) performance and generally does not require performance attire or dress-up.

> *A seventh-grade choir in the Midwest of the United States is preparing to give its first public performance during the annual Spring choral concert. The director tells the girls to show up in time for dress rehearsal. Carol, very anxiously and seemingly embarrassed, raises her hand and says that there is no way she can make it in time because she will not have time to change between the previous class and the time the rehearsal begins. Some girls giggle, others agree with Carol. At first, the teacher thinks that Carol is trying to be difficult and is about to say so. But, he suddenly realizes that he has never explained to the girls the meaning of 'dress rehearsal.' He does so and assures Carol that it was good for her to speak up. He had a constructive 'oops'-moment, a critical incident (albeit a small one) that alerted him about the importance of not presuming shared knowledge among all of his learners.*

In many critical incidents typical in education, their significance lies in the eye of the beholder. Small events can have magnifying consequences, as was the case with the choir director who realized how the presumed knowledge of what a dress rehearsal was, led to an unnecessary moment of distress in the girl. The teacher had an "aha" moment that caused him to reflect on his impact on a particular student's mental well-being. The story also illustrates that musical conventions and valued behaviors, shared by musicians but often unexplained and unquestioned, can create learning barriers among students who have little or no musical background. Most likely, all teachers have stories to tell about moments in their teaching when things did not work out as planned because their students misunderstood what was said. If used productively, such moments have the potential to expand a teacher's grasp of the consequences of her actions.

Next is a story in which a teacher's anxieties caused her to listen to herself and turn her anxiety into positive action. It is not a critical incident of the kind that occurred in the first story, but it illustrates a moment of significant change impacting subsequent pedagogic actions:

> *A high school teacher in the UK is scheduled to teach a history of popular music 'survey' course to forty students. She has taught the course for several years and has the content all worked out, including the accumulation of a huge pile of CDs and DVDs ready to bring in to school. Before teaching the course this particular year, though, she has a crisis of confidence. Suddenly*

aware of all the music she can't possibly fit in to a ten-week course, she feels paralyzed, then liberated: if she can't teach the students everything, and because the course is based almost entirely on her own musical tastes and background (surely very different from those of her diverse cohort of students), wouldn't it be better to have the students teach themselves?! Answering her own question with a resounding 'yes,' she devises a new approach and teaches the course as follows.

She begins the class by telling students that she actually doesn't know the history of popular music (because it is so vast and varied), so they'll need to figure it out among themselves. She has students dismantle the rows of chairs, sit in small groups, and play each other their favorite songs from their phones. Students then share with the rest of the class information about styles of music that are popular in their respective groups. Next, students are tasked with finding out what music and musicians influenced the music they like. For the next few weeks, the teacher establishes her role as co-learner, with students and teacher sharing what they discover. A couple of guest lecture spots are given to students who have tremendous enthusiasm for and encyclopedic knowledge of black metal and 90s electronic dance music respectively. The teacher notices that the students in class are far more collaborative and respectful with each other than in previous years, and that they remain more attentive for longer than when, in previous courses, she simply tried to fill the students with her own narrow construction of one particular history of popular music. By welcoming 'their' music into the classroom, she turned a critical moment of self-doubt into a deeper learning experience for all. The teacher democratized he learning process by allowing all knowledge and tastes in the room to be equally valued. She turned class members into researchers and learning collaborators.

Critical incidents can contribute to one's growth as an educator and thereby prove to be beneficial professionally (Tripp 1993/2012). Often puzzling (Ballenger 2009), such moments bring about heightened awareness in you about how others react to your way of seeing or acting in the world. Applied to classroom situations, the moments crystallize in unexpected, and often eye-opening ways, who your students are, how they think, and what you need to do to respond to those new insights; in other words, they tell you a lot about your own and your students' identity realization.

Personal and technical limitations are made visible and thereby help the teacher in becoming a better educator. As tools for reflection and reflective practice, critical incidents have the potential to become cornerstones in contemporary pedagogies that are directed at reaching all learners despite differences in upbringing and social, economic, and racial backgrounds. In music class, critical incidents like those mentioned earlier frequently show gaps in people's expectations between school music and life music, and as such they allow for development of learning realization and identity realization in both teacher and student. We first brought up the image of music educators as bridge builders in Chapter 2 and should add that this imagery is not unique to music education or sociology. British authors Graham Vulliamy and Edward Lee (1976, 1982/2016), American Carlos Xavier Rodríguez (2004), and many others describe how to bring popular music into school. The intentions are clear: connect and bridge the gap between school music and life music by linking the social with the musical worlds of as many learners as possible (Hull and Schultz 2002). We now explore some ways to achieve this by looking at life music and school music, informal learning and formal schooling, and learning a coveted craft.

Small Group Discussion 7.1

Think about moments in your life (in- and/or outside school) when you took for granted that others around you had the same knowledge you had, but you found that you were misunderstood. Or can you think of situations where you did not comprehend what someone else (a teacher, or a peer) was saying, but you were too afraid to speak up? Share these incidents with each other before you select one example for analysis: how did your or another's response help or hinder the situation? Note and discuss possible instances of how such moments could arise and be managed in the context of teaching music.

(Hint: Terminology could be a good place to begin.)

"Life" Music and School Music

Music teachers who understand that their students draw clear distinctions between "life" music and school music also understand that the former is used by young people to set, change, and enhance moods; to send and share messages with others; to have fun; and to "chillax" on their own terms. School music requires compliance with rules imposed by others. A sociologically informed music curriculum has the potential to bridge those two perceptual realities by diminishing appearances of being old-fashioned and void of references to students' personal socio-musical behaviors and shared cultural symbols. Anecdotal evidence and some limited systematic research would suggest that positive learning results will follow (e.g., Catterall 1997; Deasy 2002; Green 2002, 2008a; Hallam 2010; Kokotsaki and Hallam 2007). From such evidence one also might hypothesize that distinctions between life and school music lessen most readily where musical instruments are available for study. It is an issue brought up frequently, albeit anecdotally, by directors of band, choir, and string ensembles in many American high schools. Where those ensembles exist, they seem to bridge the perceived gap between in-school and out-of-school musical learning, almost from the moment when a student has opted to learn playing an instrument.

It is not uncommon that the more successful students in classical and jazz ensembles in school are usually those who also receive private music instruction. Their upbringing (primary socialization) brings them into contact with the vocabulary commonly associated with school music. When socialization experiences outside of school tend to reinforce what happens in school, and vice versa, this phenomenon has been called "home away from home" by Meghan Scully (2014, 16, see also Adderley, Kennedy, and Berz 2003). At the most, this sentiment might be shared by about 20 percent of all high school students attending public schools in the United States, where school music ensembles exist and where schools "are fortunate enough to have the means and ability to successfully continue" formal music instruction (Scully 2014, 17; see also Elpus and Abril 2011).

Informal Learning and Formal Schooling

Informal music learning happens through voluntary immersion in a music-making culture. It is perhaps most akin to what John Blacking spoke about when he lived with the Venda and fully immersed himself in their culture (see Chapter 4). Learning through immersion may also be what John Dewey (1916/2015) called "experimental logic." Applied to music education today, the focus is on the exploration of one's own craft and artistry, a type of learning that stems from improvising, composing, self-initiated listening (including and even predominantly watching videos online), peer learning with friends, and self-analysis. Such learning, while at times far removed from approaches that prevail in formal musical education in most schools around the world (e.g., Ahner 2011; D'Amore and Smith 2016; Griffin 2011; Jaffurs 2004; Vasil 2015), is not less important or, as some music teachers imagine, less focused than school learning. Rather, a majority of students tends to find what they learn outside of school more relevant to their lives and more emotionally satisfying than what they generally experience within school walls.

Research suggests that outside and inside school experiences do not have to be (and should not be) mutually exclusive. Patricia Shehan Campbell's (1998) documentation of the place of music and its meaning in children, ages five to nine, during their first years of formal schooling pointed to their intrinsic desire to learn and to affirm, if not celebrate, their primary social and musical identities. Tia DeNora (2000) concluded the same about the everyday music use of adult women. Lucy Green (2002), too, observed that "informal music learning practices and formal music education are not mutually exclusive, but learners often draw upon or encounter aspects of both" (59). Clearly, music, unlike some other subject areas in primary and secondary school curricula, has the advantage of being integral to people's lives outside of the school environment. As an important form of self-engaged *doing*, music(k)ing in all forms happens daily by way of listening, humming or playing tunes, putting together playlists, or searching for, combining, and creating the latest, newest sounds and texts on the Internet into mashups.

In the past, music educators who wanted to avoid the possible gap between informal and formal learning, included folk and ethnic songs and basic, "elemental" sounds to reach their learners; now, teachers are advised to work with songs and music learned from games, television shows, and commercials, movie theme songs, and popular hits. Such informally gained musical knowledge should become the springboard for further exploration in school. The same applies to knowledge and skills acquired in places of worship, community bands, by jamming in garage bands, listening at concerts, watching television, playing games, or streaming music at home and on their phones. Places and occasions for informal learning are, indeed, frequently different from school, but the experience of and intentions behind such learning are no less important or meaningful.

Green (2008a, 10) recommended that an informal learning approach in schools should:

- Start with music chosen by learners, thus tending to be music which they know, understand, like, and identify with.
- Feature skill acquisition primarily involving copying recordings by ear.
- Take place alone as well as alongside friends, through self-directed learning, peer-directed learning, and group learning.
- Involve the conscious and unconscious acquisition and exchange of skills and knowledge by listening, watching, imitating, and talking.
- Be characterized by skills and knowledge assimilated in haphazard, idiosyncratic, and holistic ways, starting with "whole, real-world" pieces of music (i.e., attempting to play entire pop songs from recordings in an unguided peer-learning approach, rather than having a teacher break them down into instrumental and vocal parts or song sections).
- Integrate listening performing, improvising, and composing—even as part of large ensemble instruction.

Informal learning can be integrated into formal education—a common phenomenon that Smith (2013a, 34) referred to as "hybridized learning" (see also Music Learning Profiles Project 2016). It is vital, then, to know firsthand rather than merely presume, how and to what extent students are engaged and find meaning in school music experiences (D'Amore and Smith 2016; Green 2011, 2008a).

Non-auditioned ensembles and general music courses with emphasis on listening and appreciation are often assumed to be the places where bridging differences between informally and formally gained musical knowledge is most essential. From a sociologically informed pedagogical perspective, however, this importance should also be emphasized in auditioned ensembles and one-to-one studio teaching. The more that ensemble directors and studio teachers keep in mind a young person's possible desire to connect formal learning with other aspects of their lives, the more powerful a message music can send to students of diverse musical and socio-cultural backgrounds (Wright 2010). The total of a student's music learning experiences should form and be understood as the entrance point to what follows. We hasten to add, though, that incorporating knowledge of your learners' musical lives into lesson planning may challenge you and your school administrators. Everyone will need to step outside their comfort zone by broadening their own horizons. The time-proven desire for learning to play an instrument may well prove to be the fastest way of connecting a student's learning desires with what schools have to offer.

Learning a Coveted Craft

People around the world are fascinated by physically manipulating, exploring, and experimenting with the visible mechanics of a "real" instrument rather than a toy. Associating with specific instruments and instrument choices, therefore, resonates deeply with nearly all students' sense of self, and the more a music curriculum includes the playing of musical instruments, the more it likely connects the school world with the outside world. This fact might speak against some critics' assertion that *all* formal schooling stifles curiosity, a desire to experiment, and personal involvement in active learning. Such an assertion would prove true only in cases where students' musical capabilities and the challenges imposed on them by their teachers do not match—a phenomenon philosophically and pedagogically explored by many music education scholars in many countries for many years.

Numerous reasons can explain why school music education has in some instances not yet caught up with the ways in which young people want to acquire or are developing diverse skill sets in music outside of school. School music in some parts of the world, for instance, tends to ignore that students may desire to play multiple instruments rather than focusing on one instrument alone. Although successful instrumentalists in pop, musical theater, and folk traditions play a range of instruments well, formal music education tends to leave room only for the study of one or two instruments.

What exactly constitutes an appropriate musical instrument to be included in school learning? The answer, as so often, differs among cultures, school populations, and locations. Diversification of and flexibility in choices, therefore, should be the rule, also allowing for instruments associated with "ethnic" and popular music instruments just as much as it allows for various technologies as well as (concert or marching) band and orchestral instruments. The choices might (and, many would argue, should) include music making of varying degrees of complexity on computers and smartphones, using the Internet, peers, and experimentation as the new "teachers." With digital audio workstations now so widely prevalent and affordable, young people can develop and are developing highly creative, diverse, and alternative musical virtuosities across styles, instruments, and voices—blending composition with writing lyrics, arranging parts with mixing sounds, and engaging with others in ensemble productions. Activities and opportunities should be available in equal measure to students who play traditional musical instruments and those who do not.

Examples of both systematically gathered and anecdotal evidence abound of what becomes possible when ensemble directors incorporate student-initiated, often creative activities into an ensemble rehearsal or concert setting with a concert band, choir, or orchestra (e.g., Allsup 2003; Campbell 1991; Enloe 2015; Hickey 1997; Randles and Stringham 2013; Ruthmann and Dillon 2012). Similarly, specialists who wish to showcase their students' learning progress at the primary school level have done so by including performances of children's own lyrics and song creations, dramatized song texts, and small performance groups with an assortment of instruments (e.g., Randles 2009; Wiggins 2011). Other effective performance ensembles include iPad groups and bands comprising electric guitars, drums, amplified vocals, and more (Williams and Randles 2017). Students can play cover versions and original material; teachers can play in bands with students and/or direct and facilitate ensembles to greater and lesser degrees.

Whether a highly polished concert by a top school ensemble or a showcase of work in progress, school-endorsed public performances can bring together the school community, parents, and interested public for more than musical reasons alone. Other motives for attendance include the development and reinforcement of school spirit, building up enthusiasm for formal learning, and sharing in common musical, educational, and social values. Even if not everyone equally subscribes to all of the same goals, there is something for everyone to celebrate. Each goal is as important as the other; no one value should top others in assumed importance or educational relevance.

Pedagogically and musically, concerts might well be considered the culminating point of music instructional processes. From a sociological perspective as well, public displays of musical learning in the form of traditional seasonal concerts, community "sing-alongs," and/or joint cultural/musical events between several schools are pivotal to music as an integral part of the school curriculum. Thematically structured, they may celebrate all of the arts in school or feature other subject matter areas through student-composed as well as student-performed songs, poetry, and instrumental pieces. Not everyone might notice or even care whether the performances are "spotless," but those in attendance understand what it means for each student to be involved. It is vital, and potentially very challenging, for the music teacher and students curating the event to keep a balance of musics that affirm the values of those performing and attending, however diverse these may be.

Observation Project 7.1

Attend a school concert in your neighborhood and take note of the way the program is structured. How varied is the music? How does the audience respond? How involved are the students, and in what ways? What other music(k)ing events does or could the school offer to the community?

Students Discovering and Exploring Musical Traditions

The second story told earlier in this chapter showcased how students may be encouraged to begin multi-faceted explorations into the socio-cultural and socio-historical origins of various styles of popular music. Sharing those explorations with and among students as well as with school audiences and larger communities could become fertile ground for communication and discovery across a community of learners. In-school learning in this regard need not be limited to "survey" or "appreciation" classes.

Of the many conventions symbolizing socio-musical conduct in school music settings, students in performance ensembles experience quite a few on a daily basis. Among them are rules of ensemble seating or positioning on-stage, how and when to interact with other members of an ensemble and, in classical and jazz ensembles among others, chair placement, and the resultant section dynamics and hierarchies within and across player/singer sections. These and many other conventions are highly culture-specific and require "insider" status among musicians to be shared and interpreted in context. Making such contexts, conventions, and traditions central to exploration and examination opens avenues for study beyond the learning of an instrument alone. Similarly, in certain types of ensembles (including jazz bands, samba bands, gamelan, and mariachi bands), it is essential to know when and how a piece is coming to its end or how the hierarchy of performers impacts who can play when and/or at what volume. Comparing traditions to one other might provide students with a sense of ownership about their habits of music making.

Many different performance traditions should be tried out and/or explored, if possible: the work rock band musicians do and what orchestra musicians are expected to do, the power dynamics in band line-ups and ensemble seatings, the use and place of amplification in certain styles of music and not in others. When it comes to the operation of a PA system as a necessary component in popular musics, students could learn how to set up microphone stands, coil cables, and load gear safely and efficiently into a vehicle. As mundane as such knowledge may appear to the "insider" professional, practicing these sorts of skills in the formality of schooling could provide an opportunity to turn school learning into "life" learning.

Not all students can be expected to know all instruments in a concert band, orchestra, mariachi band, or gamelan ensemble by name and function. They may also be unfamiliar with the biographies of composers (dead or alive) of songs or compositions being performed. Learning to be aware of and listen to each other while playing together, maintaining eye contact with a conductor, band leader, or rhythm-section co-member, and marking one's score for identifying tricky figures and passages are additional socio-musical behaviors that, if explicitly taught and explored rather than merely anticipated, have the potential of becoming life skills.

An added advantage of bringing socio-musical conventions to the attention of music(k)ing students lies in the opportunity to clarify classroom management and disciplinary matters during rehearsal. For instance, concert band beginners may not know that performers in the back of an ensemble (usually percussionists) are as important as a clarinetist sitting in the first row. In a large ensemble setting, the distance between the last row of students and the teacher-conductor in the front can obscure verbal comments from the teacher. When she has to raise her voice to be heard in the last row of performers, the voice may sound angry or shrill, a trait that may then be interpreted by performers as the teacher picking on the percussionists. Although the seating may be a convention useful for the desired musical results of the ensemble, an inexperienced music learner might interpret what he (mis-)hears as unwarranted criticism.

Similarly, rock musicians in class, used to playing in spaces at the typically high volumes associated with the style, may be told to "keep the noise down!" because school policies and classroom management rules demand controlling volume levels. Such restrictions may be mistakenly taken to mean that either rock music or the musicians themselves are not valued, where instead the problem lies in a collision of different socio-musical conventions in a setting that cannot easily accommodate high levels of noise. Students would need to be made aware of the suitability of the available space for the music they make, and teachers would need to familiarize themselves with the conventions of the students' musical culture, so that accommodations and explanations can be provided and no one is offended by expectations that others take for granted. Such social situations, once made an explicit topic of classroom discussion, can become vantage points from which to take music further into other social situations where similar conflicts may exist.

Pipe band & Drumline

A further example of a particular behavioral code in music with pedagogical consequences in the classroom is that of the teacher as conductor (the "maestro"). It is not uncommon that licensed music teachers feel compelled to emulate accepted and expected role behaviors associated with professional conductors in symphony orchestras, wind ensembles, and professional choirs. Aspiring to run rehearsals in the most efficient way possible, professional conductors are generally expected to be short and direct in their verbal comments, keep praises to a minimum, and be fully focused on the musical score rather than—seemingly—on the human beings delivering the performance. Especially for inexperienced students, such attention away from them personally can make the teacher-conductor appear aloof and uncaring. The behavior of the teacher as "maestro" may be interpreted by certain students as detrimental to their perception of the educator as a mentor and sensitive human being. Thus, observed differences in how a teacher acts on and off the podium can send mixed signals to inexperienced performers. To prevent such misinterpretations and in order to remove potential learning barriers, exploring the conductor role as it has evolved throughout history could prove an important addition to formal music schooling.

Inexperienced choristers are also not immune from misunderstandings derived from presumed rather than taught knowledge. For example, in the widely exported European choral tradition, singing is often based upon experiences in church choir settings. Acquired knowledge differs considerably between denominations and faith groups. Therefore, students may know how choirs act within a worship service of a particular faith, denomination, or tradition, but school choirs tend to operate in formats with other, variable traditions. At times akin to the discipline in an instrumental ensemble, choral protocol—such as warm-up exercises, singing a song in solfège or while counting in subdivisions before singing the text—are assumed normal routines by some music teachers but may be unfamiliar to many students. That unfamiliarity can make learning considerably more difficult, turning the music classroom into a bizarre place for anyone to be. Untrained singers usually find lyrics essential as a familiar guide through music. If unexplained, the use of sol-fa or other neutral syllables can hinder rather than foster a positive engagement with the music. Once any and all such practices are examined and explained, school knowledge and life knowledge have a better chance to connect.

When context-specific practices are explored firsthand and discussed in class, with increased understanding as an important educational objective, they can turn into constructive steps in learners' musical growth and toward understanding the histories and complexities of musics and knowledges that—ultimately—reflect the cultural heritage of a community or nation-state. When students are thus encouraged to explore their own identities as musicians in a socio-historical context and interdisciplinary terms, they may become socialized also into their role as active contributors to their own country's cultural future.

Thinking in Interdisciplinary Terms When Explaining Musical Matters

Worlds of musics are full of conventions that exceed the study of a specific piece of music or the learning of a particular instrument. The conventions also exceed any one musical world as they signify symbolic social gestures embedded in historical and political contexts as much as they are part of given musical contexts. To understand those contexts, many vantage points become necessary from which to examine reasons for the variety of socio-musical traditions present around the globe. These perspectives come equally from the social sciences and natural sciences, including history, language, physics, geography, mathematics, and cultural studies—not to mention sociology, psychology, and philosophy. Not only might school music be a place that enables students to explore interdisciplinary connections between cultural traditions and behaviors, but students might also be given opportunities to engage in as many of the traditions as feasible or desired.

Learning about performance etiquette in those traditions might be as important as knowing what it means to be "in tune" on a particular instrument in a given performance context or how to act appropriately as an audience member. Performance rules, routines, and regulations are situated in conventions frequently far removed from familiar cultural expectations and, therefore, can provide a glimpse into eras long gone or societal conduct of the past or from distant locales. Much of Classical music of the last 500 years, in particular, has, to many, taken on the aura of a foreign code system that seems to cloud the essence of music(k)ing itself. This becomes apparent when audience members as well as student performers wonder whether it is important to know about "movements" in Western classical instrumental music and when it is accepted conduct to clap during a concert. Why, for that matter, do jazz concerts have a different etiquette for applause than classical concerts? What is the difference between a song and a piece of music, or between a composer, songwriter, or producer? Does knowledge about these differences matter to those who perform or listen to music? Similarly, why do classical radio stations in some parts of the world provide details about opus numbers and key signatures when the equivalent information is usually not provided for popular music, and how is such knowledge relevant for listening, dancing to, or sampling excerpts of a piece? Where do these different behavioral standards come from and how important are they while listening to, re-mixing, or performing one's favorite piece of music? Or what role does the conductor play when standing on the podium in front of the performers, and how do conducting gestures impact what the audience hears? Is leadership of popular music ensembles more or less democratic than directing a classical orchestra or a jazz big band?

These questions, just a cross section of many more that address coded musical behaviors, can be appropriately answered only when viewing them through interdisciplinary lenses—a task to which the sociologically savvy music teacher is well suited. Viewing the world through a single (sociological) lens as insufficient has caused Ruth Wright (2014, 15) to call for an "integrated sociology" applied to music education. Her call is similar to the advice by sociologist John Levi Martin (2011), who cautioned against an unthinking reliance on theories and frameworks at the expense of understandings based in the real experiences of people. Instead, careful attention should be paid to what he called "the concrete relationships of interpersonal life" and the "first-person beliefs of actors" (349–350).

Affirming Students' Musical Skills and Knowledge as Cultural Assets

What, then, are the musical knowledge and skills that Basil Bernstein called *valued knowledge*, what Roger Scruton hailed, and what Pierre Bourdieu critiqued as *Cultural Capital*? In functionalist terms: what does a set of socio-musical (cultural) knowledge and music(k)ing skills look like that you, the teacher, want your students to acquire and embrace as their own? Are there agreed-upon goals and learning objectives across localities, regions, or nation-states? Can there or should there be? One of the first responses among many music educators from mostly English-speaking countries might include a reference to what music experts call "musicianship," a term that must remain broad in its definition to be applicable to music(k)ing practices in different locales and regions. A second term that especially music educators in German-speaking and Scandinavian countries might prefer to use is that of musical *Bildung*, a term already introduced as "cultural learnedness" in Chapter 4.

Without going too deeply into etymological and historical explanations of the term *Bildung* in the context of formal education in Europe, the term connotes a form of musicianship rooted more in **c/C**ultural knowledge specific to music production, distribution, history, and traditions than in the acquisition of highly developed musical skills. Close in meaning to what educators and philosophers in education think of when they speak of a liberal (arts) education (Løvlie and Standish 2002; Steinsholt and Dobson 2011), *Bildung* also exceeds that meaning (see, e.g., Byram 2010; Ehrenforth 2005; Jank 2014; Nordenbo 2002; Rolle 2008; Vogt et al. 2014). The construct might be considered an important addition, if not correlate, to musicianship through music(k)ing. Both constructs might be necessary to bring sociological thought into articulating the purpose of music in compulsory schooling. Usually germane to philosophical discourse, the following discussion of musicianship and *Bildung* is but a brief assertion that sociologies of education and music can provide important foundations for philosophical debates about the "why" and "what" of music education.

Musicianship and Musical *Bildung*

"Musicianship" consists of multi-faceted traits and skills, intended, for instance, to serve as a means to be involved with music for a lifetime. But does such involvement cement, as Bourdieu would argue, the status quo of musical doing and knowing? The answer, we believe, derives from the significance that individual teachers attach to the musicianship their students bring to formal learning experiences, the latitude that teachers give their students in developing that musicianship, and schools' curricular and programmatic willingness to fulfill students' wishes of playing instruments of various kinds (with a broad and widening definition of "instruments" as discussed earlier).

Currently in the United States, a musically educated student, graduating from high school with music as an elective course of study, may have learned to play at least one instrument and/or sing to some level of technical ability, may be able to read musical notation to an extent, and may have participated in music festivals and performance contests. In Europe, the goals are more varied, although efforts are underway to document these for future work on finding and articulating goals and objectives across member countries of the European Union (De Baets, Sammer, and Vugt 2016; Rodríguez-Quiles y García and Dogani 2011). Far more established and wide-reaching is the Associated Board of the Royal Schools of Music (ABRSM), based in the United Kingdom and operating in more than ninety countries, externally to mainstream school provision. The organization provides graded assessments in music theory and of music performance on a range of instruments to candidates from beginners up to the level required to audition for undergraduate study (along with similar pre-college-level assessment providers such as Rockschool, London College of Music, and Trinity College London).

Where they exist or are in the process of being established, curricular committees, examination boards, accrediting and awarding authorities, and musical decision-making agencies around the world play a significant role in defining what is understood by "musicianship," regardless of whether it is part of compulsory or higher education. Furthermore, geographical locations and sociocultural conditions of the communities within which schools are located also impact the ease and pace at which teachers can reach any of the officially declared musical standards of musicianship set forth by appointed or elected gatekeepers in music and education. Clearly, therefore, the diversity of musicianship levels common in general compulsory music classes demands flexibility in pedagogical approaches. School ensembles as electives, or individual (studio) lessons, can enable students to reach levels of accomplishment much different from those possible in a compulsory "general" music for all. This is why provision in one context should not and cannot become a watered-down version of what takes place in another. Educational purposes and pedagogical settings need to be aligned, with one another and with the learning and identity aspirations of the students who are to benefit from formal music schooling at any level.

Just as is the case with the educational goal of musicianship, teaching toward the goal of a general **c/C**ultural learnedness (or **c/C**ultural literacy) allows a teacher to pursue many different pedagogical avenues. The focus would lie in all cases on what the students learn beyond playing an instrument, reading music, or understanding theoretical or technological rudiments. It is here that passive and active realization of self-identity should connect with getting to know the cultures and realities of others. Here, valued knowledge held by self and others should be articulated and placed into historical and social contexts, so that musical self-fulfillment and growth can help to shape **c/C**ulturally literate individuals whose musical competencies serve them and society well beyond compulsory schooling. Sociologically, the need to step outside one's own comfort zone of beliefs and acquired musical skills and knowledge becomes evident as theoretical explorations begin to guide practical expertise and practical expertise turns into a stepping stone to exploring the theoretical.

Small Group Discussion 7.1

What elements would you consider to be important in a **c/C**ulturally literate person? How do different approaches toward the teaching of musicianship through music(k)ing enter into such considerations?

Propose strategies for different school settings that advocate educational goals of cultural literacy and musicianship by means of music(k)ing.

Embracing Theory as Integral to Practical Expertise

Personal experiences and other anecdotal evidence, along with scholarship in various academic disciplines, emphasize that mutual understanding of "how things are done" in a society is no longer (if it has ever been) common, shared knowledge among all its citizens. Societal norms, therefore, must be taught rather than merely assumed before they become shared values. Formal schooling could well be one of numerous sites where such values can be uncovered, examined, and connected to each learner's own social and musical world. Applied specifically to school music, music(k)ing of all sorts would become an important step in exploring what constitutes the **c/C**ultural habits (and habitats) in students' lives, the larger geopolitical community in which those lives are embedded, and the nation-state/s of which the community is a part.

Biographies of, blogs about, and interviews with musicians of today can be contrasted to stories of past artists and placed into knowledge about history, current affairs, politics, and sports. Any insights gained from such seemingly academic non-performance activities can serve as entry points for writing original songs or writing about music in one's life. The history of music would become alive in the stories of musicians past and present! Any questions resulting from those stories would derive from personal observations and experience rather than from textbook theory.

Ultimately (and as stated in Chapter 5), sociological thinking in both music and education seeks to combine micro perspectives of subjective experiences and observations with the worlds of macro theories and their abstractions. Between those two sets of realities lie the institutional settings within which micro actions and macro structures become visible (the meso level of analysis). Vantage points at all levels (micro, meso, and macro) are needed to examine music learning and teaching as social acts that are situated in the aesthetics of performing, appreciating, and experiencing musical works of genres and musical doings in all styles. When accepting this premise, a plethora of social and aesthetic questions follows, requiring answers (or at least warranting discussion) about school learning as an important component in life learning. In school music education settings, the most critical player in this regard is the music teacher who sets up the music(k)ing opportunities and serves as the facilitator for helping students to find answers that make them grow as musicians and citizens. In that process, the students' roles as learners change, as do the teacher's roles as musician, educator, and scholar.

In her book *Culturally Responsive Teaching*, Geneva Gay (2010, 2) observed that the dynamics of "research, theory, and practice are woven together" to produce major ideas. Her assertion applies to the musician-educator and the musician-scholar, a sentiment expressed by many critical theorists, interactionists, and functionalists in music, music education, and music therapy. There are too many of them to list by name, but all have emphasized that schooling should be about inclusion, integration, wholeness, and transparency of thought in a diverse and multi-faceted field of theory-informed practice. Therefore, the musician-performer, too, should become a questioner, someone who is curious about the craft, art, society, and **c/C**ulture/s in which he or she is engaged, and share this curiosity with students.

In conclusion, being sociologically informed also means to recognize the perennial wisdom in the statement that theory and practice are symbiotically and necessarily intertwined. The implications for you as a music educator can be powerful. They enable you to connect various discrete, sometimes overlapping, and always interacting identities in diverse musical and social contexts. As a sociologically savvy music educator, then, you are empowered similarly to enable your students to live their micro world lives fully engaged in and aware of the macro worlds of society and musics.

Reality Check 7.1

1. Where did this chapter speak to you directly, and at what points did you find it more difficult to relate?
2. What chapters seemed the most immediately relevant, and where do you see potential future applications?
3. Articulate questions that sprang up in the course of reading from this book, and outline a course of action for how you might implement some of the ideas outlined in the various chapters.

Questions for Class Discussion

1. Using the previous Reality Check box as the basis, share with each other your responses and develop a collective reaction to what you read in this book. Ask your course instructor to help you publish the response as a book review in a journal, magazine, or blog.
2. If you were to sum up the main takeaway for you from this book, what would that be? Can you articulate it in one or two short sentences? Compare your summary statement with those written by others in your class, and discuss the reasons for your respective responses.

Key Sources (for full information, see References)

Ahner, Philipp. 2011.
Ballenger, Cynthia. 2009.
Dewey, John. 1916/1953.
Gay, Geneva. 2010.
Griffin, Shelley M. 2011.
Kaplan, Max. 1966.
Tripp, David. 1993/2012.

References

Abbott, Andrew. 1988. *Professional Choices: Values at Work*. Silver Spring, MD: National Association of Social Workers.

Abbott, Stephen E., Lisa Guisbond, Jack Levy, and Meg Sommerfeld. 2014. "Hidden Curriculum." *The Glossary of Education Reform*. Accessed July 10, 2016. http://edglossary.org/hidden-curriculum.

Abeles, Hal. 1979. "Verbal Timbre Descriptors of Isolated Clarinet Tones." *Bulletin of the Council for Research in Music Education*, 59 (Summer): 1–7.

Abeles, Hal. 2009. "Are Musical Instrument Gender Associations Changing?" *Journal of Research in Music Education*, 57 (2): 127–139.

Abercrombie, Nicholas, Stephen Hill, and Bryan S. Turner. 2006. *The Penguin Dictionary of Sociology*. 5th edition, reprint, revised. New York: Penguin.

Abrahams, Frank. 2004. "The Application of Critical Theory to a Sixth Grade General Music Class." *Visions of Research in Music Education*, 4: 43–53.

Abramo, Joseph M. 2011a. "Gender Differences of Popular Music Production in Secondary Schools." *Journal of Research in Music Education*, 59: 21–43.

Abramo, Joseph M. 2011b. "Gender Differences in the Popular Music Compositions of High School Students." *Music Education Research International*, 5: 1–11.

Acker, Sandra. 1987. "Feminist Theory and the Study of Gender and Education." *International Review of Education / Internationale Zeitschrift für Erziehungswissenschaft / Revue Internationale de l'Education*, 33 (4): 419–435.

Adams, Maurianne, Lee Anne Bell, and Pat Griffin. 2007. *Teaching for Diversity and Social Justice*. 2nd edition. New York, NY: Routledge.

Addams, Jane. 1902. *Democracy and Social Ethics*. New York, NY: Macmillan.

Addams, Jane. 1912. *A New Conscience and an Ancient Evil*. New York, NY: Macmillan.

Adderley, Cecil, Mary Kennedy, and William Berz. 2003. "'A Home Away from Home': The World of the High School Music Classroom." *Journal of Research in Music Education*, 51 (3): 190–205.

Adorno, Theodor W. 1962/1976. *Introduction to the Sociology of Music*. Translated by E.B. Ashton. New York, NY: Seabury.

Aerni, April Laskey and Kim Marie McGoldrick, eds. 1999. *Valuing Us All: Feminist Pedagogy and Economics*. Ann Arbor, MI: University of Michigan Press.

Agger, Ben. 2004. *The Virtual Self: A Contemporary Sociology*. Malden, MA and Oxford: Blackwell.

Ahner, Philipp. 2011. *Wahlfach Music: Musikunterricht an Berufluichen Gymnasien in der Sekundarstufe II in Baden-Wurttemberg aus der Perspektive von Jugendlichen, Musiikpadagogik und Kultusverwalting*. Norderstedt, Germany: Books on demand.

Algan, Yann, Christian Dustmann, Albrecht Glitz, and Alan Manning. 2010. "The Economic Situation of First and Second-Generation Immigrants in France, Germany and the United Kingdom." *The Economic Journal*, 120 (February, 542): F4–F30.

Allan, Julie. 2010. "Arts and the Inclusive Imagination: Socially Engaged Arts Practices and Sistema Scotland." *Journal of Social Inclusion*, 1 (2): 111–122.

Allan, Julie, Nikki Moran, Celia Duffy, and Gica Loening. 2008. "Knowledge Exchange with Sistema Scotland." *Journal of Education Policy*, 25 (3): 335–347.

Allsup, Randall E. 2003. "Mutual Learning and Democratic Action in Instrumental Music Education." *Journal of Research in Music Education*, 51 (1): 24–37.

Allsup, Randall E. 2008. "Creating an Educational Framework for Popular Music in Public Schools: Anticipating the Second Wave." *Visions of Research in Music Education*, 12 (1): 1–12.

Antliff, Allan. 2012. "Let the Riots Begin." In *Anarchist Pedagogies: Collective Actins, Theories, and Critical Reflections on Education*, edited by Robert H. Haworth, 326–329. Oakland, CA: PM Press.

Anyon, Jean. 1980. "Social Class and the Hidden Curriculum of Work." *Journal of Education*, 162 (1): 67–92.

Apple, Michael W. 1995. *Education and Power*. 2nd edition. New York and London: Routledge.

Apple, Michael W. 2000. "The Cultural Politics of Home Schooling." *Peabody Journal of Education*, 75 (1 and 2): 256–271.

Apple, Michael W., Stephen J. Ball, and Luis Armando Gandin, eds. 2010. *The Routledge International Handbook of the Sociology of Education*. New York, NY: Taylor and Francis.

Arum, Richard, Irenee R. Beattie, and Karly Ford, eds. 2011. *The Structure of Schooling: Readings in the Sociology of Education*, 2nd edition. Thousand Oaks, CA: Pine Forge Press.

Attali, Jacques. 1985. *Noise: The Political Economy of Music*. Manchester: Manchester University Press.

Au, Wayne. 2009. *Unequal by Design: High-Stakes Testing and the Standardization of Inequality*. New York and London: Routledge.

Aukerman, Maren. 2013. "Rereading Comprehension Pedagogies: Toward a Dialogic Teaching Ethic that Honors Student Sensemaking." *Dialogic Pedagogy: An International Online Journal*, 1: A1–A31.

Auslander, Philip. 2008. *Liveness: Performance in a Mediatized Culture*. New York, NY: Routledge.

Austin, James D., Daniel S. Isbell, and Joshua A. Russell. 2010. "A Multi-Institution Exploration of Secondary Socialization and Occupational Identity among Undergraduate Music Majors." *Psychology of Music*, 40 (1): 66–83.

Baker, David. 2005. "Identities of Music Teachers: Implications for Teacher Education." *International Journal of Music Education*, 23 (3): 263–277.

Baker, Geoffrey. 2014. *El Sistema: Orchestrating Venezuela's Youth*. New York, NY: Oxford University Press.

Ball, Arnetha F. and Cynthia A. Tyson, eds. 2011. *Studying Diversity in Teacher Education*. Lanham, MD: Rowman and Littlefield.

Ball, Stephen, ed. 2004. *The RoutledgeFalmer Reader in Sociology of Education*. New York, NY: Routledge.

Ballantine, Jeanne H. and Floyd Hammack. 2009. *The Sociology of Education: A Systematic Analysis*, 6th edition. New York, NY: Pearson.

Ballantine, Jeanne H. and Joan Z. Spade, eds. 2014. *Schools and Society: A Sociological Approach to Education*. 5th edition. Thousand Oaks, CA: Sage.

Ballantyne, Julie. 2005. "Identities of Music Teachers: Implications for Teacher Education." Paper presented at the *33rd Australian Teacher Education Association Conference*, Surfers Paradise, Gold Coast, Australia, July 6–9.

Ballantyne, Julie, Jody L. Kerchner, and Jose L. Aróstegui. 2012. "Developing Music Teacher Identities: An International Multi-Site Study." *International Journal of Music Education*, 30 (3): 211–226.

Ballenger, C., 2009. *Puzzling Moments, Teachable Moments: Practicing Teacher Research in Urban Classrooms*. Practitioners Inquiry Series. New York, NY: Teachers College Press.

Banfield, William. 2010. *Cultural Codes: Makings of a Black Music Philosophy*. London: Scarecrow Press.

Barrett, Margaret S. 2011. "Towards a Cultural Psychology of Music Education." In *A Cultural Psychology of Music Education*, edited by Margaret S. Barrett, 1–16. Oxford and New York: Oxford University Press.

Bartel, Lee, ed. 2004. *Questioning the Music Education Paradigm*, Vol. 2. Waterloo, ON: Canadian Music Educators' Association.

Becker, Howard S. 1951/1980. *Role and Career Problems of the Chicago Public School Teacher*. New York, NY: Arno Press.

Becker, Howard S. 1952. "The Career of the Chicago Public School Teacher." *American Journal of Sociology*, 57 (5): 470–477.

Becker, Howard S. 1963a. *Outsiders: Studies in the Sociology of Deviance*. New York, NY: Free Press.

Becker, Howard S. 1963b. "The Culture of a Deviant Group: The Dance Musician." In *Outsiders: Studies in the Sociology of Deviance*, edited by Howard S. Becker 79–82. New York, NY: Free Press.

Becker, Howard S. 1970/1977. *Sociological Work: Method and Substance*. Chicago: Aldine; New Brunswick, NJ: Transaction Books.

Becker, Howard. 1976. "Art Worlds and Social Types." *American Behavioral Scientist*, 19: 703–718.

Becker, Howard S. 1982/1984/2008. *Art Worlds*. 25th edition, updated and extended. Berkeley, CA: University of California Press.

Becker, Howard S., Blanche Geer, and Everett Hughes. 1968/1995. *Making the Grade: The Academic Side of College Life*. New Brunswick, NJ: Transaction Publishers.

Becker, Howard S., Blanche Geer, Everett Hughes, and Anselm Strauss. 1961/1977. *Boys in White: Student Culture in Medical School*. Chicago: University of Chicago Press. New Brunswick, NJ: Transaction Books.

Beijaard, Douwe, Pauline C. Meijer, and Nico Verloop. 2004. "Reconsidering Research on Teachers' Professional Identity." *Teaching and Teacher Education*, 20 (2): 107–128.

Bell, Adam Patrick. 2015. "DAW Democracy? The Dearth of Diversity in 'Playing the Studio'." *Journal of Music, Technology and Education*, 8 (2): 129–146.

Beller, Michal L. and Naomi Gafni. 1991/1996. "International Assessment of Educational Progress in Mathematics and Sciences: The Gender Differences Perspective." *Journal of Educational Psychology*, 88 (2): 365–377.

Benedict, Cathy, Patrick Schmidt, Gary Spruce, and Paul Woodford, eds. 2015. *The Oxford Handbook of Social Justice in Music Education*. New York, NY: Oxford University Press.

Benjamin, Shereen. 2002. "'Valuing Diversity': A Cliché for the 21st Century?" *International Journal of Inclusive Education*, 6 (4): 309–323.

Bennett, Andy. 2000. *Popular Music and Youth Culture: Music, Identity and Place*. New York, NY: Macmillan.

Bennett, Andy, ed. 2006. *The Popular Music Studies Reader*. New York, NY: Routledge.

Bennett, Dawn E. 2008. *Understanding the Classical Music Profession: The Past, the Present and Strategies for the Future*. Farnham: Ashgate.

Bennett, Dawn E. 2013. "The Role of Career Creativities in Developing Identity and Becoming Expert Selves." In *Developing Creativities in Higher Music Education: International Perspectives and Practices*, edited by Pamela Burnard, 234–244. New York, NY: Routledge.

Berg, Margaret H. and Peter Miksza. 2010. "An Investigation of Preservice Music Teacher Development and Concerns." *Journal of Music Teacher Education*, 20 (1): 39–55.

Berger, Peter L. and Thomas Luckmann. 1967. *The Social Construction of Reality: A Treatise in the Sociology of Knowledge*. New York, NY: Doubleday.

Bernstein, Basil. 1977. *Class, Codes and Control*, Vol. 3. London: Routledge & Kegan Paul.

Bernstein, Basil. 1996. *Pedagogy, Symbolic Control and Identity: Theory, Research, Critique*. Washington, DC: Taylor and Francis.

Bernstein, Basil. 1996/2000. *Pedagogy, Symbolic Control, and Identity: Theory, Research, Critique*. Revised edition. Lanham, MD: Rowman and Littlefield.

Bernstein, Basil. 1971–1975/2003. *Class, Codes and Control*. London: Routledge and Kegan Paul; Vols. 1–4. New York, NY: Taylor and Francis.

Bernstein, Basil. 1990/2003. *Class, Codes, and Control, Vol. 4, The Structuring of Pedagogic Discourse*. London and New York, NY: Routledge.

Bidwell, Charles. 2000. "School as Context and Construction: A Social Psychological Approach to the Study of Schooling." In *Handbook of the Sociology of Education*, edited by Maureen T. Hallinan, 15–36. New York, NY: Kluwer Academic/Plenum Publishers.

Bidwell, Charles E., Kenneth A. Frank, and Pamela A. Quiroz. 1997. "Teacher Types, Workplace Controls, and the Organization of Schools." *Sociology of Education*, 70: 285–307.

Billingsley, Bonnie S. 1993. "Teacher Retention and Attrition in Special and General Education: A Critical Review of the Literature." *The Journal of Special Education*, 27 (2): 137–174.

Blacking, John. 1973. *How Musical Is Man?* Seattle, WA: University of Washington Press.

Blaut, James. 1993. *The Colonizer's Model of the World: Geographical Diffusionism and Eurocentric History*. New York, NY: The Guildford Press.

Blumer, Herbert. 1969/1986. *Symbolic Interactionism: Perspective and Method.* Berkeley, CA: University of California Press.

Blumer, Herbert. 2004. *George Herbert Mead and Human Conduct.* Walnut Creek, CA: AltaMira Press.

Böhnisch, Lothar. 2003. *Pädagogische Soziologie: Eine Einführung.* 2. bearbeitete Auflage. (Grundlagentexte Pädagogik).Weinheim: Beltz Juventa.

Böhnisch, Lothar and Karl Lenz. 2014. *Studienbuch Pädagogik und Soziologie.* Bad Heilbrunn: Verlag Klinkhardt.

Bolton, Sharon and Daniel Muzio. 2008. "The Paradoxical Processes of Feminization in the Professions: The Case of Established, Aspiring and Semi-professions." *Work, Employment and Society*, 22 (2): 281–299.

Bonilla-Silva, Eduardo. 2003. *Racism without Racists: Color-Blind Racism and the Persistence of Racial Inequality in the United States.* Lanham, MD: Rowman and Littlefield.

Bontinck, Irmgard. 1974. *New Patterns of Musical Behaviour of the Young Generation in Industrial Societies.* International Institute for Music, Dance and Theatre in the Audio-Visual Media. Vienna: Universal Edition.

Bontinck, Irmgard, ed. 1999. *Musik/Soziologie/ . . . Thematische Umkreisungen Einer Disziplin. Ausgewählte Beiträge aus der Arbeit des Wiener Instituts für Musiksoziologie.* Strasshof, Austria: Vier Viertel Verlag.

Bourdieu, Pierre. 1977. *Outline of a Theory of Practice.* Translated by Richard Nice. New York, NY: Cambridge University Press.

Bourdieu, Pierre. 1984. *Distinction: A Social Critique of the Judgment of Taste.* Cambridge, MA: Harvard University Press.

Bourdieu, Pierre. 1986. "The Forms of Capital." In *Handbook of Theory and Research for the Sociology of Education*, edited by John Richardson, 241–258. New York, NY: Greenwood Press.

Bourdieu, Pierre. 1993. *The Field of Cultural Production: Essays on Art and Literature.* New York, NY: Columbia University Press.

Bourdieu, Pierre. 2001. *Masculine Domination.* Translated by Richard Nice. Stanford, CA: Stanford University Press.

Bourdieu, Pierre. 2005. *The Social Structure of the Economy.* Hoboken, NJ: Wiley.

Bourdieu, Pierre and Jean-Claude Passeron. 1977. *Reproduction in Education, Society and Culture.* Translated by Richard Nice. London: Sage Publications.

Bourdieu, Pierre and Loïc J. Wacquant. 1992. *An Invitation to Reflexive Sociology.* Chicago: University of Chicago Press.

Bourn, Doug. 2008. *Development Education: Debates and Dialogue.* London: Institute of Education, University of London.

Bowles, Samuel and Herbert Gintis. 1976. *Schooling in Capitalist America: Educational Reform and the Contradictions of Economic Life*. New York, NY: Basic Books.

Bowman, Wayne D. 2007. "Who Is the 'We'? Rethinking Professionalism in Music Education." *Action, Criticism, and Theory for Music Education*, 6 (4): 109–131.

Bradley, Deborah. 2007. "The Sounds of Silence: Talking Race in Music Education." *Action, Criticism, and Theory for Music Education*, 6 (4): 132–162.

Bradley, Deborah. 2012. "Good for What, Good for Whom? Decolonizing Music Education Philosophies." In *The Oxford Handbook of Philosophy in Music Education*, edited by Wayne Bowman, and Ana Lucía Frega, 409–433. New York, NY: Oxford University Press.

Bradley, Deborah. 2015. "Hidden in Plain Sight: Race and Racism in Music Education." In *The Oxford Handbook of Social Justice in Music Education*, edited by Cathy Benedict, Patrick Schmidt, Gary Spruce, and Paul Woodford, 190–203. New York, NY: Oxford University Press.

Brookfield, Stephen. 1990. "Using Critical Incidents to Explore Learners' Assumptions." In *Fostering Critical Reflection in Adulthood: A Guide to Transformative and Emancipatory Learning*, edited by Jack Mezirov and Associates, 177–193. San Francisco: Jossey-Bass Publishers.

Brooks, Rachel, Mark McCormack, and Kalwand Bhopal, eds. 2013. *Contemporary Debates in the Sociology of Education*. 2nd edition. London: Palgrave Macmillan.

Butler, Brandon M., Yonghee Suh, and Wendy Scott. 2015. "Knowledge Transmission Versus Social Transformation: A Critical Analysis of Purpose in Elementary Social Studies Methods Textbooks." *Theory and Research in Social Education*, 43 (1): 102–134.

Butler, Judith. 1990. *Gender Trouble and the Subversion of Identity*. New York, NY: Routledge.

Byram, Michael. 2010. "Linguistic and Cultural Education for Bildung and Citizenship." *The Modern Language Journal*, 94 (2): 317–321.

Campbell, Patricia S. 1991. *Lessons from the World: A Cross-Cultural Guide to Music Teaching and Learning*. Belmont, CA: Wadsworth.

Campbell, Patricia S. 1998. "The Musical Cultures of Children." *Research Studies in Music Education*, 11 (1): 42–51.

Campbell, Patricia S. 2004. *Teaching Music Globally and Thinking Musically: Experiencing Music, Expressing Culture*. New York, NY: Oxford University Press.

Campbell, Patricia S. 2010. *Songs in their Heads: Music and Its Meaning in Children's Lives*. 2nd edition. New York, NY: Oxford University Press.

Carlsburg, Gerd-Bodo Reinert von, ed. 2009. *Enkulturation und Bildung: Fundament Sozialer Kompetenz*. Frankfurt a.M.: Peter Lang.

Carrington, Bruce and Alastair McPhee. 2008. "Boys' 'Underachievement' and the Feminization of Teaching." *Journal of Education for Teaching: International Research and Pedagogy*, 34 (2): 109–120.

Carter, Lyn. 2005. "Globalisation, Neoliberalism, and Science Education." In *Second International Handbook on Globalisation, Education and Policy Research*, edited by Joseph Zajda, 839–850. Dordrecht: Springer.

Catterall, James S. 1997. "Involvement in the Arts and Success in Secondary School." *Americans for the Arts Monographs*, 1 (9): 1–12.

The Changing Nature of Work: Implications for Occupational Analysis. 1999. Washington, DC: The National Academies Press.

Charon, Joel M. 1998. *Symbolic Interactionism: An Introduction, an Interpretation, an Integration*. 6th edition. With a chapter on Erving Goffman by Spencer Cahill. Upper Saddle River, NJ: Prentice Hall.

Chen-Hafteck, Lily. 1997. "Music and Language Development in Early Childhood: Integrating Past Research in the Two Domains." *Early Child Development and Care*, 130 (1): 85–97.

Chinn, Beverly J. 1997. "Vocal Self-Identification, Singing Style, and Singing Range in Relationship to a Measure of Cultural Mistrust in African-American Adolescent Females." *Journal of Research in Music Education*, 45 (4): 636–649.

Chong, Sylvia, Low Ee Ling, and Goh Kim Chuan. 2011. "Developing student teachers' professional identities: An exploratory study." *International Education Studies*, 4 (1): 30–38.

Christophersen, Katarina and Anna-Karin Gullberg. 2017. "Popular Music Education, Participation and Democracy: Some Nordic Perspectives." In *The Routledge Research Companion to Popular Music Education*, edited by Gareth Dylan Smith, Zack Moir, Matt Brennan, Shara Rambarran, and Phil Kirkman, 425–437. Abingdon: Routledge.

Clandinin, D. Jean, Julie Long, Lee Schaefer, C. Aiden Downey, Pam Steeves, Eliza Pinnegar, Sue McKenzie Robblee, and Sheri Wnuk. 2012. *Early Career Teacher Attrition: Problems, Possibilities, Potentials*. Alberta, Canada: Centre for Research for Teacher Education and Development, University of Alberta.

Clandinin, D. Jean, Julie Long, Lee Schaefer, C. Aiden Downey, Pam Steeves, Eliza Pinnegar, Sue McKenzie Robblee, and Sheri Wnuk. 2015. "Early Career Teacher Attrition: Intentions of Teachers Beginning." *Teaching Education*, 26 (1): 1–16.

Cloke, Paul J., Phil Crang, and Mark A. Goodwin. 2005. *Introducing Human Geographies*. New York, NY: Routledge.

Coeyman, Barbara. 1996. "Applications of Feminist Pedagogy to the College Music Major Curriculum: An Introduction to the Issues." *College Music Symposium*, 36: 73–90. Missoula, MT: College Music Society.

Coffman, James T. 1971. "Everybody Knows This Is Nowhere: Role Conflict and the Rock Musician." *Popular Music in Society*, 36: 20–32.

Cohen, Mary L., Laya H. Silber, Andrea Sangiorgio, and Valentina Iadeluca. 2012. "At-risk Youth: Music Making as a Means to Promote Positive Relationships." In *The Oxford Handbook of Music Education*. Vol. 2, edited by Gary E. McPherson and Graham F. Welch, 185–202. New York, NY: Oxford University Press.

Cole, Michael. 1996. *Cultural Psychology. A Once and Future Discipline.* Cambridge, MA: Harvard University Press.

Coleman, James. 1961. *The Adolescent Society: The Social Life of the Teenager and Its Impact on Education.* With the assistance of John Johnstone and Kurt Jonassohn. New York, NY: Free Press of Glencoe.

Coleman, James S. 1965. *Adolescents and the Schools*. New York: Basic Books.

Collins, Randall. 1979. *The Credential Society: Historical Sociology of Education and Stratification.* New York, NY: Academic Press.

Collins, Randall. 1999a. *Macrohistory: Essays in Sociology of the Long Run.* Stanford, CA: Stanford University Press.

Collins, Randall. 1999b. *The Sociology of Philosophies: A Global Theory of Intellectual Change*. Cambridge, MA: The Belknap Press of Harvard University Press.

Collins, Randall. 2004. *Interaction Ritual Chains*. Princeton, NJ: Princeton University Press.

Combe, Arno and Sylvia Buchen. 1996. *Belastung von Lehrerinnen und Lehrern: Fallstudien zur Bedeutung alltäglicher Handlungsabläufe an Unterschiedlichen Schulformen*. Weinheim und München: Juventa-Verlag.

Cooper, James M. and Amy Alvarado. 2006. *Preparation, Recruitment and Retention of Teachers.* International Academy of Education and International Institute for Educational Policy. Brussels and Paris: UNESCO. Accessed March 1, 2016. www.unesco.org/iiep/PDF/Edpol5.pdf.

Cortina, Regina and Sonsoles San Román. 2006. *Women and Teaching: Global Perspectives on the Feminization of a Profession*. Sonsoles San Román: Palgrave Macmillan.

Cox, Gordon and Robin Stevens. 2012. *The Origins and Foundations of Music Education Cross-Cultural Historical Studies of Music in Compulsory Schooling*. London: Bloomsbury Publishing.

Cremata, Radio, Joseph Pignato, Bryan Powell, and Gareth Dylan Smith. 2016. "Let's Take This Outside: Flash Study Analysis and the Music Learning Profiles Project." *Action, Criticism, and Theory for Music Education*, 15 (5), 51–80.

Crenshaw, Kimberlé, Neil Gotanda, Gary Peller, and Kendall Thomas, eds. 1995. *Critical Race Theory: The Key Writings that Formed the Movement*. New York, NY: The New Press.

Çubukçu, Zühal. 2012. "The Effect of Hidden Curriculum on Character Education Process of Primary School Students." *Educational Sciences: Theory and Practice*, 12 (2): 1526–1534.

D'Amore, Abigail and Gareth Dylan Smith. 2016. "Aspiring to Music Making as Leisure Through the Musical Futures Classroom." In *The Oxford Handbook of Music Making and Leisure*, edited by Roger Mantie and Gareth Dylan Smith, 61–80. New York, NY: Oxford University Press.

Darling-Hammond, Linda, Barnett T. Berry, David Haselkorn, and Elizabeth Fideler. 1999. "Teacher Recruitment, Selection, and Induction: Policy Influences on the Supply and Quality of Teachers." In *Teaching as the Learning Profession: Handbook of Policy and Practice*, edited by Linda Darling-Hammond and Gary Sykes, 183–232. San Francisco, CA: Jossey-Bass.

Darrow, Alice-Ann. 2015. "Ableism and Social Justice." In *The Oxford Handbook of Social Justice in Music Education*, edited by Cathy Benedict, Patrick Schmidt, and Paul Woodford, 204–220. Oxford and New York: Oxford University Press.

Dasilva, Fabio, Anthony Blasi, and David Dees. 1984. *The Sociology of Music*. Notre Dame, IN: University of Notre Dame Press.

Davies, Lynn. 2004. *Education and Conflict: Complexity and Chaos*. New York, NY: Routledge Falmer.

Davis, Robert A. 2005. "Music Education and Cultural Identity." *Educational Philosophy and Theory*, 37 (1): 47–63.

Day, Christopher, Gordon Stobart, Pam Sammons, Alison Kington, Qing Gu, Rebecca Smees, and Tamild Muitaba. 2006. *Variations in Teachers' Work, Lives and Effectiveness. Final Report of the VITAE Project*. London: Department for Education and Skills.

Deasy, Richard J. 2002. *Critical Links: Learning in the Arts and Student Academic and Social Development*. Washington, DC: Arts Education Partnership.

De Baets, Thomas, Gerhard Sammer, and Adri de Vugt, eds. 2016. *European Perspectives on Music Education: International Cooperation*. Leuven, Belgium: European Association for Music in Schools.

Deegan, Mary J., ed. 1991. *Women in Sociology: A Bio-Biographical Sourcebook*. New York, NY: Greenwood Press.

Delgado, Richard and Jean Stefanic, eds. 2000. *Critical Race Theory: The Cutting Edge*. Philadelphia, PA: Temple University Press.

Delgado, Richard and Jean Stefancic. 2012. *Critical Race Theory: An Introduction*. New York, NY: New York University Press.

Delgado, Richard, and Jean Stefancic. 2013. "Discerning Critical Moments." In *Handbook of Critical Race Theory in Education*, edited by Marvin Lynn and Adrienne D. Dixson, 23–33. New York, NY: Routledge.

DeLorenzo, Lisa C. 2015a. "Conclusion." In *Giving Voice to Democracy in Music Education: Diversity and Social Justice*, edited by Lisa C. DeLorenzo, 252–262. New York, NY: Routledge.

DeLorenzo, Lisa, ed. 2015b. *Giving Voice to Democracy in Music Education: Diversity and Social Justice*. New York, NY: Routledge.

DeNora, Tia. 2000. *Music in Everyday Life*. Cambridge: Cambridge University Press.

DeNora, Tia. 2006. "Music and Self-identity." In *The Popular Music Studies Reader*, edited by Andy Bennett, 141–147. New York, NY: Routledge.

Denzin, Norman K. and Michael D. Giardina. 2007. *Ethical Futures in Qualitative Research: Decolonizing the Politics of Knowledge*. Walnut Creek, CA: Left Coast Press.

Dewey, John. 1916/1953. *Democracy and Education*. Boston, MA: DC Heath.

Dewey, John. 1916/2015. *Essays in Experimental Logic*. Chicago, IL: University of Chicago Press.

Dewey, John. 1934. *Art as Experience*. New York, NY: Minton, Balch and Company.

Diamond, Lisa M. 2005. "'I'm Straight, But I Kissed a Girl': The Trouble with American Media Representations of Female-Female Sexuality." *Feminism and Psychology*, 15 (1): 104–110.

Dickerson, Linda W. 2007. "Postmodern View of the Hidden Curriculum." PhD diss., Georgia Southern University.

Dimitrova, Radosveta, Michael Bender, and Fons J.R. van de Vijver, eds. 2014. *Global Perspectives on Well-Being in Immigrant Families*. New York, NY: Springer.

Dines, Mike. 2015. "Learning Through Resistance: Contextualisation, Creation and Incorporation of a 'Punk Pedagogy'." *Journal of Pedagogical Development*, 5 (3): 20–31.

Diversi, Marcelo and Claudio Moreira. 2009. *Betweener Talk: Decolonizing Knowledge Production, Pedagogy, and Praxis*. Walnut Creek, CA: Left Coast Press.

Dolloff, Lori-Anne. 2007. "'All the Things We Are': Balancing Our Multiple Identities in Music Teaching." *Action, Criticism, and Theory for Music Education*, 6 (2): 1–21.

Dolton, Peter and Oscar Marcenaro-Gutierrez, with Vikas Pota, Marc Boxser, and Ash Pajpani. 2013. *Global Teacher Status Index*. London: Varkey GEMS Foundation.

Döring, Herbert. 1992. "Higher Education and Confidence in Institutions: A Secondary Analysis of the 'European Values Survey', 1981–83." *West European Politics*, 15 (2): 126–146.

Dornbusch, Sanford M. and Myra Strober, eds. 1988. *Feminism, Children, and the New Families*. New York, NY: Guilford Press.

Douglas, Susan. 2010. *Enlightened Sexism: The Seductive Message that Feminism's Work Is Done*. New York, NY: Henry Holt.

Dowling, Christopher. 2010. "The Aesthetics of Daily Life." *The British Journal of Aesthetics*, 50 (3): 225–242.

Downes, Paul. 2014. *Access to Education in Europe: A Framework and Agenda for System Change*. New York, Heidelberg, Dordrecht and London: Springer Science and Business Media.

Dreeben, Robert. 2002. *On What Is Learned in School*. Clinton Corners, NY: Eliot Werner Publications.

Drudy, Sheelag. 2008. "Gender Balance/Gender Bias: The Teaching Profession and the Impact of Feminisation." *Gender and Education*, 20 (4): 309–323.

Du Bois, W.E.B. 1899. *The Philadelphia Negro*. Philadelphia: Penn Press, University of Pennsylvania.

Du Bois, W.E.B., ed. 1910. "Efforts for Social Betterment among Negro Americans: Report of a Social Study made by Atlanta University under the Patronage of the Trustees of the John F. Slater Fund." Paper presented at the *14th Annual Conference for the Study of the Negro Problems*, Atlanta, Georgia, May 24, 1909.

Du Bois, W.E.B. 1945. *Color and Democracy: Colonies and Peace*. New York, NY: Harcourt, Brace and Co.

Du Bois, W.E.B. 2014. *The Souls of Black Folk*. Supplementary material written by Norman Harris. Series edited by Cynthia Brantley Johnson. New York, NY: Pocket Books.

Dunbar-Hall, Peter and Kathryn Wemyss. 2000. "The Effects of the Study of Popular Music on Music Education." *International Journal of Music Education*, 36: 23–34.

Durrant, Colin. 2003. *Choral Conducting: Philosophy and Practice*. London: Routledge.

Dyndahl, Petter. 2008. "Music Education in the Sign of Deconstruction." *Philosophy of Music Education Review*, 16 (2): 124–144.

Eggleston, John. 2000. *Staying on at School. The Hidden Curriculum of Selection*. Warwick Papers on Education Policy No. 9. London: Trentham Books.

Ehrenforth, Karl Heinrich. 2005. *Geschichte der Musikalischen Bildung: eine Kultur-, Sozial-und Ideengeschichte in 40 Stationen: Von den Antiken Hochkulturen bis zur Gegenwart*. Mainz: Schott.

Elkington, Sam and Robert A. Stebbins. 2014. *The Serious Leisure Perspective: An Introduction*. Abingdon: Routledge.

Elliott, David. 1995. *Music Matters: A New Philosophy of Music Education*. New York, NY: Oxford University Press.

Elliott, David and Marissa Silverman. 2015. *Music Matters: A New Philosophy of Music Education*. 2nd edition. New York, NY: Oxford University Press.

Elliott, David and Marissa Silverman. 2016. "Felt Experiences and Popular Musics." In *The Child as Musician: A Handbook of Musical Development*, edited by Gary E. McPherson, 244–264. New York, NY: Oxford University Press.

Elpus, Kenneth and Carlos R. Abril. 2011. "High School Music Ensemble Students in the United States: A Demographic Profile." *Journal of Research in Music Education*, 59 (2): 128–145.

Elwell, Frank. 1996. *The Sociology of Max Weber*. Accessed July 28, 2004. www.faculty.rsu.edu/~felwell/Theorists/Weber/Whome.htm.

Emmer, Edmund T. and Edward J. Sabornie. 2015. "Introduction to the Second Edition." In *Handbook of Classroom Management,* edited by Edmund T. Emmer and Edward J. Sabornie, 2nd edition, 3–12. New York, NY: Routledge.

Enloe, Lorie. 2015. *How to Successfully Implement Non-Performance Standards in Your Music Ensemble: Taking the Extra Step with your Music Ensemble*. Washington, DC: National Association for Music Education. Accessed May 30, 2016. www.nafme.org/how-to-successfully-implement-non-performance-standards-in-your-music-ensemble/.

Erikson, Eric H. 1950. *Childhood and Society*. New York: W.W. Norton and Co.

Etzkorn, K. Peter. 1966. "On Esthetic Standards and Reference Groups of Popular Songwriters." *Sociological Inquiry*, 36 (January): 39–47.

Etzkorn, K. Peter, ed. 1973. *Music and Society: The Later Writings of Paul Honigsheim*. New York, NY: John Wiley.

Etzkorn, K. Peter, ed. 1989. *Sociologists and Music: An Introduction to the Study of Music and Society*. New Brunswick, NJ: Transaction Publishers.

Faulkner, Robert. 1971. *The Hollywood Studio Musician*. Chicago, IL: Aldine-Atherton Press.

Faulkner, Robert. 1973. "Career Concerns and Mobility Motivations in Orchestra Musicians." *Sociological Quarterly*, 14 (3): 334–349.

Ferreira, Francisco H.G. and Jérémie Gignoux. 2014. "The Measurement of Educational Inequality: Achievement and Opportunity." *The World Bank Economic Review*, 28 (2): 210–248.

Fowler, Charles. 1991. "Finding the Way to be Basic: Music Education in the 1990s and Beyond." In *Basic Concepts in Music Education, II*, edited by Richard Colwell, 88–122. Niwot, CO: University Press of Colorado.

Fox, Karen. 2016. "Entering into an Indigenous Cypher: Indigenous Music-Dance Making Sings to Western Leisure." In *The Oxford Handbook of Music Making and Leisure*, edited by Roger Mantie and Gareth Dylan Smith, 519–540. New York, NY: Oxford University Press.

Frederickson, Jon and James F. Rooney. 1988. "The Free-lance Musician as a Type of Non-person: An Extension of the Concept of Non-personhood." *Sociological Quarterly*, 29 (2): 221–239.

Freire, Paulo. 1968/1970/2000. *Pedagogy of the Oppressed*. Translated by M. Ramos; 30th anniversary edition. New York, NY: Continuum.

Frith, Simon. 1981. *Sound Effects; Youth, Leisure, and the Politics of Rock 'n' Roll*. New York, NY: Pantheon Books.

Frith, Simon. 1996/2011. "Music and Identity." In *Questions of Cultural Identity*, edited by Stuart Hall and Paul Du Gay, 108–127. London: Sage.

Froehlich, Hildegard C. 2007a. *Sociology for Music Teachers: Perspectives for Practice*. New York, NY: Pearson/Prentice-Hall/Routledge.

Froehlich, Hildegard C. 2007b. "Gateopeners One Step at a Time: Thoughts about Mentoring Doctoral Students in Music Education." In *Kunskapens konst: Vänbok till Börje Ståhlhammar*, edited by Eva Georgii-Hemming, 115–130. Skriftserie Forskning, 2007:1, Musikvetenskap Musikhögskolan, Őrebro Universitet, Örebro, Sweden.

Froehlich, Hildegard C. 2015. *A Social Theory for Music Education: Symbolic Interactionism in Music Learning and Teaching*. Lewiston, NY: The Edwin Mellen Press.

Froehlich, Hildegard C. and Lucy Green. 2014. "Music Education, Sociology of." *New Grove Dictionary for Music and Musicians*. Accessed March 13, 2014. http://libproxy.library.unt.edu:2081/subscriber/search_results?q=Froehlich+and+Green&button_search.x=33&button_search.y=8&button_search=search&search=quick.

Fryer, Roland G. Jr. and Steven D. Levitt. 2004. "Understanding the Black-White Test Score Gap in the First Two Years of School." *The Review of Economics and Statistics*, 86 (2): 447–464.

Fussell, Paul. 1983/1992. *Class: A Guide through the American Status System*. New York, NY: Ballantine Books.

Gatto, John T. 2005. *Dumbing Us Down: The Hidden Curriculum of Compulsory Schooling*. Gabriola Island, BC: New Society Publishers.

Gay, Geneva. 2010. *Culturally Responsive Teaching: Theory, Research, and Practice*. New York, NY: Teachers College Press.

Gaztambide-Fernández, Rubén A. and James T. Sears, eds. 2004. *Curriculum Work as a Public Moral Enterprise*. Lanham, MD: Rowman and Littlefield.

Gebesmair, Andreas. 2006. "Von der Kultur Für Alle zur Allesfresser-Kultur. Unintendierte Folgen der Kulturpolitik?" In *Soziale Ungleichheit—Kulturelle Unterschiede, Verhandlungen des 32. Kongresses der Deutschen Gesellschaft für Soziologie in München*, edited by Karl-Siegbert Rehberg, 882–897. Frankfurt and New York, NY: Campus.

Gebesmair, Andreas. 2009. "The Transnational Music Industry." In *The Ashgate Research Companion to Popular Musicology*, edited by Derek Scott, 467–484. Aldershot: Ashgate.

Gerth, H. and C. Wright Mills, eds. 1946. *From Max Weber: Essays in Sociology*. Translated and edited by Hans Heinrich Gerth and Charles Wright Mills. New York, NY: Oxford University Press.

Gillborn, David and Gloria Ladson-Billings. 2010. "Education and Critical Race Theory." In *The Routledge International Handbook of the Sociology of Education*, edited by Michael W. Apple, Stephen, J. Ball, and Luis Armando Gandin, 37–47. New York, NY: Routledge.

Gilligan, Carol. 1982. *In a Different Voice*. Cambridge, MA: Harvard University Press.

Gilman, Charlotte P. 1898. *Women and Economics: A Study of the Economic Relation between Men and Women as a Factor in Social Evolution*. Boston, MA: Small, Maynard and Co.

Gilman, Charlotte P. 1903/1910. *The Home: Its Work and Influence*. New York, NY: Charlton Company.

Giroux, Henry A. 1983. *Critical Theory and Educational Practice*. Geelong, Victoria: Deakin University Press/Hyperion Books.

Giroux, Henry A. 1988. *Teachers as Intellectuals: Toward a Critical Pedagogy of Learning*. South Hadley, MA: Bergin and Garvey Publishers.

Giroux, Henry A. 2001. *Theory and Resistance in Education: Towards a Pedagogy of the Opposition*. Westport, CT: Bergin and Garvey.

Giroux, Henry A. 2007. "Utopian Thinking in Dangerous Times: Critical Pedagogy and the Project of Educated Hope." In *Utopian Pedagogy: Radical Experiments against Neoliberal Globalization*, edited by Mark Coté, Richard J.F. Day, and Greig de Peuter, 25–42. Toronto, ON: University of Toronto Press.

Giroux, Henry A. 2014. *Neoliberalism's War on Higher Education*. Chicago, IL: Haymarket.

Giroux, Henry A. 2016. *America's Addiction to Terrorism*. New York, NY: Monthly Review Press.

Giroux, Henry A. and Anthony Penna. 1983. "Social Education in the Classroom: The Dynamics of the Hidden Curriculum." In *The Hidden*

Curriculum and Moral Education, edited by Henry Giroux and David Purpel, 100–121. Berkeley, CA: McCutchan Publishing Corporation.

Goffman, Erving. 1959/1973. *The Presentation of Self in Everyday Life*. Woodstock, NY: Overlook Press.

Goldstein, Harvey. 2004. "Education for All: The Globalization of Learning Targets." *Comparative Education*, 40 (1): 7–14.

Gorard, Stephen and Emma Smith. 2004a. "An International Comparison of Equity in Education Systems." *Comparative Education*, 40 (1): 15–28. Accessed January 28, 2016. http://search.proquest.com/docview/195147945?accountid=7113.

Gorard, Stephen and Emma Smith. 2004b. "(Mis)understanding underachievement: A Response to Connolly." Accessed August 24, 2016. http://citeseerx.ist.psu.edu/viewdoc/download?doi=10.1.1.690.4698&rep=rep1&type=pdf

Gorski, Paul C. and Julie Landsman. 2013. *The Poverty and Education Reader: A Call for Equity in Many Voices*. Herndon, VA: Stylus Publishing, LLC.

Gould, Carol C. 2004. *Globalizing Democracy and Human Rights*. Cambridge, MA: Cambridge University Press.

Gould, Elizabeth S. 1992. "Music Education in Historical Perspective: Status, Non-Musicians, and the Role of Women." *College Music Symposium*, 32: 10–18. www.jstor.org/stable/40374199.

Gould, Elizabeth. 2007. "Social Justice in Music Education: The Problematic of Democracy." *Music Education Research*, 9 (2): 229–240.

Gould, Elizabeth. 2008. "Devouring the Other: Democracy in Music Education." *Action, Criticism, and Theory for Music Education*, 7 (1): 29–44.

Gouzouasis, Peter, Rita L. Irwin, Emily Miles, and Alexandra Gordon. 2013. "Commitments to a Community of Artistic Inquiry: Becoming Pedagogical Through A/r/tography in Teacher Education." *International Journal of Education and the Arts*, 14 (1). Retrieved March 20, 2014. www.ijea.org/v14n1/.

Gracyk, Theodore. 2007. "Searching for the 'Popular' and the 'Art' of Popular Art." *Philosophy Compass*, 2:380–395. doi:10.1111/j.1747-9991.2007.00085.x

Gray, David E. 2007. "Facilitating Management Learning Developing Critical Reflection through Reflective Tools." *Management Learning*, 38 (5): 495–517.

Green, Lucy. 1997. *Music, Gender, Education*. Cambridge: Cambridge University Press.

Green, Lucy. 2002. *How Popular Musicians Learn: A Way Ahead for Music Education*. Aldershot: Ashgate.

Green, Lucy. 2008a. *Music, Informal Learning, and the School: A New Classroom Pedagogy*. Aldershot, UK and Burlington, VT: Ashgate.

Green, Lucy. 2008b. *Music on Deaf Ears: Musical Meaning, Ideology, Education.* London: Abramis.

Green, Lucy, ed. 2011. *Learning, Teaching and Musical Identity: Voices across Cultures*. Bloomington: Indiana University Press.

Green, Lucy. 2014. *Music Education as Critical Theory and Practice: Selected Essays*. Farnham: Ashgate.

Greiner, Lena. 2013. "Weltweite Umfrage zu Status: Lehrer Werden in Deutschland Kaum Respektiert. Schulspiegel." *Spiegelonline* (Donnerstag, 3–10–2013). Accessed March 18, 2016. www.spiegel.de/schulspiegel/ausland/weltweite-umfrage-deutsche-lehrer-werden-kaum-respektiert-a-925826.html.

Griffin, Shelley M. 2011. "Reflection on the Social Justice behind Children's Tales of In-and Out-of-School Music Experiences." *Bulletin of the Council for Research in Music Education,* 188: 77–92.

Gruhn, Wilfried. 1999. "Music Education in Postmodernism: About the Difficulties to Move Knowledge into Action, Theory into Practice." *International Journal of Music Education,* 34 (1): 57–63.

Gullberg, Anna-Karin. 2010. "Boom Town Music Education: An Introduction." In *Music, Education and Innovation: Festschrift for Sture Brändström*, edited by Cecilia Thorgersen Ferm and Sidsel Karlsen, 123–144. Luleå Tekniska Universitet, Department of Music and Media.

Gunnarsson, Victoria, Peter F. Orazem, and Mario A. Sánchez. 2006. "Child labor and school achievement in Latin America." *The World Bank Economic Review* 20 (1): 31–54. Accessed August 22, 2016 from https://academic.oup.com/wber/article/20/1/31/1680454/Child-Labor-and-School-Achievement-in-Latin

Hall, Stuart. 1996. "Introduction: Who Needs 'Identity'?" In *Questions of Cultural Identity*, edited by Stuart Hall and Paul du Gay, 1–17. London: Sage Publications.

Hallam, Susan. 2001. "The Development of Expertise in Young Musicians: Strategy Use, Knowledge Acquisition and Individual Diversity." *Music Education Research*, 3 (1): 7–23.

Hallam, Susan. 2010. "The Power of Music: Its Impact on the Intellectual, Social and Personal Development of Children and Young People." *International Journal of Music Education*, 28 (3): 269–289.

Hallam, Susan and Helena Gaunt. 2012. *Preparing for Success: A Practical Guide for Young Musicians*. London: University of London, Institute of Education.

Hallinan, Maureen T. 2000. *Handbook of the Sociology of Education.* London: Springer.

Hamilton, David and Gaby Weiner. 2000. "Subjects, Not Subjects: Curriculum Pathways, Pedagogies and Practices in the United Kingdom." Paper presented at the *Internationalization of Curriculum Studies Conference*, Louisiana Baton Rouge, USA, April, 2000. Accessed December 14, 2004. www.educ.umu.se/~gaby/subjects_not_subjects.html.

Hammel, Lina. 2011. *Selbstkonzepte Fachfremd Unterrichtender Musiklehrerinnen und Musiklehrer an Grundschulen: Eine Grounded-Theory-Studie*. Berlin: LIT Verlag.

Hansen, Richard K. 2005. *The American Wind Band: A Cultural History*. Suffolk, UK and Rochester, NY: Boydell and Brewer Ltd.

Hanson, Barbara. 2001. "Systems Theory and the Spirit of Feminism: Grounds for a Connection." *Systems Research and Behavioral Science*, 18 (6): 545–556.

Haraway, Donna. 2004. *The Haraway Reader*. New York, NY: Routledge.

Hargreaves, David J., Ross M. Purves, Graham F. Welch, and Nigel A. Marshall. 2007. "Developing Identities and Attitudes in Musicians and Classroom Music Teachers." *British Journal of Educational Psychology*, 77 (3): 665–682.

Hargreaves, Linda, Mark Cunningham, Anders Hansen, Donald McIntyre, and Caroline Oliver. 2007. *The Status of Teachers and the Teaching Profession in England: Views from Inside and Outside the Profession. Final Report of the Teacher Status Project*. Cambridge, UK: The Chancellor, Masters and Scholars of the University of Cambridge.

Hartsock, Nancy C.M. 1998. *The Feminist Standpoint Revisited and Other Essays*. Boulder, CO: The Westview Press.

Haston, Warren and Joshua A. Russell. 2012. "Turning into Teachers: Influences of Authentic Context Learning Experiences on Occupational Identity Development of Preservice Music Teachers." *Journal of Research in Music Education*, 59 (4): 369–392.

Hawkins, Denise. 2015. "The 'Moral Value' of Teaching: The Missing Link in Teacher Preparation?" *National Education Association*. Accessed October 7, 2016. http://neatoday.org/2015/03/17/moral-value-teaching-missing-link-teacher-preparation/.

Heath, Anthony F., Catherine Rothon, and Elina Kilpi. 2008. "The Second Generation in Western Europe: Education, Unemployment, and Occupational Attainment." *Annual Review of Sociology*, 34 (August): 211–235.

Hebert, David G. 2015. "Another Perspective: Militarism and Music Education." *Music Educators Journal*, 101 (3): 77–84.

Hebert, David G., Joseph P. Abramo, and Gareth Dylan Smith. 2017. "Sociological Issues in Popular Music Education." In *The Routledge Research Companion to Popular Music Education*, edited by Gareth Dylan Smith, Zack Moir, Matt Brennan, Shara Rambarran, and Phil Kirkman, 451–478. Abingdon: Routledge.

Hebert, David G. and Alexandra Kertz-Welzel. 2012. *Patriotism and Nationalism in Music Education*. Farnham: Ashgate.

Hegel, Georg Wilhelm Friedrich. 1977. *The Phenomenology of Spirit*. Translated by Arnold V. Miller. Oxford: Oxford University Press.

Hehir, Thomas. 2002. "Eliminating Ableism in Education." *Harvard Educational Review*, 72 (1):1–33.

Heyer, Robert, Sebastian Wachs, and Christian Palentien, eds. 2013. *Handbuch Jugend—Musik—Sozialisation*. Cambridge, MA: Harvard University Press.

Hickey, Maud. 1997. "Teaching Ensembles to Compose and Improvise." *Music Educators Journal*, 83 (6): 17–21.

Higgins, Lee. 2012. *Community Music in Theory and in Practice*. New York, NY: Oxford University Press.

Hill Collins, Patricia. 2000/2002. *Black Feminist Thought: Knowledge, Consciousness, and the Politics of Empowerment*. 2nd edition. New York, NY: Routledge.

Hines, Sally. 2013. *Gender Diversity, Recognition and Citizenship: Towards a Politics of Difference*. New York, NY: Palgrave Macmillan.

Hjelm, Titus. 2014. *Social Constructionisms: Approaches to the Study of the Human World*. London: Palgrave Macmillan.

Hodges, Donald A. 2017. *A Concise Survey of Music Philosophy*. New York, NY: Routledge.

Holland, Dorothy, Debra Skinner, William Lachicotte, Jr., and Carol Cain. 2001. *Identity and Agency in Cultural Worlds*. Cambridge, MA: Harvard University Press.

Holz, Oliver and Margarete Grimus, eds. 2013. *EDucation & GEnder Gendergerechte Bildung und Erziehung in ausgewählten Ländern Historische Aspekte – aktuelle Trends*. Münster: Waxmann.

hooks, bell. 1984. *Feminist Theory: From Margin to Centre*. London: Pluto Press.

hooks, bell. 2000. *Feminism Is for Everybody: Passionate Politics*. London: Pluto Press.

Hornberg, Sabine. 2010. *Schule im Prozess der Internationalisierung von Bildung*. Münster: Waxmann Verlag.

Horsley, Stephanie. 2015. "Facing the Music: Pursuing Social Justice through Music Education in a Neoliberal World." In *The Oxford Handbook of Social Justice in Music Education*, edited by Cathy Benedict, Patrick Schmidt, Gary Spruce, and Paul Woodford, 62–77. New York, NY: Oxford University Press.

Howard, Tyrone C. 2014. *Black Male(d): Peril and Promise in the Education of African American Males*. New York, NY: Teachers College Press.

Hoyle, Eric. 2001. "Teaching Prestige, Status and Esteem." *Educational Management and Administration*, 29 (2): 139–152.

Hudak, Glenn M. and Paul Kihn. 2001. *Labeling: Pedagogy and Politics*. Hove, UK: Psychology Press.

Hull, Glynda A. and Katherine Schultz, eds. 2002. *School's Out: Bridging Out-of-School Literacies with Classroom Practice*. Vol. 60. New York, NY: Teachers College Press.

Illich, Ivan. 1971. *Deschooling Society*. New York, NY: Harper and Row.

Ingersoll, Richard M. and David Perda. 2008. "The Status of Teaching as a Profession." In *Schools and Society: A Sociological Approach to Education*. 3rd edition, edited by Jeanne H. Ballantine and Joan Z. Spade, 107–118. Los Angeles, CA: Pine Forge Press.

Institut für Musiksoziologie. 2016. Institut für Musiksoziologie Berichte und Informationen Nr. 32 2014–2015. Vienna, Austria: mdw – Universität für Musik und darstellende Kunst Wien.

Isbell, Daniel S. 2008. "Musicians and Teachers: The Socialization and Occupational Identity of Preservice Music Teachers." *Journal of Research in Music Education*, 56 (2): 162–178.

Isbell, Daniel S. 2009. "The Socialization of Undergraduate Music Majors in the United States." *Music Education Research International*, 3: 13–28.

Jaffurs, Sheri E. 2004. "The Impact of Informal Music Learning Practices in the Classroom, or How I Learned How to Teach from a Garage Band." *International Journal of Music Education*, 22 (3): 189–200.

Jank, Werner. 2014. "Didaktik, Bildung, Content: On the Writings of Frede V. Nielsen." *Philosophy of Music Education Review*, 22 (2): 113–131.

Jarman-Ivens, Freya. 2006. "Queer(ing) Masculinities in Heterosexist Rap Music." In *Queering the Popular Pitch*, edited by Sheila Whiteley and Jennifer Rycenga, 199–219. New York, NY: Routledge.

Jay, Michelle. 2003. "Cultural Race Theory, Multicultural Education, and the Hidden Curriculum of Hegemony." *Multicultural Perspectives*, 5 (4): 3–9.

Jerald, Craig D. 2006. "The Hidden Costs of Curriculum Narrowing. Issue Brief." *Center for Comprehensive School Reform and Improvement*. Accessed January 8, 2017. http://files.eric.ed.gov/fulltext/ED494088.pdf

Johansen, Geir. 2010. "Musikdidaktik and Sociology." In *Sociology and Music Education*, edited by Ruth Wright, 207–222. Aldershot: Ashgate.

Jorgensen, Estelle. 1998. *In Search of Music Education*. Chicago, IL: University of Illinois Press.

Jorgensen, Estelle. 2003. *Transforming Music Education*. Bloomington, IN: Indiana University Press.

Jorgensen, Estelle R. 2008. *The Art of Teaching Music*. Bloomington, IN: Indiana University Press.

Kadushin, Charles. 1969. "The Professional Self-Concept of Music Students." *American Journal of Sociology*, 75 (November): 389–404.

Kaiser, Hermann J., Eckhard Nolte, and Michael Roske. 1993. *Vom pädagogischen Umgang mit Musik*. Mainz: Schott.

Kallio, Alexis A. 2015. "Navigating (Un)popular Music in the Classroom: Censure and Censorship in an Inclusive, Democratic Music Education." PhD Diss., University of the Arts, Helsinki.

Kamerman, Jack and Rosanna Martorella. 1983. *Performers and Performances: The Social Organization of Artistic Work*. New York, NY: Praeger.

Kaplan, Max. 1951. "The Musician in America: A Study of His Social Roles (Introduction to a Sociology of Music)." PhD diss., University of Illinois.

Kaplan, Max. 1966. *Foundations and Frontiers in Music Education*. New York, NY: Holt, Rinehart and Winston.

Kaplan, Max. 1990. *The Arts: A Social Perspective*. Rutherford, NJ: Fairleigh Dickinson University Press.

Karlsen, Sidsel. 2010. "BoomTown Music Education and the Need for Authenticity: Informal Learning Put into Practice in Swedish Post-compulsory Music Education." *British Journal of Music Education*, 27 (1): 35–46.

Karsenti, Thierry and Simon Collin. 2013. "Why Are New Teachers Leaving the Profession? Results of a Canada-wide Survey." *Education*, 3 (3): 141–149.

Kealy, Edward R. 1974. "The Real Rock Revolution: Sound Mixers, Social Inequality, and the Aesthetics of Popular Music Production." PhD diss., Northwestern University.

Kealy, Edward R. 1980. "From Craft to Art: The Case of the Sound Mixers and Popular Music." *Sociology of Work and Occupations*, 6 (September): 3–29.

Keil, Charles. 1966. *Urban Blues*. Chicago: University of Chicago Press.

Keil, Charles. 1979. *Tiv Song: The Sociology of Art in a Classless Society*. Chicago: University of Chicago Press.

Keil, Charles. 2002. "They Want the Music But They Don't Want the People." *City and Society*, 14 (1): 37–57.

Keil, Charles and Steven Feld. 1994. *Music Grooves*. Chicago, IL: The University of Chicago Press.

Kelleher, Fatimah, Francis O. Severin, Meera Samson, Anuradha De, Tepora Afamasaga-Wright, and Upali M. Sedere. 2011. *Women and the Teaching Profession: Exploring the Feminisation Debate*. London: Commonwealth Secretariat and UNESCO.

Kellner, Douglas. 2011. "Cultural Studies, Multiculturalism, and Media Culture." In *Gender, Race, and Class in Media: A Critical Reader*, edited by Gail Dines and Jean M. Humez, 7–18. Thousand Oaks, CA: Sage.

Kelly, Stephen. 2009. *Teaching Music in American Society: A Social and Cultural Understanding of Music Education*. New York, NY: Routledge.

Kentli, Fulya D. 2009. "Comparison of Hidden Curriculum Theories." *European Journal of Educational Studies*, 1 (2): 83–90.

Kertz-Welzel, Alexandra. 2004. "Didaktik of Music: A German Concept and its Comparison to American Music Pedagogy." *International Journal of Music Education*, 22 (3): 277–286.

Kertz-Welzel, Alexandra. 2013a. "Two Souls, Alas, Reside within My Breast: Reflections on German and American Music Education Regarding the Internationalization of Music Education," *Philosophy of Music Education Review*, 21 (1): 52–65.

Kertz-Welzel, Alexandra. 2013b. "Comparative Music Education in Times of Globalization." Paper presented at the *9th International Symposium on the Philosophy of Music Education*, New York, NY, June 5–8.

Khadaroo, Stacy T. 2013. "'A Nation at Risk': How Much of 'Apocalyptic' Education Report Still Applies?" *The Christian Science Monitor*. Accessed April 24, 2014. www.csmonitor.com/USA/Education/2013/0426/A-Nation-at-Risk-How-much-of-apocalyptic-education-report-still-applies.

Kincheloe, Joe L., and Raymond A. Horn, eds. 2007. *The Praeger Handbook of Education and Psychology*. Vol. 1. Westport, CT: Greenwood.

King, Elizabeth M., Peter F. Orazem, and Elizabeth M. Paterno. 1999. "Promotion With and Without Learning: Effects on Student Dropout." Paper No. 18 in the working papers series on impact evaluation of education reforms. Washington, DC: World Bank.

Kingsbury, Henry. 1988/2010. *Music Talent and Performance: Conservatory Cultural System*. Philadelphia, PA: Temple University Press.

Kirschner, Tony. 1998. "Studying Rock: Towards a Materialist Ethnography." In *Mapping the Beat: Popular Music and Contemporary Theory*, edited by Thomas Swiss, John Sloop, and Andrew Herman, 247–268. Oxford: Blackwell.

Kivy, Peter. 2004. "Continuous Time and Interrupted Time: Two-timing in the Temporal Arts." *Musicae Scientiae*, 8 (1 suppl): 141–155.

Kivy, Peter, ed. 2009. *The Blackwell Guide to Aesthetics*. Malden, MA: John Wiley and Sons.

Knörzer, Lisa, Robin Stark, Babette Park, and Christian Rolle. 2015. "'I Like Reggae and Bob Marley is Already Dead': An Empirical Study on

Music-Related Argumentation." *Psychology of Music*, 44 (5): 1158–1174. doi:10.1177/0305735615614095.

Kokotsaki, Dimitra and Susan Hallam. 2007. "Higher Education Music Students' Perceptions of the Benefits of Participative Music Making." *Music Education Research*, 9 (1): 93–109.

Konieczka, Joanna. 2013. "The Hidden Curriculum as a Socialization of Schooling Is in Process at All Times, and Serves to Transmit Messages to Students about Values, Attitudes and Principles." *Proceedings in ARSA-Advanced Research in Scientific Areas*, 1 (December 2–6, 2013): 1–3.

Koza, Julia Eklund. 1991. "Music and the Feminine Sphere: Images of Women as Musicians in 'Godey's Lady's Book', 1830–1877." *The Musical Quarterly*, 75 (2): 103–129.

Kozol, Jonathan. 1991. *Savage Inequalities. Children in America's Schools.* New York, NY: Crown Publishers.

Kozol, Jonathan. 2012. *Fire in the Ashes: Twenty-five Years Among the Poorest Children in America.* New York, NY: Random House.

Kratus, John. 2007. "Music Education at the Tipping Point." *Music Educators Journal*, 94 (2): 42–48.

Krikun, Andrew. 2009. "Mixing Memphis Soul into the Community College Curriculum Stew." *Journal of Popular Music Studies*, 21 (1): 76–89.

Kruse, Adam J. 2016a. "Featherless Dinosaurs and the Hip-hop Simulacrum: Reconsidering Hip-hop's Appropriateness for the Music Classroom." *Music Educators Journal*, 102 (4): 13–21.

Kruse, Adam J. 2016b. "Toward Hip-hop Pedagogies for Music Education." *International Journal of Music Education*, 34 (2): 247–260.

Ladd, Helen F. 2007. "Teacher Labor Markets in Developed Countries." *The Future of Children*, 17 (1): 201–217.

Ladson-Billings, Gloria. 2015. "You Gotta Fight the Power: The Place of Music in Social Justice Education." In *The Oxford Handbook of Social Justice in Music Education*, edited by Cathy Benedict, Patrick Schmidt, Gary Spruce, and Paul Woodford, 406–419. New York, NY: Oxford University Press.

Lamb, Roberta. 1994. "Feminism as Critique in Philosophy of Music Education." *Philosophy of Music Education Review*, 2 (2): 59–74.

Lamb, Roberta. 2010. "Mind the Gap!" *Action, Criticism, and Theory for Music Education*, 9 (1): 44–53.

Lamb, Roberta. 2014. "A Wild Passion? A Wild Patience? A Wild Flower? Cultivating In The Feminist Theory And Music Garden." Reprint of *GEMS (Gender, Education, Music, & Society)*, 1 (1) in 7 (3): 5–11.

Lamb, Roberta and Niyati Dhokai. 2015. "Disjunctured Feminisms: Emerging Feminisms in Music Education." In *The Oxford Handbook of Social Justice in Music Education*, edited by Cathy Benedict, Patrick Schmidt, Gary Spruce, and Paul Woodford, 122–139. New York, NY: Oxford University Press.

Lapidaki, Eleni. 2016. "Uncommon Grounds: Preparing Students in Higher Music Education for the Unpredictable." *Philosophy of Music Education Review*, 24 (1): 65–83.

Lareau, Annette. 2011. *Unequal Childhoods: Class, Race, and Family Life*. 2nd edition. With an Update a Decade Later. Berkeley, CA: University of California Press.

Lather, Patti. 1988. "Feminist Perspectives on Empowering Research Methodologies." *Women's Studies International Forum*, 11 (6): 569–581.

Laurence, Felicity and Olivier Urbain, eds. 2011. *Music and Solidarity: Questions of Universality, Consciousness, and Connection*. New Brunswick, NJ: Transaction Publishers.

Lavy, Ilana, and Aharon Yadin. 2010. "Team-Based Peer Review as a Form of Formative Assessment: The Case of a Systems Analysis and Design Workshop." *Journal of Information Systems Education*, 21 (1): 85–98.

Leavitt, Howard B. 1992. *Issues and Problems in Teacher Education: An International Handbook*. Santa Barbara, CA: Greenwood Publishing Group.

Leavitt, Howard B. 2013. "Worldwide Issues and Problems in Teacher Education." *Journal of Teacher Education*, 42 (5): 323–331.

Lebler, Don. 2008. "Popular Music Pedagogy: Peer Learning in Practice." *Music Education Research*, 10 (2): 193–213.

Leddy, Thomas. 2012. *The Extraordinary in the Ordinary: The Aesthetics of Everyday Life*. Buffalo, NY: Broadview Press.

Lee, Valerie E. and Douglas D. Ready. 2009. "The U.S. High School Curriculum: Three Phases of Contemporary Research and Reform." *The Future of Children*, 19 (1): 135–156.

Lemert, Charles. 2005. *Social Things: An Introduction to the Sociological Life*. Lanham, MD: Rowman & Littlefield.

Lengermann, Patricia M. and Gillian Niebrugge. 1998/2007. *The Women Founders: Sociology and Social Theory 1830–1930. A Text/Reader*. Long Grove, IL: Waveland Press.

Leppert, Richard and McClary, Susan. 1987. *Music and Society: The Politics of Composition, Performance and Reception*. Cambridge: Cambridge University Press.

Levinson, Jerrold. 1996. *The Pleasures of Aesthetics: Philosophical Essays*. New York, NY: Cornell University Press.

Levinson, Jerrold. 2006. *Contemplating Art: Essays in Aesthetics: Essays in Aesthetics*. New York, NY: Oxford University Press.

Lewis, Jenny and John Leach. 2006. "Discussion of Socio-scientific Issues: The Role of Science Knowledge." *International Journal of Science Education*, 28 (11): 1267–1287.

Leyshon, Andrew. 2011. "Toward a Non-economic, Economic Geography? From Black Boxes to the Cultural Circuit of Capital in Economic Geographies of Firms and Managers." In *The SAGE Handbook of Economic Geography*, edited by Andrew Leyshon, Roger Lee, Linda McDowell, and Peter Sunley, 383–398. Los Angeles, CA: Sage.

Lieb, Kristin J. 2015. "Pop Stars Perform 'Gay' for the Male Gaze." In *Production Studies, the Sequel! Cultural Studies of Global Media Industries*, edited by Miranda Banks, Bridget Cnor, and Vicki Mayer, 59–72. New York, NY: Routledge.

Lindqvist, Per, Ulla Karin Nordänger, and Rickard Carlsson. 2014. "Teacher Attrition the First Five Years: A Multifaceted Image." *Teaching and Teacher Education*, 40: 94–103.

Liu, Dilin, Gil-Soon Ahn, Kyung-Suk Baek and Nan-Ok Han. 2004. "South Korean High School English Teachers' Code Switching: Questions and Challenges in the Drive for Maximal Use of English in Teaching." *TESOL Quarterly* (December): 605–638.

Lortie, Dan. 1959. "Laymen to Lawmen: Law School, Careers, and Socialization." *Harvard Educational Review*, 29: 155–171.

Lortie, Dan. 1975/2002. *Schoolteacher: A Sociological Study*. 2nd edition. Chicago, IL: University of Chicago Press.

Løvlie, Lars and Paul Standish. 2002. "Introduction: Bildung and the Idea of a Liberal Education." *Journal of Philosophy of Education*, 36 (3): 317–340.

L'Roy, DiAnn. 1983. "The Development of Occupational Identity in Undergraduate Music Education Majors." PhD diss., North Texas State University [University of North Texas], Denton, Texas.

Luhmann, Niklas. 2006. "System as Difference." *Organization*, 13 (1): 37–57.

Luhmann, Niklas. 2012. *Theory of Society*, Vol. 1. Translated by Rhodes Barrett. Stanford, CA: Stanford University Press.

Lynn, Marvin and Adrienne D. Dixson. 2013. *Handbook of Critical Race Theory in Education*. New York, NY: Routledge.

Lysaker, Judith T. and Shelly Furuness. 2011. "Space for Transformation Relational, Dialogic Pedagogy." *Journal of Transformative Education*, 9 (3): 183–197.

McCall, George and Jerry L. Simmons. 1978. *Identities and Interactions: An Examination of Human Associations in Everyday Life*. New York, NY: The Free Press.

McCarthy, Marie. 2002. "Social and Cultural Contexts of Music Teaching and Learning: An Introduction." In *The New Handbook of Research on Music Teaching and Learning: A Project of the Music Educators National Conference*, edited by Richard Colwell and Carol Richardson, 563–565. New York, NY: Oxford University Press.

McCarthy, Marie. 2004. *Toward a Global Community: The International Society for Music Education*. Perth, WA: International Society for Music Education.

McClary, Susan. 1991. *Feminine Endings: Music, Gender and Sexuality*. Minneapolis, MN: University of Minnesota Press.

McClary, Susan. 2016. "Afterword by Susan McClary. Remembering Neville Braithwaite." In *The Christopher Small Reader,* edited by Robert Walser, 230–232. Middletown, CT: Wesleyan University Press.

McClintock, Anne. 1995. *Imperial Leather: Race, Gender, and Sexuality in the Colonial Contest*. New York, NY: Routledge.

Macdonald, Doune. 1999. "Teacher Attrition: A Review of Literature." *Teaching and Teacher Education*, 15 (8): 835–848.

MacDonald, Raymond A.R., David J. Hargreaves, and Dorothy Miell, eds. 2002. *Musical Identities*. New York, NY: Oxford University Press.

McLaughlin, Janice, Mark E. Casey, and Diane Richardson. 2006. "Introduction: At the Intersections of Feminist and Queer Debates." In *Intersections between Feminist and Queer Theory*, edited by Diane Richardson, Janice McLaughlin, and Mark E. Casey, 1–18. London: Palgrave MacMillan.

McPherson, Gary and Graham Welch, eds. 2012. *The Oxford Handbook of Music Education*. New York, NY: Oxford University Press.

Majno, Maria. 2012. "From the Model of El Sistema in Venezuela to Current Applications: Learning and Integration through Collective Music Education." *Annals of the New York Academy of Sciences*, 1252 (1): 56–64.

Majzub, Rohati and Muhammad Rais. 2010. "Teachers' and Parents' Perception on Effective Strategies for Dropout Prevention." *Procedia— Social and Behavioral Sciences*, 9: 1036–1041. doi:10.1016/j.sbspro.2010.12.282

Manning, Alan. 2010. "The Integration of Immigrants and Their Children in Europe: Introduction." *Economic Journal*, 120 (542): F1–F3.

Mantie, Roger. 2015. "Liminal or Lifelong: Leisure, Recreation, and the Future of Music Education." In *Music Education: Navigating the Future*, edited by Clint Randles, 167–182. New York, NY: Routledge.

Mantie, Roger. 2016. "Leisure Grooves: An Open Letter to Charles Keil." In *The Oxford Handbook of Music Making and Leisure*, edited by Roger Mantie and Gareth Dylan Smith, 621–640. New York, NY: Oxford University Press.

Mantie, Roger and Gareth Dylan Smith. 2016. *The Oxford Handbook of Music Making and Leisure*. New York, NY: Oxford University Press.

Mantie, Roger and Brent C. Talbot. 2015. "How Can We Change Our Habits If We Don't Talk about Them?" *Action, Criticism, and Theory for Music Education*, 14 (1): 128–153.

Marcuse, Herbert. 1978. *The Aesthetic Dimension: Toward a Critique of Marxist Aesthetics*. English version translated and revised by Herbert Marcuse and Erica Sherover. Boston, MA: Beacon Press[0].

Martin, John Levi. 2011. *The Explanation of Social Action*. New York, NY: Oxford University Press.

Martin, Peter J. 1995. *Sounds and Society: Themes in the Sociology of Music*. Manchester: Manchester University Press.

Martin, Peter J. 2005. "The Jazz Community as an Art World: A Sociological Perspective." *Jazz Research Journal*, 2 (1): 5–13.

Martin, Peter J. 2006. *Music and the Sociological Gaze: Art Worlds and Cultural Production*. Manchester: Manchester University Press.

Martindale, Don, Johannes Riedel, and Gertrude Neuwirth. 1958. "Max Weber's Sociology of Music: Introduction." In *The Rational and Social Foundations of Music*, edited by Don Martindale, Johannes Riedel, and Gertrude Neuwirth, xi–lii. Carbondale, IL: Southern Illinois University Press. www.scribd.com/doc/110976463/Max-Weber-The-Rational-and-Social-Foundations-of-Music

Mead, George H. 1938. *The Philosophy of the Act*. Chicago, IL: University of Chicago Press.

Melchionne, Kevin. 2013. "The Definition of Everyday Aesthetics." *Contemporary Aesthetics 11*. Accessed April 5, 2014. http://hdl.handle.net/2027/spo.7523862.0011.026.

Merton, Robert. 1957. *Social Theory and Social Structure: Toward the Codification of Theory and Research*. Glencoe, IL: Free Press.

Merton, Robert. 1967. *Social Theory and Social Structure. Part I. On Theoretical Sociology; Five Essays, Old and New*. New York, NY: Free Press.

Mezirow, Jack. 2003. "Transformative Learning as Discourse." *Journal of Transformative Education*, 1 (1): 58–63.

Michaelis-Jähnke, Karin. 2006. *Vom Nutzen der Grauen Theorie. Pädagogik und Psychologie für Referendare und Lehreranwärter an Beruflichen Schulen und Institutionen der Weiterbildung*. Hohengehren, Germany: Schneider Verlag GmbH.

Milner, H. Richard. 2004. "African American Graduate Students' Experiences: A Critical Analysis of Recent Research." *A Long Way to Go: Conversations About Race by African American Faculty and Graduate Students*, edited by Darrell Cleveland, 19–31. New York, NY: P. Lang.

Milner, H. Richard IV. 2010. *Start Where You Are, But Don't Stay There: Understanding Diversity, Opportunity Gaps, and Teaching in Today's Classrooms*. Cambridge, MA: Harvard Education Press.

Moore, Allan F. 2001. *Rock: The Primary Text.* Farnham: Ashgate.

Moore, Allan F., ed. 2003. *Analyzing Popular Music.* Cambridge: Cambridge University Press.

Mora, Manolete. 2008. "Lutes, Gongs, Women and Men: (En)gendering Instrumental Music in the Philippines." *Ethnomusicology Forum*, 17 (2): 225–247.

Moran, Anne and Lesley Abbott. 2006. *The Development of Inclusive Schools in Northern Ireland: A Model of Best Practice.* Research Report. Department of Education, Northern Ireland Statistics and Research Agency. Accessed June 21, 2016. https://core.ac.uk/download/files/3/309083.pdf.

Morgan, Gareth. 1983. "Social Science and Accounting Research: A Commentary on Tomkins and Groves." *Accounting, Organizations and Society*, 8 (4): 385–388.

Morgan, J. Graham. 1980. "Women in American Sociology in the 19th Century." *Journal of the History of Sociology*, 2 (2): 1–34.

Morgan, Stephen L. 2005. *On the Edge of Commitment: Educational Attainment and Race in the United States.* Stanford, CA: Stanford University Press.

Mueller, John. 1958. "Music and Education: A Sociological Approach." In *Basic Concepts in Music Education*, edited by Harld Spivacke and Nelson B. Henry, 88–122. Chicago, IL: National Society for the Study of Education.

Museus, Samuel D. 2014. *Asian American Students in Higher Education.* New York, NY: Routledge.

Musicians' Union. 2012. *The Working Musician.* London: DHA Communications.

Nash, Dennison. 1954. "The American Composer. A Study in Social Psychology." PhD diss., University of Pennsylvania.

Nash, Dennison. 1957. "The Socialization of an Artist: The American Composer." *Social Forces*, 35 (Spring): 307–313.

Nash, Dennison. 1961. "The Role of the Composer." *Ethnomusicology*, 5 (September): 81–94.

National Education Association. 2015. *Students Affected by Achievement Gaps.* Accessed January 8, 2017. www.nea.org/home/20380.htm

National Union of Teachers. 2014. *Teacher Recruitment and Retention.* Accessed July 15, 2016. www.teachers.org.uk/edufacts/teacher-recruitment-and-retention.

Nettl, Bruno. 1995. *Heartland Excursions: Ethnomusicological Reflections on Schools of Music.* Chicago, IL: University of Illinois Press.

Nielsen, Frede V. 2009. "What Is the Significance of Research for Music Education in Practice? On Relations between the Practice of and the Scientific Approach to Music Education." *Philosophy of Music Education Review*, 17 (1): 22–40.

Nielsen, Klaus N. 1999. "Musical Apprenticeship. Learning at the Academy of Music as Socially Situated." PhD diss., Aarhus University, Institute of Psychology, Aarhus.

Nieto, Sonia. 2000. "Placing Equity Front and Center: Some Thoughts on Transforming Teacher Education for a New Century." *Journal of Teacher Education*, 51 (3): 180–187.

Nieto, Sonia. 2004. *Affirming Diversity: The Sociopolitical Context of Multicultural Education.* 4th edition. New York, NY: Pearson/Allyn and Bacon.

Noddings, Nel. 1984. *Caring, a Feminine Approach to Ethics & Moral Education.* Berkeley, CA: University of California Press.

Nordenbo, Sven Erik. 2002. "Bildung and the Thinking of Bildung." *Journal of Philosophy of Education*, 36 (3): 341–352.

Norton, William. 2014. *Human Geography*. 8th edition. New York, NY: Oxford University Press.

Nyberg, Johan. 2015. "Music Education as an Adventure of Knowledge: Student and Teacher Experience as Conceptualizations of Musical Knowledge, Learning and Teaching." Doctoral diss. Luleå University of Technology.

O'Flynn, John. 2009. *The Irishness of Irish Music*. Aldershot: Ashgate.

Oldenburg, Ray. 1999. *The Great Good Place: Cafes, Coffee Shops, Bookstores, Bars, Hair Salons, and Other Hangouts at the Heart of a Community*. 3rd edition. New York, NY: Marlowe and Company.

O'Leary, Jared and Evan Tobias. 2016. "Sonic Participatory Cultures within, through, and around Video Games." In *The Oxford Handbook of Music Making and Leisure*, edited by Roger Mantie and Gareth Dylan Smith, 543–566. New York, NY: Oxford University Press.

O'Loughlin, Michael and Marilyn Charles. 2015. *Fragments of Trauma and the Social Production of Suffering: Trauma, History, and Memory*. Lanham, MD: Rowman and Littlefield.

Organisation for Economic Co-operation and Development. 2015. *PISA 2015 Assessment and Analytical Framework: Science, Reading, Mathematic and Financial Literacy*. Biggleswade, UK: Turpin Distribution Services (OECD).

Ostinelli, Giovanni. 2009. "Teacher Education in Italy, Germany, England, Sweden and Finland." *European Journal of Education*, 44 (2): 291–308.

Parkinson, Tom. 2017a. "Being Punk in Higher Education: Subcultural Strategies for Academic Practice." *Teaching in Higher Education*, 22 (2): 143–157. doi:10.1080/13562517.2016.1226278

Parkinson, Tom. 2017b. "Teaching the Devil's Music: Some Intersections of Popular Music, Education and Morality in a Faith School Setting." In *The Routledge Research Companion to Popular Music Education*, edited by Gareth Dylan Smith, Zack Moir, Matt Brennan, Shara Rambarran, and Phil Kirkman, 382–394. Abingdon: Routledge.

Parkinson, Tom and Gareth Dylan Smith. 2015. "Towards an Epistemology of Authenticity in Higher Popular Music Education." *Action, Criticism, and Theory for Music Education*, 14 (1): 93–127.

Parsons, Talcott. 1937. *The Structure of Social Action: A Study in Social Theory with Special Reference to a Group of Recent European Writers*. New York, NY: McGraw-Hill.

Parsons, Talcott. 1951. *The Social System*. Glencoe, IL: Free Press.

Parsons, Talcott. 2015. "The School Class as a Social System." In *Schools and Society: A Sociological Approach to Education*, edited by Jeanne Ballantine and Joan Z. Spade, 5th edition, 335–339. Los Angeles, CA: Sage.

Partti, Heidi. 2012. "Cosmopolitan Musicianship under Construction: Digital Musicians Illuminating Emerging Values in Music Education." *International Journal of Music Education*, 32 (1): 3–18.

Pavalko, Ronald M. 1971. *Sociology of Occupations and Professions*. Itasca, IL: F.E. Peacock.

Pavalko, Ronald M. 1972. "Recruitment to Teaching: Patterns of Selection and Retention." In *Sociological Perspectives on Occupations*, edited by Ronald M. Pavalko, 239–249. Itasca, IL: F.E. Peacock.

Peragine, Vito, Flaviana Palmisano, and Paolo Brunori. 2014. "Economic Growth and Equality of Opportunity." *The World Bank Economic Review*, 28 (2): 247–281.

Peretti, Burton William. 2009. *Lift Every Voice: The History of African American Music*. Lanham, MD: Rowman and Littlefield.

Picart, Caroline Joan S. 2013. *Critical Race Theory and Copyright in American Dance: Whiteness as Status Property*. New York, NY: Palgrave Macmillan.

Pike, Graham. 2000. "Global Education and National Identity: In Pursuit of Meaning." *Theory into Practice*, 39 (2): 64–73.

Pinson, Halleli, Madeleine Arnot, and Mano Candappa. 2010. *Education, Asylum and the "Non-Citizen" Child: The Politics of Compassion and Belonging*. London: Palgrave Macmillan.

Pitts, Stephanie. 2012. *Chances and Choices: Exploring the Impact of Music Education*. Oxford: Oxford University Press.

Plößer, Melanie. 2005. *Dekonstruktion, Feminismus, Pädagogik. Vermittlungsansätze zwischen Theorie und Praxis*. Königstein/Taunus: Ulrike Helmer Verlag.

Powell, Bryan and Scott Burstein. 2017. "Popular Music and Modern Band Principles." In *The Routledge Research Companion to Popular Music Education*, edited by Gareth Dylan Smith, Zack Moir, Matt Brennan, Shara Rambarran, and Phil Kirkman, 243–254. Abingdon: Routledge.

Prengel, Annedore. 2006. *Pädagogik der Vielfalt: Verschiedenheit und Gleichberechtigung in Interkultureller, Feministischer und Integrativer Pädagogik (Schule und Gesellschaft)*. Wiesbaden: VS Verlag für Sozialwissenschaften.

Rambarran, Shara. 2016. "'DJ Hit That Button': Amateur Laptop Musicians in Contemporary Music and Society." In *The Oxford Handbook of Music Making and Leisure*, edited by Roger Mantie and Gareth Dylan Smith, 587–602. New York, NY: Oxford University Press.

Randles, Clint. 2009. "'That's My Piece, that's My Signature, and It Means More . . . ': Creative Identity and the Ensemble Teacher/Arranger." *Research Studies in Music Education*, 31 (1): 52–68.

Randles, Clint. 2012. "Music Teacher as Writer and Producer." *Journal of Aesthetic Education*, 46 (3): 35–52.

Randles, Clint and David Stringham, eds. 2013. *Musicianship: Composing in Band and Orchestra*. Chicago, IL: GIA Publications.

Ratcliffe, Mary, and Marcus Grace. 2003. *Science Education for Citizenship: Teaching Socio-scientific Issues*. London: McGraw-Hill Education.

Reay, Diane. 2010. "Sociology, Social Class and Education." In *The Routledge International Handbook of the Sociology of Education*, edited by Michael W. Apple, Stephen J. Ball, and Luis Armando Gandin, 396–404. Abingdon: Routledge.

Regelski, Thomas A. 1998. "Critical Theory as a Foundation for Critical Thinking in Music Education." *Studies in Music from the University of Western Ontario*, 17: 1–21.

Regelski, Thomas A. 2004. *Teaching General Music in Grades 4–8: A Musicianship Approach*. New York, NY: Oxford University Press.

Regelski, Thomas A. 2016. *A Brief Introduction to a Philosophy of Music and Music Education as Social Praxis*. New York, NY: Routledge.

Regelski, Thomas A. and J. Terry Gates, eds. 2009. *Music Education for Changing Times: Guiding Visions for Practice*. Dordrecht, Netherlands: Springer.

Reich, Robert B. 2012. *Beyond Outrage: What Has Gone Wrong with Our Economy and Our Democracy, and How to Fix It.* New York, NY: Vintage Books, a Division of Random House.

Reimer, Bennett. 1970. *A Philosophy of Music Education*. Englewood Cliffs, NJ: Prentice-Hall.

Reimer, Bennett. 1989. "A Comprehensive Arts Curriculum Model." *Design for Arts in Education*, 90 (6): 2–16.

Reimer, Bennett. 2003. *A Philosophy of Music Education: Advancing the Vision*. Englewood Cliffs, NJ: Prentice Hall.

Reimer, Bennett. 2009. *Seeking the Significance of Music Education: Essays and Reflections.* Published in Partnership with MENC, the National Association for Music Education. Lanham, MD: Rowman & Littlefield.

Reynolds, Larry T. and Nancy J. Herman-Kinney, eds. 2003. *Handbook of Symbolic Interactionism*. Lanham, MD: Rowman and Littlefield.

Rhein, Stefanie, and Renate Müller. 2006. "Musikalische Selbstsozialisation Jugendlicher. Theoretische Perspektiven und Forschungsergebnisse." *Diskurs Kindheits-und Jugendforschung*, 1 (4): 551–568.

Rhodes, Stephen Lawrence. 2007. *A History of the Wind Band.* Lipscomb University. Accessed December 1, 2007. www.lipscomb.edu/windbandhistory/index.htm.

Richards, Janet and Kristien Zenkov, eds. 2016. *Social Justice, the Common Core, and Closing the Instructional Gap: Empowering Diverse Learners and Their Teachers*. Charlotte, NC: Information Age.

Rieger, Eva. 1981. *Frau, Musik und Männerherrschaft. Zum Ausschluss der Frau aus der deutschen Musikpädagogik, Musikwissenschaft und Musikausübung.* Ullstein Materialien. Frankfurt: Ullstein.

Rivas-Caicedo, Luz. 2017. "University Music Education in Colombia: The Multidimensionality of Teaching and Training." In *The Routledge Research Companion to Popular Music Education*, edited by Gareth Dylan Smith, Zack Moir, Matt Brennan, Shara Rambarran, and Phil Kirkman, 313–327. Abingdon: Routledge.

Rizvi, Fazal, Bob Lingard, and Jennifer Lavia. 2006. "Postcolonialism and Education: Negotiating a Contested Terrain." *Pedagogy, Culture & Society*, 14 (3): 249–262.

Roberts, Brian A. 1991a. *A Place to Play: The Social World of University Schools of Music*. St John's, NFLD: Memorial University of Newfoundland, Faculty of Education.

Roberts, Brian A. 1991b. *Musician: A Process of Labelling*. St John's, NFLD: Memorial University of Newfoundland, Faculty of Education.

Roberts, Brian A. 1993. *I, Musician: Towards a Model of Identity Construction and Maintenance by Music Education Students as Musicians*. St. John's, NFLD: Memorial University of Newfoundland Faculty of Education.

Roberts, Brian A. 2000. "Gatekeepers and the Reproduction of Institutional Realities: The Case of Music Education in Canadian Universities." *The Education of the Professional Musician: Musical Performance*, 2 (3): 63–80.

Roberts, Brian A. 2004. *Who's in the Mirror? Issues Surrounding the Identity Construction of Music Educators*. Accessed August 8, 2004. www.siue.edu/MUSIC/ACTPAPERS/v3/Roberts04b.htm.

Roberts, Brian A. 2007. "Making Music, Making Selves, Making It Right: A Counterpoint to Rhoda Bernard." *Action, Criticism & Theory for Music Education*, 6 (2): 2–13.

Roberts, Celia and Raewyn Connell. 2016. "Feminist Theory and the Global South: Introduction to Special Issue on Southern Feminisms." *Feminist Theory*, 17 (2): 135–140.

Robinson, Kathy. 2006. "White Teacher, Students of Color: Culturally Responsive Pedagogy for Elementary General Music in Communities of Color." In *Teaching Music in the Urban Classroom, Volume I: A Guide to Survival, Success, and Reform*, edited by Carol Frierson-Campbell and MENC, 35–56. Lanham: Rowman and Littlefield.

Rodríguez, Carlos Xavier. 2004. *Bridging the Gap: Popular Music and Music Education*. Lanham, MD: Rowman & Littlefield.

Rodríguez-Quiles y García, José A. and Konstantina Dogani. 2011. "Music in Schools Across Europe: Analysis, Interpretation and Guidelines for Music Education in the Framework of the European Union." In *Music Inside and Outside the School*, edited by Airi Liimets and Marit Mäesalu, 95–122. Series: Baltische Studien zur Erziehungs und Sozialwissenschaft, Vol. 21. Frankfurt a.M.: Peter Lang.

Rodríguez-Silva, Ileana M. 2012. *Silencing Race: Disentangling Blackness, Colonialism, and National Identities in Puerto Rico*. New York, NY: Palgrave Macmillan.

Roediger, David R. 2007. *The Wages of Whiteness: Race and the Making of the American Working Class*. Revised edition. New York, NY: Verso.

Rolle, Christian. 2008. "Musikalische Bildung durch Kompetenzerwerb? Überlegungen im Anschluss an den ‚Entwurf eines Kompetenzmodells‹ Musik wahrnehmen und kontextualisieren." *Zeitschrift für Kritische Musikpädagogik*, 2 (Sonderedition): 42–59.

Rolle, Christian. 2013. "Argumentation Skills in the Music Classroom: A Quest for Theory." In *European Perspectives in Music Education II: Artistry and Craftsmanship*, edited by Isolde Malmberg and Adri de Vugt, 51–64. Vienna: Helbling.

Rosabal-Coto, Guillermo. 2016. *Music Learning in Costa Rica: A Postcolonial Institutional Ethnography*. Studia Musica 68. Helsinki: The Sibelius Academy of the University of the Arts Helsinki.

Rose, David and Eric Harrison, eds. 2014. *Social Class in Europe: An Introduction to the European Socio-economic Classification*. New York, NY: Routledge.

Rudolph, Thomas and James Frankel. 2009. *YouTube in Music Education*. Kindle edition. Milwaukee, WI: Hal Leonard Books.

Rumbelow, Allan Stuart. 1969. "Music and Social Groups: An Interactionist Approach to the Sociology of Music." PhD diss., University of Minnesota.

Russell, Joshua A. 2012. "The Occupational Identity of In-service Secondary Music Educators: Formative Interpersonal Interactions and Activities." *Journal of Research in Music Education*, 60 (2): 145–165.

Ruthmann, Alex and Steven Dillon. 2012. "Technology in the Lives and Schools of Adolescents." In *The Oxford Handbook of Music Education*. Vol. 1, edited by Gary E. McPherson and Graham F. Welch, 529–550. New York, NY: Oxford University Press.

Sadler, Troy D. 2009. "Situated Learning in Science Education: Socio-scientific Issues as Contexts for Practice." *Studies in Science Education*, 45 (1): 1–42.

Sadler, Troy D., ed. 2011. *Socio-Scientific Issues in the Classroom: Teaching, Learning and Research*. New York, NY: Springer Science and Business Media.

Savage, Mike. 2015. *Social Class in the 21st Century*. London: Penguin.

Scarlett, W. George, ed. 2015. *The SAGE Encyclopedia of Classroom Management*. Los Angeles, CA: SAGE Publications. Accessed January 8, 2017. http://now.tufts.edu/articles/caring-classrooms

Scheib, John W. 2006. "Policy Implications for Teacher Retention: Meeting the Needs of the Dual Identities of Arts Educators." *Arts Education Policy Review*, 107 (6): 5–10.

Schippers, Huib. 2009. *Facing the Music: Shaping Music Education from a Global Perspective*. New York, NY: Oxford University Press.

Schippers, Huib. 2010. *Facing the Music: Shaping Music Education from a Global Perspective*. Oxford and New York: Oxford University Press.

Schön, Donald A. 1983. *The Reflective Practitioner: How Professionals Think in Action*, Vol. 5126. New York: Basic Books.

Schugurensky, Daniel. 2015. "On Informal Learning, Informal Teaching and Informal Education: Addressing Conceptual, Methodological, Institutional and Pedagogical Issues." In *Measuring and Analyzing Informal Learning in the Digital Age*, edited by Olutoyin Mejiuni, Patricia Cranton, and Olufemi Taiwo, 18–36. Hershey, PA: IGI Global.

Schwartz, Jessica A. 2016. "Listening in Circles: Punk Pedagogy and the Decline of Western Music Education." *Punk and Post-Punk*, 4 (2 and 3): 141–158.

Scott, John and Gordon Marshall. 2009. *A Dictionary of Sociology*. New York, NY: Oxford University Press.

Scruton, Roger. 2000. *An Intelligent Person's Guide to Modern Culture*. South Bend, IN: St. Augustine's Press.

Scully, Meghan K. 2014. "High School Music Students' Music Participation in- and outside of School and Plans For Future Music Participation." Masters Thesis, University of Delaware.

Seeger, Charles. 1977. *Studies in Musicology, 1935–1975*. Berkeley, CA: University of California Press.

Seeger, Charles. 1994. *Studies in Musicology II, 1929–1979*. Edited by Ann M. Pescatello. Berkeley, CA: University of California Press.

Seidman, Alan, ed. 2012. *College Student Retention: Formula for Student Success.* 2nd edition. Lanham, MD: Rowman & Littlefield.

Sensoy, Özlem and Robin DiAngelo. 2012. *Is Everyone Really Equal? An Introduction to Key Concepts in Social Justice Education.* New York and London: Teachers College Press.

Shepherd, John. 1991. *Music as Social Text*. Cambridge: Polity Press.

Shepherd, John and Kyle Devine. 2015. *The Routledge Reader on the Sociology of Music*. New York and London: Routledge.

Shepherd, John, Phil Virden, Graham Vulliamy, and Trevor Wishart. 1977/1980. *Whose Music? A Sociology of Musical Languages*. London: Transaction Books.

Shepherd, John and Peter Wicke. 1997. *Music and Cultural Theory*. Cambridge: Polity Press.

Shibutani, Tamotsu. 1987. *Society and Personality: An Interactionist Approach to Social Psychology*. New Brunswick, NJ: Transaction Books.

Shulman, Lee. 1987. "Knowledge and Teaching: Foundations of the New Reform." *Harvard Educational Review*, 57 (1): 1–23.

Shusterman, Richard. 2000. *Performing Live: Aesthetic Alternatives for the Ends of Art*. Ithaca, NY: Cornell University.

Shusterman, Richard. 2008. *Body Consciousness: A Philosophy of Mindfulness and Somaesthetics*. New York, NY: Cambridge University Press.

Siedenburg, Ilka. 2016. "Populäre Musik, Gender und Musikpädagogik: Wirkungsweisen der Kategorie Geschlecht und Perspektiven für die Forschung." Accessed August 24, 2016. URN: urn:nbn:de:0111-pedocs-115723.

Silbermann, Alphons. 1957/1963. *Sociology of Music*. Translated by Corbet Stewart. London: Routledge and Kegan Paul.

Slee, Roger. 2010. "A Cheese-slicer By Any Other Name? Shredding the Sociology of Inclusion." In *The Routledge International Handbook of the Sociology of Education*, edited by Michael W. Apple, Stephen J. Ball, and Luis Armando Gandin, 99–108. New York, NY: Routlege.

Sloboda, John A. and Jane Davidson. 1996. "The Young Performing Musician." In *Musical Beginnings*, edited by Irène Deliège and John Sloboda, 171–190. Oxford: Oxford University Press.

Small, Christopher. 1977/1996. *Music–Society–Education: A Radical Examination of the Prophetic Function of Music in Western, Eastern and African Cultures with Its Impact on Society and Its Use in Education*. New York, NY: Schirmer.

Small, Christopher. 1987/1998. *Music of the Common Tongue: Survival and Celebration in African American Music*. London: Calder.

Small, Christopher. 1998. *Musicking: The Meanings of Performing and Listening*. Hanover, NH: University Press of New England.

Small, Christopher. 2010. "Afterword." In *Sociology and Music Education,* edited by Ruth Wright, 283–290. Farnham: Ashgate.

Small, Christopher. 2011. "Prologue: Misunderstanding and Reunderstanding." In *Music and Solidarity: Questions of Universality, Consciousness and Connections*, edited by Felicity Laurence and Olivier Urbain, vii–xviii. New Brunswick, NJ: Transaction Publishers.

Smith, Dorothy E. 2005. *Institutional Ethnography: A Sociology for People*. Lanham, MD: Altamira.

Smith, Gareth Dylan. 2013a. *I Drum, Therefore I Am: Being and Becoming a Drummer*. Farnham: Ashgate.

Smith, Gareth Dylan. 2013b. "Seeking 'Success' in Popular Music." *Music Education Research International*, 6: 26–37. Accessed October 6, 2016. www.arts.usf.edu/content/articlefiles/3985-MERI06pp26–37Smith.pdf.

Smith, Gareth Dylan. 2015. "Neoliberalism and Symbolic Violence in Higher Music Education." In *Giving Voice to Democracy: Diversity and Social Justice in the Music Classroom*, edited by Lisa DeLorenzo, 65–84. New York, NY: Routledge.

Smith, Gareth Dylan. 2016. "(Un)popular Music Making and Eudaimonia." In *The Oxford Handbook of Music Making and Leisure*, edited by Roger Mantie and Gareth D. Smith, 151–170. New York, NY: Oxford University Press.

Smith, Gareth Dylan. in press. "Informal Learning and the Creative Process." In *The Oxford Handbook of the Creative Process in Music*, edited by Nicolas Donin. New York, NY: Oxford University Press.

Smith, Gareth Dylan, Mike Dines, and Tom Parkinson, eds. in press. *Punk Pedagogies in Practice*. New York, NY: Routledge.

Smith, Gareth Dylan and Colin Durrant. 2006. "Mind Styles and Paradiddles—Beyond the Bell Curve: Towards an Understanding of Learning Preferences, and Implications for Instrumental Teachers." *Research Studies in Music Education*, 26: 51–62.

Smith, Gareth Dylan and Atar Shafighian. 2013. "Creative Space and the 'Silent Power of Traditions' in Popular Music Performance Education." In *Developing Creativities in Higher Music Education: International Perspectives and Practices*, edited by Pamela Burnard, 256–267. London: Routledge.

Smith, Peter K. and Craig H. Hart, eds. 2010. *The Wiley-Blackwell Handbook of Childhood Social Development*, 2nd edition. Hoboken, NJ: Wiley-Blackwell.

Snell, Karen, and Johan Söderman. 2014. *Hop-hop Within and Without the Academy*. Lanham, MD: Lexington Books.

Söderman, Johan and Ove Sernhede. 2016. "Hip-hop–What's in It for the Academy? Self-Understanding, Pedagogy and Aesthetical Learning Processes in Everyday Cultural Praxis." *Music Education Research*, 18 (2): 142–155.

Sormus, Megan. 2016. "'I Could Scream My Truth Right through Your Lies if I Wanted': Bikini Kill's Sound-Collage and the Subversive Rhetoric of Grrrlhood." *Punk and Post-Punk*, 4 (2 and 3): 159–174.

Southern, Eileen. 1971/1983/1997. *The Music of Black Americans: A History*. 3rd edition. New York, NY: Norton.

Spring, Joel. 2016. *American Education*. 17th edition. New York, NY: Routledge.

Stebbins, Robert A. 1964. "The Jazz Community: The Sociology of a Musical Sub-Culture." PhD diss., University of Minnesota.

Stebbins, Robert A. 1966. "Class, Status, and Power among Jazz and Commercial Musicians." *Sociological Quarterly*, 7: 197–213.

Stebbins, Robert A. 1992. *Amateurs, Professionals, and Serious Leisure*. Montreal: McGill-Queen's Press.

Stebbins, Robert A. 2001. "Serious Leisure." *Society*, 38 (4): 53–57.

Stebbins, Robert A. 2006/2011. *The Serious Leisure Perspective (SLP) Website*. Accessed March 3, 2016. www.seriousleisure.net.

Stebbins, Robert A. 2007. *Serious Leisure: A Perspective For Our Time*. New Brunswick and London: Transaction Publishers.

Stebbins, Robert A. 2010. *A History of the Serious Leisure Perspective (SLP)*. Accessed July 5, 2016. www.seriousleisure.net/

Stebbins, Robert A. 2014. *Careers in Serious Leisure: From Dabbler to Devotee in Search of Fulfillment*. Basingstoke: Palgrave Macmillan.

Steinsholt, Kjetil and Stephen Dobson, eds. 2011. *Bildung: Introduction to an [sic] Diffuse Educational Landscape*. Trondheim: Tapir Publishers.

Stewart, Carolee. 1992. "Who Takes Music? Investigating Access to High School Music as a Function of Social and School Factors (Social Factors)." PhD diss., University of Michigan.

Supičić, Ivo. 1964/1971/1987. *Music in Society: A Guide to the Sociology of Music*. New York, NY: Pendragon Press.

Suša, Rene. 2009. "With Global Education to Global Solidarity: Building Global Citizenship and Intercultural Competencies in Schools." Conference Report. SLOGA supported by the North-South Centre of the Council of Europe. Accessed January 7, 2017. www.nscglobaleducation.org/images/Resource_center/2009_Slovenia-REPORT.pdf

Suša, Rene and Nina Vodopivec. 2011. "National Identity in the Context of Global Citizenship: Central and South Eastern Europe and the EU Mediterranean Countries." Conference Report. SLOGA: Ljubljana. Accessed January 8, 2017. www.coe.int/t/dg4/nscentre/Resources/Publications/SLOGA_publikacija_National_Identity_splet.pdf

Swanwick, Keith. 1999/2012. *Teaching Music Musically*. Classic edition. New York, NY: Routledge.

Swennen, Anja, Monique Volman, and Mineke van Essen. 2008. "The Development of the Professional Identity of Two Teacher Educators in the Context of Dutch Teacher Education." *European Journal of Teacher Education*, 31 (2): 169–184.

Talbot, Marion. 1910. *The Education of Women*. Chicago: The University of Chicago Press.

Talley, Simeon. 2010. "The 'Browning' of America." *The Daily Iowan*, April 12, 2010. Accessed August 24, 2016. www.dailyiowan.com/2010/04/12/Opinions/16657.html

Teddlie, Charles, and David Reynolds, eds. 2000. *The International Handbook of School Effectiveness Research*. London and New York: Falmer Press.

Terhart, Ewald, Hedda Bennewitz, and Martin Rothland, eds. 2014. *Handbuch der Forschung zum Lehrerberuf*. Münster: Waxmann Verlag.

Tichenor, Mercedes S. and John M. Tichenor. 2004–2005. "Understanding Teachers' Perspectives on Professionalism." *Professional Educator*, 27 (1–2): 89–95.

Tierney, John McDonnell. 2003. *Making Sense in the Field of Time and Space: Reflections on the Education of Young Human Beings*. Shelburne Falls, MA: JKPty.

Tobias, Evan S. 2014. "Solo, Multitrack, Mute? Producing and Performing (Gender) in a Popular Music Classroom." *Visions of Research in Music Education*, 25. Accessed February 2, 2016. www.rider.edu/~vrme.

Tønsberg, Knut. 2013. "Value Changes in Norwegian Music Education: From Increased Acceptance of Rock to a Reduced Status for Classical Music?" *Nordic Yearbook for Research in Music Education*, 14: 145–166.

Torrez, Estrella. 2012. "Punk Pedagogy: Education for Liberation and Love." In *Punkademics: The Basement Show in the Ivory Tower*, edited by Zack Furness, 131–142. Brooklyn, NY: Minor Compositions.

Tripp, David. 1993/2012. *Critical Incidents in Teaching: Developing Professional Judgement*. Milton Park, UK: Routledge.

Trumbull, Elise, Carrie Rothstein-Fisch, Patricia M. Greenfield, and Blanca Quiroz. 2001. *Bridging Cultures between Home and School: A Guide for Teachers*. New York, NY: Routledge.

Tuan, Yi-F. 1977. *Space and Place: The Perspective of Experience*. Minneapolis, MN: University of Minnesota Press.

Turner, Bryan S. 2006. *The Cambridge Dictionary of Sociology*. Cambridge: Cambridge University Press.

Tyson, Lois. 2014. *Critical Theory Today: A User-Friendly Guide*. 3rd edition. New York, NY: Routledge.

UNESCO. 2014a. *Teaching and Learning. Achieving Quality for All: EFA Global Monitoring Report*. Paris: UNESCO. Accessed March 20, 2016. http://unesdoc.unesco.org/images/0022/002256/225660e.pdf.

UNESCO. 2014b. *Sustainable Development Post-2015 Begins with Education*. 2nd edition. Paris: UNESCO. Accessed March 20, 2016. https://sustainable development.un.org/content/documents/21252030%20Agenda%20for%20 Sustainable%20Development%20web.pdf.

UNESCO. 2015a. *Transforming Our World: The 2030 Agenda for Sustainable Development*. A/RES/70/1. Accessed November 18, 2015. https://sustainable development.un.org/content/documents/21252030%20Agenda%20for%20 Sustainable%20Development%20web.pdf.

UNESCO. 2015b. *Education For All 2000–2015: Achievements and Challenges*. EFA Global Monitoring Report. Paris: UNESCO Publishing. Accessed March 20, 2016. http://unesdoc.unesco.org/images/0023/002322/232205e.pdf.

UNESCO. 2015c. *Re-thinking Education. Towards a Global Common Good?* Paris: UNESCO Publishing. Accessed March 20, 2016. www.unesco.org/new/fileadmin/MULTIMEDIA/FIELD/Cairo/images/RethinkingEducation.pdf.

Uy, Michael Sy. 2012. "Venezuela's National Music Education Program El Sistema: Its Interactions with Society and Its Participants' Engagement in Praxis." *Music and Arts in Action*, 4 (1): 5–21.

Väkevä, Lauri. 2006. "Teaching Popular Music in Finland: What's Up, What's Ahead?" *International Journal of Music Education*, 24 (2): 126–131.

Väkevä, Lauri. 2009. "The World Well Lost, Found: Reality and Authenticity in Green's 'New Classroom Pedagogy'." *Action, Criticism, and Theory for Music Education*, 8 (2): 7–34.

Väkevä, Lauri. 2010. "Garage Band or GarageBand®? Remixing Musical Futures." *British Journal of Music Education*, 27 (1): 59–70.

Valdez, Avelardo and Jeffrey A. Halley. 1996. "Gender in the Culture of Mexican American Conjunto Music." *Gender and Society*, 10 (2): 148–167.

Vallance, Elizabeth. 1973/1974. "Hiding the Hidden Curriculum: An Interpretation of the Language of Justification in Nineteenth-century Reform." *Curriculum Theory Network*, 4 (1): 5–22.

Vasil, Martina. 2015. "Integrating Popular Music and Informal Music Learning Practices: A Multiple Case Study of Secondary School Music Teachers Enacting Change in Music Education." PhD diss., West Virginia University.

Vogt, Jürgen. 2003. "Philosophy–Music Education–Curriculum: Some Casual Remarks on Some Basic Concepts." *Action, Criticism, and Theory for Music Education*, 2 (1): 1–25.

Vogt, Jürgen, Frauke Heß and Markus Brenk, eds. 2014. (Grund-)Begriffe musikpädagogischen Nachdenkens. Entstehung, Bedeutung, Gebrauch. Sitzungsbericht 2013 der Wissenschaftlichen Sozietät Musikpädagogik. *Wissnchaftliche Musikpädagogik* Band 6. Münster (Germany): LIT. [Basic Defining Terms for Thinking about Music Education, its Origins, Meaning and Uses. Proceedings of the 2013 meeting of the Wissenschaftlichen Sozietät Musikpädagogik/freely translated: *Society of Scholars in Music Education*].

Vogt, Jürgen, Frauke Heß, and Christian Rolle, eds. 2012. *Musikpädagogik und Heterogenität*. Vol. 5. Münster: LIT Verlag.

Vohs, Kathleen D. and Roy F. Baumeister. 2011. "What's the Use of Happiness? It Can't Buy You Money." *Journal of Consumer Psychology*, 21 (2): 129–131.

Vulliamy, Graham and Edward Lee, eds. 1976. *Pop Music in School*. Cambridge: Cambridge University Press.

Vulliamy, Graham and Edward Lee. 1982/2016. *Popular Music: A Teacher's Guide*. New York, NY: Routledge.

Vulliamy, Graham and John Shepherd. 1984. "Sociology and Music Education: A Response to Swanwick." *British Journal of Sociology of Education*, 5 (1): 57–76.

Waldron, Janice L. and Kari K. Veblen. 2008. "The Medium Is the Message: Cyberspace, Community, and Music Learning in the Irish Traditional Music Virtual Community." *Journal of Music, Technology and Education*, 1 (2–3): 99–111.

Wallace, Susan, ed. 2015. *A Dictionary of Education*. 2nd edition. Oxford: Oxford University Press.

Wallbaum, Christopher. 2000. *Produktionsdidaktik im Musikunterricht: Perspektiven zur Gestaltung Ästhetischer Erfahrungssituationen*. Regensburg and Kassel: Bosse.

Ward, Irene. 1994. *Literacy, Ideology, and Dialogue: Towards a Dialogic Pedagogy*. New York, NY: SUNY Press.

Warner, Michael. 1991. "Introduction: Fear of a Queer Planet." *Social Text*, 29: 3–17.

Weber, Max. 1921/1958. *The Rational and Social Foundations of Music*. Translated and edited by Don Martindale, Johannes Riedel, and Gertrud. Neuwirth. Carbondale, IL: Southern Illinois University Press.

Welch, Graham F. 2001. *The Misunderstanding of Music: An Inaugural Lecture*. London: Institute of Education.

Westerlund, Heidi M. 2006. "Garage Rock Bands: A Future Model for Developing Musical Expertise?" *International Journal of Music Education*, 24 (2): 119–125.

Wiggins, Jackie. 2011. "When the Music Is Theirs: Scaffolding Young Songwriters." In *A Cultural Psychology of Music Education*, edited by Margaret S. Barrett, 83–114. New York, NY: Oxford University Press.

Willemse, Martijn, Mieke Lunenberg, and Fred Korthagen. 2005. "Values in Education: A Challenge for Teacher Educators." *Teaching and Teacher Education*, 21 (2): 205–217.

Williams, David and Clint Randles. 2017. "Navigating the Space Between Spaces: Curricular Change in Music Teacher Education in the United States." In *The Routledge Research Companion to Popular Music Education*, edited by Gareth Dylan Smith, Zack Moir, Matt Brennan, Shara Rambarran, and Phil Kirkman, 46–59. Abingdon: Routledge.

Winner, Ellen, Thalia R. Goldstein, and Stéphan Vincent-Lancrin. 2013. *Art for Art's Sake? The Impact of Arts Education, Educational Research and Innovation*. OECD Publishing. Accessed January 5, 2017. www.keepeek.com/Digital-Asset-Management/oecd/education/art-for-art-s-sake_9789264180789-en#.WGFO6vArLcs#page3

Woodford, Paul. 2012. "Dewey's Bastards: Music, Meaning, and Politics." In *The Oxford Handbook of Music Education*. Vol. 2, edited by Gary McPherson and Graham Welch, 698–702. Oxford: Oxford University Press.

Wright, Ruth, ed. 2010. *Sociology and Music Education*. Farnham: Ashgate.

Wright, Ruth. 2014. "The Fourth Sociology and Music Education: Towards a Sociology of Integration." *Action, Criticism, and Theory for Music Education*, 13 (1): 12–39.

Yanow, Dvora and Haridimos Tsoukas. 2009. "What Is Reflection-in-Action? A Phenomenological Account." *Journal of Management Studies*, 46 (8): 1339–1364.

Index